HOW TO EARN A LIVING SELLING USED BOOKS ONLINE Internet Bookselling Made EASY!

Joe Waynick

Small Business Press, LLC

Internet Bookselling Made Easy! How to Earn a Living Selling Used Books Online

First Edition. First Printing.

For information about this title or to order other books and/or electronic media, contact the publisher:

Small Business Press, LLC
P.O. Box 1800
Litchfield Park, AZ 85340
(602) 233-2721
http://www.smallbusinesspress.com

Waynick, Joe.
    Internet bookselling made easy! : how to earn a
living selling used books online / Joe Waynick. — 1st
ed.
    p. cm.
    Includes index.
    LCCN 2010916397
    ISBN-13: 978-0-9831296-0-8
    ISBN-10: 0-9831296-0-6

    1. Small business—Management. 2. New business
enterprises—Management. 3. Internet bookstores—
Management. I. Title.

    HD62.7.W39 2011   658.02'2
                               QBI11-600044

Printed in the United States of America.

10 9 8 7 6 5 4 3 2 1   11 12 13

Table of Contents

Warning and Disclaimer

This book is based on the author's personal experiences. It's sold with the understanding that the publisher and author are not rendering legal, accounting or other professional services or advice. If legal or other expert assistance is required, the services of a competent professional should be retained.

It's not the purpose of this book to reprint all the information available to the reader from other sources, but to complement, amplify and supplement existing works. For more information about other books on this subject see the many references in the Appendix.

Internet bookselling is not a get-rich-quick scheme. Anyone who decides to try Internet bookselling must expect to invest substantial time and effort with no guarantee of success. Books do not find themselves nor do they list themselves for sale. People must locate, grade, and list books to earn income.

Every effort has been made to make this book as complete and accurate as possible. However, it may contain typographical and factual errors. Therefore, this text should be used only as a general guide and not as the ultimate source of Internet bookselling information. Furthermore, this book contains information about Internet bookselling that is current only up to the publication date.

The purpose of this book is to educate and entertain. The author and/or publisher shall have neither liability nor responsibility to any person or entity for loss or damages caused or alleged to be caused directly or indirectly by the information contained in this book.

Trademarks

All trademarks are the property of their respective owners. Due to the volume of products, businesses, and websites noted and referenced in this book it would be cumbersome to acknowledge individual trademarks. However, the absence of such acknowledgment should not be regarded as affecting the legal status of any trademark or tradename.

Acknowledgments

This book couldn't have been published without help from some amazingly talented and supportive individuals. In particular, I want to express my sincere thanks to:

—My small army of proofreaders, Pamela Vasquez, Christina Vasquez, Ronald Laeremans, Loretta Humble, Paul Stevens, Eric Waynick, Teresa Diyaolu, and Lee Pool. Your keen insights and constructive criticisms made this project far better than it would have been without you.

—The team from 1106 Design, LLC who created an awesome cover as well as typeset and designed the interior of the book. They provided the creative talent I lack in the mechanics of producing a professional work of art. If your publishing house needs first-rate designers then they are the ones to contact. Take a look at samples of their work at *http://www.1106design.com.*

—Laird Brown, my photographer from Laird Brown Photography, who set up and snapped the photo you see on the front cover. He patiently tolerated me when I tripped all over his equipment, hovered over his shoulder and cast shadows on the shot, and refused to smile when he tried to photograph me. In short, he's a real professional and he's someone you should consider hiring. Contact him at *http://www.smallbusinessphoto.com.*

—Doran Hunter, my incredibly insightful editor who repeatedly challenged me to make this book a stronger work. He asked the questions I failed to ask, and showed me how to turn a phrase in ways I never realized. He rightfully won the majority of battles, but I managed to win an occasional victory, however few they may have been. Thanks for keeping me honest!

—My readers from around the world, past, present, and future. Thank you for supporting me in my mission to help others reach their financial and personal goals.

—Finally, my wife Sylvia, without whom this book would have been impossible.

Introduction

If you've ever dreamed of owning your own business, then this book is for you. I explain in clear, easy-to-understand language how to start an Internet bookselling business and begin earning income in as little as 48 hours.

In today's troubled economy, many families find themselves struggling to make ends meet. It's my sincere desire to help as many of them as possible achieve their financial dreams. I've sold tens of thousands of books on the Internet and made a comfortable living doing so. I'm still a full-time Internet bookseller, and I believe the Internet offers one of the greatest business opportunities available to the average person. I'm thrilled to have the opportunity to share my knowledge and experience.

Just a few short years ago my wife and I were only a paycheck away from financial hardship, but you would have never known it. We both had busy lives and earned decent money. I was a 20 year veteran of the information technology industry, and she was a project manager in the banking industry. The good times kept rolling, so our standard of living rose with each salary increase. We built a brand new 3,500 sq. ft. home in a beautiful resort community in a quiet suburb of Phoenix, Arizona; a picturesque community complete with two golf courses, restaurants, tennis courts, clubhouses, swimming pools, and—well, you get the idea.

Two car payments, a 60-inch wide-screen TV, all new furniture, and a one hour commute each way to and from work convinced us we were living the good life. But beneath the slick veneer of our picture-perfect lifestyle was a house of cards about to be swept away in a torrential rain storm.

Realizing that the only way to true wealth and prosperity was to run our own business, we bought a printing and graphics company in an attempt to take control of our financial lives. It was a complete disaster.

We barely exited the printing business with the shirts on our backs. Worse yet, for the first time in my life, at 46 years old I suddenly found myself unemployed. Our once-abundant bank account was nearly depleted. Early retirement was not only out of the question, but just making ends meet at the end of the month was a struggle.

We knew we'd never achieve financial independence punching a time clock, and we still believed running our own business was the way to achieve financial freedom. We just needed the right opportunity. However, we were both in our late 40s and nearly broke. We simply couldn't afford to take a lot of risk. Determined not to repeat past mistakes, we decided to find a business that could lead us to financial security.

> *Over the years I spent thousands of dollars buying books simply because I loved to read. I never once imagined I could sell them myself.*

Our criteria were challenging. It had to be a business in which we could both participate. It had to be relatively easy to operate and not require a large cash investment to start. It also had to have the potential to grow large enough to add substantially to our net worth.

I spent more than a year investigating various home-based business opportunities, but nothing seemed to fully meet our requirements. I read all the business opportunity magazines I could find. I spent countless hours in the public library, painstakingly reviewing every business book available.

Similarly, I camped out in bookstores that carried large selections of business books and absorbed as much information about small business opportunities as humanly possible. I scoured the Internet and bought dozens of books about starting and running various types of businesses, but nothing seemed to appeal to us.

One day after purchasing yet another business book off a website called Half.com, I thought to myself, "With all the money I spend buying books from these guys, I should get a commission." Suddenly, I had an epiphany.

"Why NOT sell books on the Internet?"

Over the years I spent thousands of dollars buying books simply because I loved to read. I never once imagined I could sell them myself. Now instead of randomly researching every business opportunity I happened to stumble on, I focused my attention on gathering all the information I could about selling books online.

As with most business opportunities I expected to find a barrage of information on Internet bookselling, and I was ready to dive in head first. However, I was sorely disappointed. In fact, I found little quality information about how to get into the business. Still, I got my hands on everything in sight, meager as it was.

I immersed myself in every article, book, newsletter, website, and blog that even remotely mentioned bookselling. It took a considerable amount of digging, but I gradually developed an understanding of the business. After months of research, I was ready to launch my new venture.

In my first month as an Internet bookseller, I eked out $1,700 in sales. Within eight months, I was generating monthly sales of $7,500. Within a year, I easily grossed $10,000 each and every month. By the end of my first year in business, I racked up $115,000 in sales. In my second year, I grossed more than $177,000. During this whole time, I managed to maintain a 50-percent gross profit margin. Not bad for what started out as a part-time home-based business opportunity!

In retrospect, I realize that if I had an established business model I could have done better. Although I had the benefit of having read several books by knowledgeable authors about selling online, there were still large gaps in the available literature. Clearly, there was room for another source of information to answer the many questions I had when I started my business. That's why I decided to make my own contribution to the body of knowledge on this subject.

You can start a low risk, low investment operation and grow as large as you want without taking unnecessary chances. Financial stability is well within your grasp if you're willing to try.

While writing this book, I left nothing to the imagination. Every step I took to get my business off the ground was carefully documented and organized into what you now hold in your hands. I can't guarantee you'll achieve the same results as me. But I can guarantee that I've included everything I did to achieve the results of my first few years of selling books online.

You have the benefit of learning from my mistakes and not being condemned to repeat them. For example, you don't have to learn through trial and error how to jump-start your business. I've already covered that ground for you. In fact, I'll show you how you can start earning money within 48 hours of finishing this book! How's that for fast results?

This is not your run-of-the-mill "how to" book. This is a road map that shows you the exact steps I took to reach my goal of earning a living selling books, DVDs, CDs, and vintage VHS tapes online. What you decide to do with this information is up to you. Will you use it to improve your financial future or set it on your bookshelf to gather dust? I sincerely hope the former.

You can start a low risk, low investment operation and grow as large as you want without taking unnecessary chances. Financial stability is well within your grasp if you're willing to try. All you have to do is reach out and grab it to achieve your dreams—starting today!

—Joe Waynick
March 2011

CHAPTER 1

So You Want to Be an Internet Bookseller?

More than 700,000 small businesses are started in the United States each year.[1] If you ask small business owners why they became entrepreneurs, there will be many reasons. But if there's one common thread connecting this motley crew it's the desire to take charge of their own lives.

Many entrepreneurs are seduced by the allure of not having to report to a boss, punch a time clock, or work according to someone else's priorities. Being your own boss is freedom in the truest sense of the word. It's freedom to control your time and money; freedom to control your life.

Like any worthwhile endeavor, Internet bookselling requires determination and commitment. But the beauty of selling online is that you can customize your business to suit your own circumstances. Sound easy? In a word—yes, it is. In another word—no, it's not.

It's easy because getting your inventory listed online for sale is a snap. But to sell thousands of dollars of books per month you must first locate adequate sources of supply, acquire it, and then get it online for sale (the easy part again).

Finding inventory takes time and effort. Depending on how much money you want to earn it might take a *considerable* amount of time and effort. But I can assure you it's doable, no matter how busy you are. You simply need to be realistic about your income goals and put forth the level of effort needed to achieve them.

The World of Internet Bookselling

Why is selling books on the Internet such an exciting prospect for large and small businesses alike? Because books are as close to being the perfect product for Internet sales as you can get. Consider these advantages books have over other products sold online:

- Everyone is familiar with books, hence they're easy to describe and market via the Internet.
- Books are easy to ship anywhere in the world.
- Books are plentiful and resellers can acquire them at a reasonable cost.
- No single retailer, or cartel of retailers, controls the market (although Amazon is the dominant force).
- Internet booksellers have a worldwide market with virtually unlimited inventory available to them.

Internet bookselling is fast becoming the small business opportunity of choice for many people seeking to change their lives. Bookselling giant Amazon .com reported 2009 revenue of $24.51 BILLION.[2] Of course those sales come from all product categories, including books, CDs, DVDs, and VHS tapes. However, Amazon goes on to report that 30 percent of its revenue came from third-party sellers—that's you and me.

To put things in perspective, here's a direct quote from Jeff Bezos, founder and CEO of Amazon:

> "Sales of products by third party sellers on our websites represented 30 percent of unit sales in 2009. Active seller accounts increased 24 percent to 1.9 million for the year."[3]

Just think what that means.

Amazon generates $67,123,288 in revenue per day, $2,768,804 per hour, or $46,613 per minute, 24-hours per day, 7 days per week, 365 days per year—just under a third of which is generated by 1.9 million third-party sellers.

How would you like to leverage the power of the Amazon.com brand to boost your own success? This book shows you how.

The good news doesn't stop there. Did you know that mega bookseller Barnes & Noble sells tens of millions of dollars worth of books over the Internet each year? You betcha. Once again, you can leverage the brand name recognition, capital investment, and marketing genius of the largest physical bookstore chain in America to your benefit.

Do the math. There's a vast online market out there and there's no reason why you shouldn't get your share.

Anyone Can Make Money Selling Books on the Internet

Do you have what it takes to sell books on the Internet? If you have average intelligence, are self motivated, willing to work hard, and not afraid of computers, I believe the answer is yes. No matter who you are, where you're from, or how much you earn, you can augment your existing income with this business.

Furthermore, if you choose to, you can even grow your part-time venture into a full-time business. All you do is learn a few basic concepts that have worked for others and apply them daily. Don't try to reinvent the wheel. Doing what others have already successfully done increases your own chances for success. Learn the basics until it becomes second nature. Repeat what works well for you, discard the rest, and the money will follow.

I consider myself an unlikely candidate to have succeeded in this business. I came from a poor family and was raised in government subsidized housing known as "the projects." I grew up in the inner city where rampant crime, a poor educational system, and constant hunger dogged my every step.

My father passed away when I was eight years old. Consequently, my mother was forced to work 16 hours a day as a nurse to put food on the table and keep a roof over our heads. From my earliest years I had a lot of unsupervised time on my hands due to my circumstances.

Miraculously, instead of hanging out with the neighbor kids I chose to spend the majority of my time sequestered in my room reading stacks of books. As a child I always had two dreams. One was becoming an astronaut, and the other was running my own mail order business. I spent countless hours absorbing everything I could read about my two passions. Eventually, my interest in business dominated my thoughts and all other interests in future professions faded.

From those humble beginnings I got involved in various business ventures over the years, from computer shareware and, computer consulting, to printing and graphics, but nothing quite "clicked" for me. However, I never gave up my dream. At the time of this writing, I own and operate a successful Internet bookselling business complete with a large shipping and receiving warehouse, several employees, and thousands of unique titles online for sale with more on the way.

By all conventional metrics, you can say I run a successful operation. I finally achieved my dream, and now I want to help you achieve yours.

Start Small and Grow Slowly

The beauty of Internet bookselling is that you don't have to bet the farm to make money. The Internet is unique in its ability to accommodate the financial constraints of just about any budget. You can earn a living selling books online, but how much and how fast depends entirely on your personal circumstances.

Until you've gotten your feet wet, start slowly. Like Bill Murray in the hit movie *What About Bob?* take baby steps at first. Learn the business from the ground up. Develop your contacts, organize your resources, work your plan, and success can be yours.

The month before I officially went into business, I was eager to get my feet wet. I used what I now call the 48-hour Fast Track method and tested the waters. During my self-imposed trial, I sold nine books for a total of $83. I can tell you without hesitation that initial $83 gave me a bigger thrill than the first time I skydived.

Operating on the fringes of the business totally risk free gave me the motivation and confidence to go all the way. Over the following weekend I found 100 more books and put them online that Sunday night. I was then an official member of the Internet bookselling community.

For the next month, I "scouted" (hunted for books) an hour or two per day, listed my finds each afternoon, and raked in another $1,700. After those two small successes, I knew there was no turning back.

The Potential of Selling on the Internet

How much money can you make selling books on the Internet? That depends entirely on you. As mentioned previously, you can start small and earn a few hundred dollars per month. In fact, many Internet booksellers only want to sock enough money away each month for a nice Christmas fund to spend on their children or grandchildren every year.

For others, it's a car payment, boat payment, medical bill, money for mom and dad, or other financial obligation. For others still, stashing a few hundred dollars away each month finances the annual family vacation, or fattens their retirement account.

For the more daring among us, an enterprise ringing up $50,000–$100,000 a year in sales is the stuff of which dreams are made. Operated part-time out of the home, such an operation can easily net a 40- to 50-percent before-tax profit.

The truly adventurous entrepreneur desiring financial and personal freedom from the drudgery of corporate life can build a full-time business with annual sales of hundreds of thousands of dollars. For that ambitious group, I urge you to study the contents of this book until it becomes second nature. This book contains everything you need to start and operate a home-based Internet bookselling business that earns $500 to $5,000 per month. When you're ready, buy a copy of my follow-up book, *Advanced Internet Bookselling Techniques: How to Take Your Online Bookselling Business to the Next Level*, visit *http://www.internetbookselling .com* for additional information.

Your education shouldn't end with my books. I encourage you to read books published by other authors too. In addition, actively participate on bookselling message boards and blogs, attend book shows, trade shows, seminars, and of course, book sales. Throughout this book, I recommend many ways you can increase your bookselling knowledge. Please take advantage of them. Never stop learning for as long as you're in business.

Operating your own bookselling business can be personally and financially rewarding, but you don't have to rush in and bet the farm. Start small and grow from there. It's the safest possible route.

Get your feet wet by selling a few dozen books to learn a tiny piece of the business. Then sell a few hundred to learn another piece. When you're comfortable, sell a few thousand more before expanding any further. Take it one step at a time and you'll soon discover the overwhelming joy of being captain of your own ship.

Chapter 2

Getting Started

Internet bookselling is not a complicated business. And there are no secret tricks that will help you get rich quick. But it certainly is a way for the average person to earn a few hundred to a few thousand dollars each and every month.

In this chapter, I'm going to put you on the fast track to getting your bookselling business up and running with minimal effort. It won't make you rich overnight, but it will show you just how easy and how quickly you can earn a living in this business.

Peri H. Pakroo hit the nail on the head when she wrote in her book, *The Women's Small Business Start-Up Kit: A Step-by-Step Legal Guide,*

> ". . . there's no question that working for yourself provides an excellent opportunity to live a more satisfying, authentic life on your own terms."[1]

Internet bookselling certainly gives you a tremendous opportunity to live the kind of life you want and on your own terms too. Now let's get down to business as you take your first steps toward true authenticity.

The Not-So-Secret—Secret!

Okay, maybe there *is* a little secret that savvy Internet booksellers know that goes unnoticed by the masses. But it's not much of a secret because it's talked about on all the major and minor bookselling forums daily. The difference, and here's the secret, is that instead of just *talking* a good game, the savvy Internet bookseller *applies* the "not-so-secret—secret" every day in his or her business.

Just what is this oxymoron I keep talking about? Common sense really. If you want a wildly successful Internet bookselling business, you only need do five simple things well:

1. Scout daily.
2. List daily.
3. Ship daily.
4. Answer correspondence daily.
5. Reprice often.

I'll explain each step in detail below. But if anyone tells you this business is more complicated than that I suggest you find a new advisor. Anyone can make good money doing those simple things alone. Applying the not-so-secret—secret every single day builds synergy in your business that produces results far beyond each individual effort. Believe me, I've been there and I've done it. You can too if you apply this principle.

I know you're skeptical. "It can't be that easy," you may be saying to yourself. In Chapter 8 I'll show you exactly why it works so elegantly. For now, let's do a little test.

The Fast Track Method to Starting Your Business

When I decided to become an Internet bookseller I wanted to test the waters risk-free before putting my hard-earned savings on the line. I had to be sure that bookselling was for me, so I used what I now call the Fast Track Business Start-Up Method. I wish I could claim credit for inventing it. In truth, I read about similar processes from several different sources and customized what I read to fit my circumstances. When I wrote this book I customized it further to a "one size fits all" approach for my readers to use.

It's deceptively simple, yet powerful in its ability to give you the confidence to move forward with your Internet bookselling dream. Fast tracking your dream doesn't take a great deal of money. It's ideal for people who want to test the waters or who have more time than money in the start-up phase of their business.

Step 1: Make two lists of all of the books sitting on your personal bookshelf. On the first list, include the title, ISBN (more about those in Chapter 3), the publisher's name, and publication date. The second list is for books without ISBNs. Record the title, publisher, and publication date. All of this information can usually be found on the copyright page. Your only cost is your time. Total expenditure: $0.

Step 2: Log onto a price comparison website such as Addall.com and look up each of your books to determine their value. Most of your books won't be selling for much. Many of them may sell for as little as a penny! If that's the case, simply move on to the next book. You're bound to have a few titles that retained part of their value or even increased in value over the years.

Return books with a resale value of less than $5 back to your bookshelf. The remaining books should be set aside for sale. This is your inventory. Total expenditure: $0.

Step 3: Establish a seller's account with one of the larger no-fee venues like Half.com. You'll be ready to handle a fee-based account soon enough, but for now, you just want to get your feet wet so keep expenses to the bare minimum. Total expenditure: $0.

Step 4: Gather your shipping supplies. Before listing your books you need an adequate amount of shipping supplies on hand. The reason is that low-ranking and scarce books often sell in as little as one hour after going online when competitively priced. Be prepared to deliver fast, professional customer service for those first few sales. The last thing you want is to delay shipment and receive negative feedback from the start. Negative feedback can kill your business before it even gets off the ground.

Visit your local office supply superstore and purchase enough size #0, #2, and #6 bubble envelopes to ship at least one third of your available inventory. Alternatively, you can visit your local supermarket and collect enough free cardboard boxes to make your shipping containers from scratch. Total expenditure: $0–$50.

Step 5: List your books. That's right. Put your inventory up for sale. Make sure you accurately describe each item using the suggestions found later in this book. Take care to disclose all significant flaws to potential buyers. Don't list any of the books as "new," regardless of how good the condition. The only proper conditions are "Very Good" and "Good," with ex-library books falling into the good category.

Price your books to match the lowest-price competitor whose book is in the same or better condition as yours. For example, if your book is "Good" or "Very Good," give it the same price as the lowest-price book in the same condition. Total expenditure: $0.

Step 6:   Fulfill your orders. Make sure you promptly respond to all customer correspondence the same day it's received. Ship all orders within 24-hours. Use delivery confirmation! When you receive an order, send the customer an eMail acknowledging that the order was received. Total expenditure: $0.

Follow the above instructions and you can try the Internet bookselling business almost risk-free. There's simply no easier way to sell books online.

How the Fast Track Worked for Me

I got my own feet wet by selling my personal books. In fact I did extremely well with them. I only listed a handful of my personal books and I grossed $83. Then I went through the remainder of my books and found a few real gems.

For example, in 1990 I purchased a copy of *Smart Trust Deed Investment in California*, by George Coats for about $25 (including tax), thinking I wanted to learn more about buying and selling trust deeds. For a number of reasons, with available start-up capital being the major one, I never gave the business a try. The book sat in my personal library until 2007 when I checked Addall.com and discovered several copies selling on Amazon for $250! I timidly listed my copy for $175 thinking, "Who would ever pay that much money for this old book?" Three days later, to my astonishment, the book sold.

Great news, you think? I didn't think so. I was in a total panic! All I could imagine was somehow I was going to be defrauded out of my merchandise *and* the $175. You see, I didn't have the benefit of the information in this book to guide me. Fortunately, a few Internet-savvy friends helped me handle the transaction and the rest, as the mysterious "they" always say, is Internet bookselling history.

I actually found several other gems on my bookshelf I could have listed for nice money. For example, my first edition 1934 copy of Benjamin Graham's *Security Analysis,* and my copy of *Poor Charlie's Almanack: The Wit and Wisdom of Charles T. Munger,* autographed by Charlie Munger himself. There are others, but you get the point. There are some books I won't part with for any price . . . on second thought, maybe there is a price. Let's not be ridiculous.

Maintain Your Momentum

These first few sales are meant to demonstrate how easy it is to generate income selling books on the Internet. Depending on what books you currently possess, you may get sales the very same day, especially if you list a fairly current title. What if you don't have any recently published books to sell right away? Go get some!

In Chapter 3 you'll learn about dozens of sources of books to sell. Pick one and buy a few books for less than a dollar each that were published in the last 12 months. List those right away and watch your sales pop.

Like I said before, this business boils down to doing a few simple things well. Buy new inventory every day, put it online immediately, respond to your customers daily, ship orders within 24 hours, and keep your books competitively priced. That's it. If you want, I can make it more complicated. But why would you want me to do that? Remember the KISS principle, Keep It Simple and Straightforward.

CHAPTER 3

How and Where to Find Books

A s an Internet bookseller, one of your most important activities is locating salable inventory. Finding books that are in good condition, have strong demand, and command high prices is critical to your success.

More than 170,000 new books are published every year in the United States.[1] Those books can have a print run of just a few hundred copies each to several million for runaway bestsellers. Ever wonder where all those books go? The answer is just about everywhere. Almost everyone owns a few books. Most people occasionally buy books. Unfortunately, not enough people actually read them, but that's another story.

Sourcing: The Keys to the Kingdom

If you're fortunate enough to live in or near a large urban area you'll find a seemingly inexhaustible supply of books all around you. If you reside in a rural area there are sourcing techniques that can work well for you too. In this chapter, you'll learn several techniques for buying the right kind of *quality* books before thinking about *quantity*.

Just because books are all around you doesn't mean they all have value. You need to learn how to identify titles most likely to sell in a reasonable amount of time and for decent prices. But first, it's necessary to understand what types of books are available.

To stay focused on your target market you'll find it helpful to separate Internet booksellers into purveyors of three distinct groups of books:

1. Antiquarian books and modern first editions.
2. Recently published and moderately aged books.
3. Penny books.

Antiquarian Books and Modern First Editions

This group of books is considered the cream of the crop of the industry; the crème de la crème of bookselling. Antiquarian bookselling requires a great deal of skill, keen judgment, and possibly deep pockets to be successfully practiced. Ian C. Ellis describes antiquarian booksellers in *Book Finds* this way:

> "Antiquarian book lovers seek out classic old volumes—editions of Scott, Wordsworth, Shakespeare, the *Bay Psalm Book,* examples of fine printing and binding from centuries past, such as books from the Doves or Ashendene Presses."[2]

Generally speaking, the first edition of a book is the first time the book is made available for sale commercially, as identified by the publication date. A more coveted first edition is called a "first, first edition," meaning that not only is it a first edition by publication date, but it's also the first print run. A book can still be considered a first edition even though it may have been reprinted 100 times, so long as no significant revisions have been made to the content. Therefore, a true first, first edition, is the first edition, first printing of the title.

True purists take it one step further, and look for the first edition, first printing, and first *state*. While a book is still considered a first edition through multiple printings, minor errors can be corrected without it being considered a new edition. For example, misspellings, dropped words, adjustments to the Table of Contents, and so on, can all be corrected without affecting the status of the edition.

However, the state of a first edition is how it appeared when originally published, including errors. It's the closest one can get to the mind of the author when the book was first written, except for the original typed or handwritten manuscript—which is the most coveted first edition of them all.

I'm personally interested in developing my skills as an antiquarian book collector; I spent nearly three years studying that aspect of the business before dipping my toe in the water. Becoming a collector of fine books is certainly a worthy goal but one that should be pursued only after you've gained enough experience to avoid getting burned.

Recently Published and Moderately Aged Books

I consider recently published titles to be books published within the last three years. By moderately aged, I mean titles published since 1972, but more than three years ago. Why arbitrarily choose 1972 as my staring point, you ask? That's about when ISBNs became widely used in printed books and you'll understand why that's so important in just a few pages.

Another cool thing about post-1972 titles is that they're plentiful and inexpensive to acquire. If antiquarian books are the cream of the crop in the industry, then post-1972 books are its bread-and-butter. You're going to learn how to generate thousands of dollars in sales each and every month selling bread-and-butter books.

Penny Books

Can you really buy books for a penny? Sure. Several Internet marketplaces offer thousands of books for sale for a penny plus a reasonable fee for shipping, but why would *you* want to sell them? I wouldn't sell them and I can't think of a legitimate reason why you would want to either. However, there are plenty of sellers who seemingly make a profit selling books for a penny.

How does one sell books for a penny and earn a living? With great difficulty, I can assure you. As you become familiar with the online haunts frequented by fellow booksellers, you'll inevitably stumble across this question being asked by newbies all the time. Therefore, I'll lay out the business model right here so you can answer those newbies with authority and conviction, and (hopefully) discourage them from engaging in this profit destroying practice.

Penny sellers typically find ways to acquire books for free or nearly free. How do you get free books? Most often by being a non-profit entity, and taking book donations from the public. Otherwise, profit seeking businesses can literally buy tons of salvage books and pay by the pound to launch a penny book operation.

With little or no cash invested in their inventory, it's easier for penny sellers to squeeze a tiny profit out of shipping fees by literally giving away books because it's all based on volume. By selling thousands of books per day penny sellers are able to qualify for lower presorted shipping rates from USPS. Therefore, between free inventory and reduced postage a penny seller can squeeze 25¢ to 50¢ from each sale.

Multiply those quarters by a thousand or two books per day and they can clear $250 to $1,000 per day in profits. The following analysis demonstrates the economics of penny book selling using current shipping allowances and presorted postage rates.

The presorted shipping figure is for shipping a one-pound book. I don't know of a penny seller that profitably sells books weighing more than 16 ounces. Packing materials are usually cobbled together from recycled paper and cardboard. Labor is based on a minimum wage employee processing at least 200 books per hour. If you're doing your own packing and shipping, the labor number can be zero. Processing tasks include sorting, inspecting, listing, and packing for shipment. Profits can be increased by obtaining the majority of packing materials for free, and increasing the productivity of employees.

Revenue:

Sale price of book	$0.01
Shipping allowance	$3.99
Total revenue	$4.00

Expenses:

Commission	$0
Closing fee	$1.35
Presorted postage	$2.22
Packing materials	$0
Labor	$0.18
Total expenses	$3.75
Profit:	$0.25

Mounting a penny book operation takes a massive infrastructure investment in personnel, storage facilities, equipment, and computer software to ensure the most efficient workflow possible. In addition, there must be a steady supply of free or almost free inventory. Needless to say, building a penny book business efficient enough to turn a profit is not for the timid.

Now you too know the secrets of the penny book sellers! However, there are far easier ways to make a living with Internet bookselling. I sincerely hope I've thoroughly discouraged you from pursuing penny books as your business model.

A Humble Suggestion

As a new Internet bookseller, your primary focus should be recently-published and moderately-aged nonfiction titles; at least at first. I suggest you spend a year or two learning the industry before venturing into the antiquarian market if you're interested in that business.

As far as penny books are concerned—don't go there. I can't think of a more difficult and less rewarding aspect of Internet bookselling than being a penny bookseller. But that's just me. I'm sure the penny book sellers of the world are fine people, but that side of the business simply isn't my cup of tea.

Post-1972 books are where I cut my teeth in this business and it's where you should start your business too. As you gain experience, you'll start recognizing and buying higher priced inventory. Until then, your first objective is to learn how to select books you can sell quickly to generate immediate cash flow. In essence, to be successful with post-1972 books, learn how to leverage condition, demand, and price to select profitable titles.

Condition

Each marketplace has a slightly different way of expressing the condition of a book. On Amazon you grade books as New, Like New, Very Good, Good, or Acceptable. We'll discuss how to judge the condition of a book a little later, but for now just remember you only want to sell books rated "Good" or better. Books rated below Good are just plain bottom fishing, and you don't want to be in that kind of business. You don't want to run the risk of receiving negative feedback because a buyer failed to carefully read the description of an "Acceptable" book. It just isn't worth the hassle.

Judging the condition of a book is nothing more than exercising common sense. When deciding whether or not to purchase a particular book, always give it the "yuck factor" test. Does the book have a dust jacket? If so, is it torn and tattered? Believe it or not, the dust jacket represents up to 80 percent of the value of modern first editions (sometimes called "firsts") and older collectible books. If the dust jacket on these kinds of books is missing or tattered beyond recognition, you might consider not making the purchase unless it's a truly valuable book and still commands a decent price even with a missing or severely damaged dust jacket. For most bread-and-butter, post-1972 titles the dust jacket is far less significant.

Avoid books that are water damaged, have severely torn or missing pages, are heavily highlighted, underlined, or contain extensive note taking in the margins. Don't buy books that are musty smelling, have visible signs of mold and mildew, or reek of cigarette smoke. Books with even a hint of mold should be discarded without remorse. Moldy books not only pose a health risk if you breathe their spores; mold can spread throughout your entire inventory and ruin your business.

In short, when you look at the book, if it makes you think to yourself, "Yuck!"—don't buy it. Follow these guidelines and you'll be rewarded with higher feedback scores and more profitable inventory.

Demand

The easiest way to determine demand for a book is to look up its Amazon sales ranking. We'll cover sales ranking more thoroughly later. For now I just want to introduce you to a few basic concepts.

Amazon keeps hourly sales statistics on every book sold on their website. Each book is ranked according to its relative popularity based on the number of copies sold. Amazon doesn't reveal exactly how it calculates the sales rank, but booksellers have come to rely on it as a valuable indicator of how fast a particular book will sell. In general, the lower the sales rank number, the more popular the book. Conversely, the higher the sales rank number the less popular the book. The only exception is when a book has a sales rank of zero.

When a book has a sales rank of zero, many interpret that to mean there's no demand for it. Actually, it means Amazon has no record of ever selling a copy of that title. In reality, you'll regularly sell books with a sales rank of zero. I account for part of that phenomenon by reasoning that demand is hidden until a bookseller actually lists a zero-ranked book for sale. At that time a buyer becomes aware of the availability of the book and purchases it. However, don't purposely load up on zero-ranked books. Yes, they sell, but they sell s-l-o-w-l-y.

You decide whether to buy a book for resale or not by considering the sales rank in conjunction with the asking price. For example, if you find a book with a price of $10 and a sales rank below 100,000 and only three other copies are available for sale, it has a high probability of selling within 90 days.

A book ranked above two million may take many months if not years to sell, especially with 20 copies available from other sellers. Books with a sales rank below 50,000 often sell within a matter of weeks if priced competitively. Books with a sales rank below 10,000 sell in hours or a just a few days if competitively priced. Generally, books with a sales rank below 500,000 are consistent sellers, and their sales velocity increases as the number gets smaller.

You may be thinking, "That settles it. I'll only sell books with a sales rank below 100,000." You can do that, but you'll severely limit your income potential because there are only so many low ranking books available. In addition, the sale price of your books closely correlates with the sales rank. Let me explain.

High demand books have lower sales ranks, but tend to attract fierce competition and prices drop like a rock. Thus the lower ranking books sell for lower and sometimes rapidly declining prices due to competition. Books with low demand have higher sales ranks but often command higher prices because there's less competition from other sellers.

What's a poor bookseller to do? That depends on your business model. In general, you want to minimize the number of books in your inventory that have a high sales rank or books with a sales rank of zero. However, if a book with a high sales rank has a high price—$30 or more—and you can snag it for a buck or two, buy it. The wait is worth the phenomenal profit you'll receive.

While acquiring my first 2,000 books I maintained a 70/30 balance between purchasing faster selling, low ranking books and slower selling, higher ranking books. I wanted the fast sellers to generate cash flow and I wanted the slower sellers to raise my average sale price per book. I was able to generate a nice income almost immediately while slowly building a higher quality, higher priced inventory for long-term "residual sales." Residual sales are the percentage of books sold from your total inventory month after month over an extended period of time. I'm going to thoroughly explain residual sales in Chapter 8.

Price

Obviously, you want to buy books as inexpensively as possible that sell for high prices. You'll find lots of those, but you'll soon learn selling lower priced books with slim profit margins serve an important role in your overall profit picture. Later, you'll get a purchasing strategy that makes your profits soar.

For now, suffice it to say that to avoid tying up an excessive amount of cash in your inventory, don't buy books with a sales rank higher than 500,000 you can't sell for at least $8 and which represent more than four times your cost. Therefore, an $8 book shouldn't cost you more than $2 to purchase. Books with a sales rank between 10,000 and 500,000 should fetch a minimum $6 sale price representing at least three times your cost. Below 10,000 you can buy books with a $5 minimum sale price that's at least twice your cost.

Before buying books, large sellers use far more sophisticated analyses than these decision points. But for small sellers the above guidelines are all that's needed to minimize their cash outlay while generating steady and profitable sales.

Another important point is that there are certain categories of books that sell better than others. For starters, most nonfiction is king in my book (no pun intended) as long as it's reasonably current. Why? For the simple reason that there's always an active market for titles that educate readers about a particular subject rather than merely entertain them. Most "How-To" titles less than three years old fall into the education category.

For example, recently published computer books of all kinds, self-help, business, cookbooks, health, exercise, and diet subjects do well. I've also found higher mathematics, chemistry, psychology, and medical books less than two years old to be profitable. Art, World War I, World War II, Civil War, and other military history books are popular with brick and mortar stores as trades, but tend to do poorly on the Internet, unless they're collectible. Art and military history books are often coffee table books and can't be shipped economically, thereby making them better suited for trading.

Undergraduate and, to a lesser degree, graduate textbooks that are still in common use in colleges and universities can hold significant online value. Some booksellers actually specialize in textbook sales and go to great lengths to maintain solid contacts with university professors and campus bookstores.

Recently published titles are the low hanging fruit in this business. They usually have lower sales rankings and as such sell relatively quickly. Unfortunately, they also tend to have lower prices, usually under $15, but not always. You can find recently published books all day long and generate good cash flow. However, you want to watch out for higher ranking books that sell for $30 to $300 too. You'll learn to recognize unusual nonfiction titles selling in the higher price ranges soon enough.

For example, I once came across a copy of *Metal-Ceramics: Principle and Methods of Makoto Yamamoto* for which I paid 75¢. After checking the demand for the book I discovered only two other copies for sale on the entire Internet. I listed my copy for $440 and it sold within a week. How sweet it is.

Four days later I listed a copy of *The Plot Genie: Index* by Wycliffe A. Hill for which I paid $1 and sold it in eight days for $300 plus shipping. These are just two examples of many diamonds I've sold. You can do the same after developing an eye for the unusual. But acquiring that skill takes time in the trenches. Meanwhile, load up on all the low hanging fruit you can find and generate a consistent cash flow while honing your skills spotting diamonds and building your cash reserves.

Books to Avoid

Just like there are certain books to seek out, there are certain books to avoid like the plague. At the top of my list is fiction of all kinds published more than 18 months ago. The reason fiction exists is for pure entertainment. After the initial release, a fiction title experiences a spurt of sales, then interest quickly declines as readers move on to the next hot novel. Therefore, fiction titles don't hold their value for long and prices start dropping soon after publication. It's possible to find fiction titles that sell, but the amount of effort needed to weed them out is ten times what's needed to pick up an equivalent number of good nonfiction books. As a general rule don't waste your time on fiction. There's lower hanging fruit for you to pick.

Having said that, it's possible to find valuable fiction published within the last 12 months and make a fair profit. Many of those books are still salable and when acquired at the right price they can be a decent buy. Keep an eye on the *New York Times* best seller list and you'll know which titles to watch out for.

Another fact to keep in mind is that fiction made into a feature film tends to do well when the film is released. My copies of *Marley and Me* by John Grogan did remarkably well when the movie by the same title became a hit.

One further exception to this rule about ignoring fiction is when you're having a bad scouting day. The process of hunting for salable inventory using the techniques in this book is called scouting. I didn't coin the phrase. It's an industry standard term. Some days you'll find lots of books. On other days, not so much.

If you're turning up goose eggs everywhere you go, you may resort to looking at fiction as a last act of desperation before leaving each stop on your route. Quickly eyeball the fiction section for titles you recognize. Next, go over the section a second time and selectively pull books with the newest looking dust jackets, and scan them with your barcode scanner (more about scanners in a moment), keeping in mind that newer looking books are more likely recently published. Occasionally, you'll be pleasantly surprised with a decent find. As an added bonus, a few good nonfiction books are sometimes improperly shelved with the fiction.

You can increase your yield by several books per location during tough times by scouting for fiction in this manner. When nonfiction books are plentiful you can safely bypass fiction titles unless you're determined to maximize the total number of books you buy from each location at all times.

Generally, other books to avoid are Book Club Editions, National Geographic titles, Readers Digest condensed books, used college textbooks more than two years old, any of the Time-Life series, and magazines. Books by magazine publishers such as Rodale Press, Popular Science, Outdoor Life, and so on, tend to not sell well on the Internet because they're so plentiful. Keep in mind that many of these same books and magazines sell quite well on eBay as collector sets. But that's an entirely different business model.

Also, stay away from books written by celebrities unless you can get them hot off the press or if they're autographed and you can snag them for pennies on the dollar, which is highly unlikely for small sellers—but it happens. I know because it's happened to me. I once bought a copy of *Don't Block the Blessings* by Patti LaBelle for $3.50 at a library sale. It had a book plate autograph on the front endpaper (the front and rear blank pages of a book) and I sold it for $35 five weeks later.

How Much Should You Pay for Books?

It's ridiculously easy to score good inventory when scouting for post-1972 books. That's exactly where you should start your business to grab the low hanging fruit. Those books can be bought for about 25¢ to $5 and sold for around $5 to $300 each.

If you carefully follow the business model in this book your average cost for inventory should be about $2. If your overall cost per book creeps higher than $2.50 you need to exercise more buying discipline. This doesn't mean you never pay more than $2.50 for a book. It simply means your average cost should not exceed $2.50 over an extended period of time using this business model. One reason your average cost may go higher than your targeted maximum for a month or so is if you attend a book sale and purchase a large number of books with a higher average cost.

On the revenue side you want your average sale price to land somewhere north of $10 per book. If your average sale price slips below $8.50 for an extended period of time you're leaving money on the table. This price range is what I call the "sweet spot" for profitable bookselling because it roughly represents prices that are low enough to make them attractive to buyers but high enough to generate strong profits. Using the business model I outline, you'll find that most of your books will be priced in this range.

Again, this guideline isn't an outright prohibition against selling books for less than $10. You may go through a spell where you find large numbers of books with sales rankings below 10,000 and sell a ton of books for $5 to $8 over a couple of months. It's happened to me, so don't sweat it. The key is to find a delicate balance between quick cash flow and premium sale prices. Your specific financial circumstances dictate the proper ratio of fast and slow sellers you buy for your inventory.

If you eventually choose to specialize in higher priced books, say $15 and above, then all these numbers go out the window. You'll find yourself paying more than $2 per book, and your average sale price will be much higher than $10. There's nothing wrong with that, but make sure you're fully aware of what you plan to pay for books before diving into the deep end of the pool.

For example, I once found a public library that maintained two entire bookcases of what they called "critic" books. These were books publishers gave to local book critics who would review them in major regional and perhaps national newspapers. After reviewing the books the critics donated them to the local library. These books were barely skimmed and were in perfect condition. I would pay $3.40 for paperbacks and $6.80 for hardcovers. In like-new condition these books sold for $10 to $12 for paperbacks and $12 to $18 for hardcovers. All of them had a sales rank below 100,000 and more than half of them always had a sales rank below 10,000.

Mind you these were *not* Advance Reading Copy titles or Uncorrected Proofs (see Appendix 1). They were full-fledged post publication books that were released within the previous few weeks. Whenever these books became available I would buy as many as I could get my hands on because they sold like hotcakes. One afternoon a critic had just dropped off a new batch of books when I happened along. I went crazy and bought more than 80 of them in less than an hour. The library personnel freaked out because they felt my buying deprived other patrons of the pleasure of having access to the best titles. Consequently, they placed a ten book per week limit on my buying. Six months later, new management further restricted my buying to four books per week.

Setting aside the roller coaster policy restricting my purchases, my point is that there are exceptions to every rule. If you can buy a book with a sales rank between 1 and 10,000 and you can make a profit, no matter how small, *buy it!* It's as close as you'll ever come to a guaranteed return on your investment. It's called the "quick flip," and we'll cover it in more detail later.

Conversely, the higher end antiquarian book market requires a considerable amount of expertise that only comes with time and serious study. Therefore, antiquarian book buying and selling is beyond the scope of this book. If you seri-ously want to learn about the antiquarian book market three excellent resources to get you started are *Slightly Chipped* by Lawrence and Nancy Goldstone, *Book Finds* by Ian C. Ellis, and *Among the Gently Mad* by Nicholas A. Basbanes.

Wireless Look-up and Scanning Devices

If there's one absolutely essential investment to make right from the beginning, it's purchasing a look-up device. If you can't afford one right away, your income prospects are greatly reduced. All your efforts should be geared toward building up enough capital until you can afford one. If money is a challenge, I recommend you closely read Chapter 7 and pay particular attention to the section covering readers starting with limited capital.

The thing that makes Internet bookselling possible for the average person is the ability to easily check book prices on the web while scouting for inventory when the book has either an ISBN or barcode. Unless you deal exclusively in the higher end antiquarian market, you're crippled without the use of a look-up device. Before we get into how look-up devices work, you need to understand a little bit about ISBNs and barcodes.

What are ISBNs and Barcodes?

ISBN stands for "International Standard Book Number." An ISBN is either a 10-digit or 13-digit number that uniquely identifies a book. The 10-digit code is the old standard and is currently being replaced by the 13-digit standard, which came into effect January 1, 2007. You'll find the ISBN on the copyright page and back cover of most books. Here's what you'll normally see:

ISBN-13: 978-0-9831296-0-8

ISBN-10: 0-9831296-0-6

Widespread use of ISBNs didn't occur until about 1972. Prior to that date, few books have an ISBN and throughout this book I refer to them as "pre-ISBN" books. As modern book publishing proliferated, a standard means to identify specific books by librarians, publishers, retailers, wholesalers, distributors, and universities became essential.

Not long after the adoption of ISBNs came barcodes. A barcode is a series of machine-readable vertical lines or bars varying in width that are printed on the back cover or dust jacket of a book. The book industry adopted what's known as the "Bookland EAN." EAN is short for "European Article Number," and is essentially a machine-readable representation of the ISBN-13.

ISBN 978-0-9831296-0-8

This is a Bookland EAN barcode which graphically represents the ISBN-13.

The reason why ISBNs and barcodes are important is because they paved the way for the adoption of wireless look-up and barcode scanning devices. Armed with such a device a book scout can simply key the ISBN into the device or scan the barcode printed on the back of the book to instantly access all of the competitive information needed to make a buy or don't buy decision. When the information returned indicates the book can be profitably sold in a reasonable amount of time, that's considered a "buy signal."

Imagine yourself at a library sale or thrift store holding what you believe is a valuable book in your hands. Wouldn't it be nice if you knew the following information before making your purchase?

- What is the current lowest price online for the book?
- How many copies are available for sale online?
- What is the sales rank of the book?
- What other conditions of the book are available for sale?
- If the book sells, is it profitable?

All of the above information and more are readily available with a wireless look-up device.

Think about it. Much of the risk in buying and selling books on the Internet can be eliminated by knowing in advance that the book you're examining stands an excellent chance of selling within the next few days, weeks, or months at a handsome profit. As you can see, a look-up tool takes most of the risk out of Internet bookselling.

Cell Phone vs. PDA Scanning

There are two types of look-up devices on the market: cell phone services and Personal Data Assistant (PDA) devices. There are advantages and disadvantages to both. For example, cell phone services are extraordinarily inexpensive; as little as $5 to $10 per month. PDA scanners typically run $25 to $50 per month.

Conversely, PDA scanners are lightening fast, giving you a significant advantage over the cell phone user during the heat of battle at a book sale. Let's take a closer look at the differences between the two.

Cell Phone Scouting

Most cell phones can be used to look up prices on the Internet if you install the proper software. In fact, you can save money on hardware if your current phone is Internet capable. With a subscription to a wireless look-up service you enter the ISBN or UPC code into your cell phone keypad. After a minute or so it returns real-time pricing, sales ranking, and other detailed information from the Amazon marketplace for display on your phone screen.

Since the data being returned is real-time, you get up-to-the-minute accuracy and know precisely what's selling online. As previously mentioned, cell phone look-up subscriptions are inexpensive, but don't forget to factor in the cost of wireless Internet access to make a fair comparison.

PDA Scouting

Scouting with a PDA device is completely different. Stored on your PDA is a database containing ISBNs for books, UPC codes for DVDs, CDs, VHS tapes, software, and games, with prices for each item. You periodically download refreshed data from your host provider to your PDA.

You scan a book by pointing the PDAs laser at the barcode on the back of a book, much like the way you scan grocery items in a supermarket. After scanning the barcode the pricing information is instantly displayed on the screen. In addition, you can turn on optional sound notification and hear a special tone signaling you to buy the item you just scanned. All this takes place in about one second.

For books without a barcode you have the option of punching the ISBN or UPC code into a touch keypad display, but the data retrieval still takes less than a split second.

Why PDA Scouting Is Superior

I'm going to ask you to use your imagination one more time. Try to project yourself into a mega book sale. There are hundreds of people shoulder to shoulder with you. You're standing there furiously punching ISBN numbers into your cell phone as you look up prices of books you want to buy. Suddenly, I walk up and stand next to you with a barcode scanner and for every ISBN you punch into your cell phone I scan ten books. Zip, zip, zip, KA-CHING! I found one.

While you're busy punching in ISBN codes, my scanner instantly retrieves all the information needed to make a buy decision. It's safe to say that when it comes to scouting, taking a cell phone look-up tool to a book sale is like taking a knife to a gun fight. Trust me, you'll get killed.

Where to Buy Books Every Single Day

Earlier I told you that books can be found almost anywhere. I wasn't kidding. Start looking at book scouting like hunting for buried treasure. If you look in the right places, you'll find diamonds fairly consistently. Many of these sources can be found in your neighborhood and some can't. You may also feel more comfortable scouting in certain venues than others.

The list is in alphabetical order, but I make special mention of my favorite venues. Experiment with them all to discover which ones work for you best. Some sources are more opportunistic because you'll stumble across books when you least expect it, so carry your scanner with you at all times. For example, if you happen to be shopping at one of the big box stores, you can often find a manager's special in the bargain bin that may sell like hotcakes on the Internet. Having your scanner allows you to exploit those unexpected opportunities.

Some venues require more advanced skills to master and are best left until after you've gained more experience. Those venues are listed under the "Advanced Book Sourcing" heading and only receive a brief explanation because they are covered far more comprehensively in *Advanced Internet Bookselling Techniques: How to Take Your Online Bookselling Business to the Next Level*. Check out my website, *http://www.internetbookselling.com* for more information.

Big Box Super Stores

One of the most surprising sources of inventory I ever found is the so-called "big box" store like Wal-Mart, K-Mart, Best Buy, Costco, and Sam's Club, to name a few. This list doesn't even include the dozens of local and regional stores serving limited geographical areas.

The big box stores almost always carry bargain bins where they mark down books, DVDs, and CDs as loss leaders (products sold at or below cost to encourage new customers to visit a store) or because they're overstocked and want to move the merchandise off their shelves. You may feel a little odd scanning merchandise in a Wal-Mart and you may even get a few curious stares, but don't sweat it.

Most likely you'll have mixed success with these sources, but occasionally you'll find a few good buys. It probably won't pay to go out of your way to hit these places regularly unless you happen to live near a particularly lucrative store. Occasionally, you'll be pleasantly surprised when you whip out your scanner while shopping and find a few special deals. It certainly doesn't cost anything to try.

Bulletin Boards

Every community has public bulletin boards where you can legally post flyers or 4 × 6 index card ads announcing your willingness to buy unwanted books. The most common locations of these bulletin boards are grocery stores, laundry mats, and big box stores.

Posting your announcement is free, but you must abide by certain restrictions such as the size of your message. In addition, not all stores allow commercial messages and restrict the use of the bulletin board to sales by individuals and "lost and found" messages.

There are different ways to use this technique. One is to openly advertise that you want to buy books for resale in those locations that allow commercial ads. Since it's free advertising it never hurts to carry around a supply of 4 × 5 or 4 × 6 index cards you can pin up whenever you run across a board that permits commercial messages. You can buy professionally printed flyers or postcards inexpensively from VistaPrint. If you get on their mailing list you can be notified of special sales. Visit them at *http://www.vistaprint.com.*

Another method is to ask for donations and pledge to give a percentage of the profits to charity when they sell. I personally know someone who uses this method, and she reports that while it's not a major source of new inventory, it's steady. There are significant legal, ethical, and logistical issues involved with taking donations. Sellers who get it wrong (and many who try this do get it wrong) hurt themselves and the industry.

I researched and tried both these techniques with limited results. Some booksellers swear by it, but I've found it's only useful as a third- or fourth-tier source of supply. The primary problem is that you get a lot of curiosity seekers wasting your time. It helps tremendously if you develop a phone script to screen out unpromising leads.

No doubt you can find books this way, but until you learn to screen your prospects before making a trip to inspect the merchandise, it'll require a disproportionate amount of your time. The law of averages suggests that you're bound to occasionally find valuable inventory.

Business Cards

For cheap advertising consider having a supply of business cards printed with your name, eMail address, phone number, and a catchy slogan like "Used Books Wanted," or "We Buy Used Books for CASH!" Give them away like candy to anyone and everyone you meet. Eventually, you'll meet people willing to sell you their personal library at deep discounts. You'll gain a reputation in the community as the person to call when people have books to sell.

You can get 250 "free" professional-looking business cards online from Vista Print. Free means you pay around $10 shipping and the cards contain a tagline on the back that says, "Business cards are free at *http://www.vistaprint.com.*" If you're going to try this (and I recommend that you do) go ahead and pop for an additional $4.99 and Vista Print won't put their ad on the back. So for less than $15 you get 250 snazzy cards for about $0.06 each. Cheap.

To give my business an extra boost I once printed 5,000 business cards advertising that I buy books. I pledged to myself that I'd give away at least 1,000 cards per month until I ran out. I was determined to become the go-to guy for anyone wanting to sell their books, no matter how large or small their inventory. After giving away just a few hundred cards I had more referrals than I could handle, so I started referring leads to bookstore owner friends to cultivate more goodwill.

Church Fund Raisers

You may have good success using this technique. Churches periodically hold fundraising drives and the members bring all sorts of stuff to sell. I've found terrific bargains in boxes of books donated to a church.

Look for sale announcements in your local paper and try to hit as many as possible in a single day to increase your odds of finding salable books. Pay particular attention to ads that mention books as part of the sale. Usually, books won't be mentioned unless there are quite a few of them. If a phone number is included in the ad call the number and ask if there are any books for sale. Or, if books are mentioned, ask how many and for what price. No matter what they tell you about price, it's almost always negotiable when you arrive at the event.

Colleges and Universities

Some colleges regularly consign pallets of books to online auction houses. Typically, these pallets can be purchased relatively inexpensively. I've gotten reports of sellers buying them for $200 to $300 each. However, always exercise caution when bidding on pallets where you don't know exactly what you're getting until after the (real or virtual) gavel drops and you've won the bid. You could end up with a skid of out-of-date technical journals holding little value.

If at all possible, try to get a preview of the pallets, even from a distance. Take a pair of binoculars to get a better look if you're not allowed to get up close and personal. If you're able to recognize a few high priced books in the lot that you've sold previously, you may do well.

Consignment Sales

There are people sitting on a cache of books they know have value and either can't or don't want to be bothered selling them. You can offer to sell them on consignment and split the proceeds—usually 60/40 in your favor. You have no money tied up in the arrangement because you only pay when the books sell.

You can assure a favorable outcome for both parties by limiting yourself to the fastest selling books with a minimum sale price of $10. Earlier, we briefly discussed how to identify fast selling books based on sales rank, and we'll cover the topic in greater detail later. For now, it's important to understand that only accepting books you expect to sell within six months maximizes your profit potential and eliminates a great deal of risk.

Write your agreement so the split is based on gross *profit* and not gross *revenue* or *sales*. Your cost structure should be similar to this:

Sales Revenue	
Sale Price	$10.00
Shipping Credit	3.99
Gross Revenue	$13.99
Expenses	
Shipping Cost (Actual)	($ 2.95)
Marketplace Commissions	(1.50)
Marketplace Closing Fee	(1.35)
Packaging Materials	(0.40)
Book Cost	0.00
Total Expenses	$ (6.20)
Gross Profit	$ 7.79

In the above example, 60 percent of $7.79 is $4.67. That's your share of the sale. The reason you require 60 percent is because your fulfillment costs must be covered (for example, labor and overhead). It costs money to pull stock, clean, pack, and then haul the packages to the post office for shipping, and you don't work for free.

If after a pre-determined length of time the books don't sell, the original owner can take them back, you can buy out the owner at a predetermined price like 20 percent of current list value, or you can donate them to charity if that's your arrangement.

> *Caution:* **NEVER** dispose of someone else's books
> without his or her consent, or you could end up paying
> for a cord of deadwood at grossly inflated prices!

All consignment agreements should be in writing to establish clear expectations and responsibilities of the parties involved, from payment terms upon sale to who's responsible for getting rid of stale inventory. Keep good records and behave ethically and fairly with your sources and you can generate good cash flow with this idea.

Estate Sales

This is a lucrative method of acquiring books, DVDs, CDs, and even VHS tapes that command nice prices. I've used this method with great success over the years. The first estate sale I ever attended was a total accident. One of my friends sold postcards on eBay and was a frequent attendee of estate sales. One Sunday afternoon I got a call from her out of the blue and she told me there were a lot of books at a particular sale she was attending and suggested I come down to take a look.

Although I was a bit skeptical, the event wasn't far from my home so I hopped into my car and paid the place a visit. What I found was a private collection of several hundred books, DVDs, and VHS tapes. My timing couldn't have been better. It was the last day of the sale (it actually started on Friday) and there hadn't been much interest in those items.

As usual I started scanning, cherry picking an item here and there, when the sale organizer approached me and announced he would gladly sell me everything for a flat price. Trying not to appear too stunned, I covertly glanced at the pile of 15 or so items for which I already owed $30 after scanning about one third of the books. I surmised I'd eventually end up with about 50 items so I offered $75 for everything. The organizer accepted my offer without blinking an eye.

I spent the next several hours packing everything into boxes the organizer provided and hauled away more than 300 items in my Toyota Camry. My trunk was full; the back seats were laid down and piled to the roof with boxes. In addition, six boxes occupied the front passenger floor and seat. My car must have looked like a low-rider from the weight of the books as it inched down the freeway.

After getting it all stacked up in my garage I began to painstakingly sort and price each item, listing everything that sold for $5 or more. To my astonishment, within a week I'd sold nearly $500 worth of merchandise. One item was a vintage VHS tape of *An Evening With Danny Kaye* conducting the New York Philharmonic

Symphony that sold for $229! Needless to say I became a big believer in estate sales from that day forward.

To find estate sales in your area go to *http://www.estatesales.net* and subscribe. You'll get weekly eMail announcements of upcoming estate sales near you. If you want more information about what's available for sale, click the sale link in the eMail and you're taken to a pictorial view of the home hosting the sale. You can buy many beautiful things including furniture, power tools, art, tableware, electronics—you name it.

When you get your announcements, always eMail the sale organizer and ask if there are books for sale. If not, skip the sale unless there's something else you want.

Flea Markets and Swap Meets

Most of the regular sellers you find at flea markets and swap meets sell online themselves and are pretty savvy about the market price of their inventory. However, special situations occasionally crop up that can be profitable if you're alert. The occasional or first-time seller isn't nearly so price conscious and may simply want to get rid of a lot of unwanted items that have accumulated in the garage or attic over the years. Seek out those sellers first because they tend to offer the best bargains.

Another special situation that occasionally occurs is the regular or professional flea market seller who wants to unload his or her entire inventory. This kind of arrangement isn't for the inexperienced. If you're offered the opportunity to buy out a booth, quickly eyeball the inventory for diamonds. If you can't spot a few valuable titles with the potential of returning the majority of your cash outlay in a short period of time, then insist on getting an inventory list of ISBN and maybe UPC codes you can take home and evaluate before making an offer. Buying large lots is an advanced technique best left to more experienced dealers.

Freebie Newspapers

Most reasonably sized towns and small cities have at least one free newspaper. You usually grab one at your local supermarket or video rental store. Not only is the paper free, but consumers can place a free ad to sell personal items. The free consumer ads attract readers and the paper makes its money selling advertising to commercial businesses.

If you watch the paper on a regular basis you'll find ads for yard sales, estate sales, moving sales, and going out of business sales. Commercial advertising in these papers is inexpensive and you might consider running an ad of your own. You never know who may respond and considering the reasonable cost it could prove to be a worthwhile investment.

Garage and Yard Sales

Scouting at garage and yard sales with your scanner is no different than scouting anywhere else. However, I have a few definite ideas about how to make the most effective use of your time going this route. I also think yard sales are an excellent way to build your inventory with minimal risk if you can't afford a scanner right away.

On Thursday of each week collect the various newspapers in your area and scan the classifieds for upcoming weekend yard sales. Maximize your time by starting with multi-family or church fundraising sales that are farthest away but still within your travel distance. Then work your way back home by mapping your route to hit as many sales as possible. The process of mapping your route for the weekend sales usually takes about an hour to an hour and a half each week using Google maps.

If you don't have a scanner, familiarize yourself with book values and develop an eye for spotting diamonds most likely to sell. Otherwise, buying books at yard sales, garage sales, and swap meets is a crapshoot. Not knowing what books to purchase that are salable may make you nervous. If so, you might want to try using the following system to give yourself an edge.

On the day of the sales start out early enough to reach your first destination by 6 a.m. You have a lot of ground to cover and you don't want to waste time or lose good inventory to the early birds. Upon arrival at each sale, inspect the books for their suitability for online selling. Stay focused on interesting nonfiction books of all kinds. Make sure the dust jackets and paperback covers are as clean as possible. The interior pages should not be torn, crumpled, folded, highlighted, faded, underlined, or have notes written in the margins. Also, don't buy books more than three or four years old until you've gained more experience spotting diamonds. In short, you're looking for relatively current books in "Good" to "Like New" condition.

After a month or two when you have more experience you'll also want to look for older nonfiction titles that appear interesting. Set aside all the books meeting these minimum criteria.

After making your selections offer 25¢ each for all the books in your pile. Make your lowball offer regardless of the prices sellers place on the books. Right around 75 percent of the time your offer will be accepted. If a seller refuses and there are titles in the bunch you believe are particularly promising, counter by doubling your offer to 50¢ each for hard cover books, but maintain your 25¢ offer for paperbacks. About a third of the holdouts usually accept your revised offer, but if the seller still refuses to sell at those prices, smile politely, thank the seller for his or her time, and walk away.

Having the discipline to walk away ensures you never loose sight of the fact that profits are made in this business when you *buy* books, not when you *sell* them. You can't make money over-paying for books at the outset. This hard-nosed approach takes into account that many of the books you buy are going to be penny books online. Without a scanner you don't know for sure most of the time. Buying "right" protects you from your inevitable mistakes by maintaining a healthy "margin of safety," as the legendary Benjamin Graham would say.

As you gain experience spotting diamonds, you'll feel comfortable paying the seller's asking price. It's one thing to lowball offers when you have no idea if there's value in a box of books. It's quite another when you know you've got winners. If you're familiar with an author or title and you know for a fact you can fetch $50 for a book and the seller is asking for $3, don't be a cheapskate and offer 25¢. The ethics of such tactics stink to high heaven and anyone playing that game should be ashamed.

After hitting every major (and sometimes minor) sale within your prospecting area, return home and immediately begin listing your treasures online. Books selling online for less than $3 should be set aside. As your inventory grows and cash flow becomes more consistent, gradually increase your minimum list price to $5.

The next step is to take the unlisted books to a used bookstore for trade. This is where your buying discipline pays off. If you trade four books for one that sells for at least $20 and you paid 25¢ to 50¢ for the traded books, you're trading $1 to $2 of inventory plus one quarter retail for a $20 sale. You'll frequently find used bookstore books priced from $8 to $15 that you can buy for $4 to $7.50 cash plus your trade. Under those circumstances your cost averages around $5 or $6 for books you sell online for $20 or more. Those are good economics any day of the week!

You'll increase your chances of successfully trading with bookstore owners by learning what type of books they generally carry. Try to only bring those types of books for trade. You also want to find out if the store has any immediate needs, and keep a sharp eye out for those books as well. For example, the store may want military history, art, or regional specialty books.

Don't limit yourself to just one bookstore for trading. Always have several stores where you have a relationship with an owner willing to accept your books in trade. Inventory that used bookstore owners are unwilling to accept can be donated to a local charity and you'll be entitled to a tax deduction equal to the cost of the books.

You can get the same tax benefit by hauling unwanted books to the dump and deducting the cost of the discards. However, why trash perfectly readable books when you can do a bit of civic good by donating them? Consult your CPA for professional advice about taking business deductions on your tax return.

Buying large quantities of books at garage and yard sales for as little as possible is how I started buying and selling books. There's no guarantee you'll achieve the exact same results as described above, but I've never lost money using this approach. Your costs are the price of the books, about a quarter tank of gas, and your time.

Yard sales take place all over the country every single weekend. There are plenty of books to be found and it's the perfect way to start your business with little risk. If you don't have a scanner and you have more time than money to invest in your business you can quickly generate cash flow with this strategy.

Library Sales

Periodically, your local public library holds a book sale as a fundraising event. They are commonly know as "Friends of the Library" sales, or "FOL" sales for short. They display books donated by generous library patrons, as well as discarded titles officially removed from library shelves, and sell them to the general public. Depending on your location, you'll attend sales with as few as 2,000 books and sales with as many as 500,000 books. Needless to say, the larger the sale the larger the crowd attracted to the event.

Libraries tend to put reasonable prices on their books, anywhere from 50¢ to $5 each. Large quantities of potential inventory and low prices make library sales fertile ground for aspiring Internet booksellers. Books are typically displayed on a long table with the spines up. This makes it easy to run your finger along the spines to aid in selecting titles you instantly recognize. It also makes it easy to pull the book toward you just far enough to expose the barcode for scanning.

At larger sales you'll often find the books stored on metal shelving displayed like books in a public library, standing upright with the spine facing outward. Again, it's easy to pull the book toward you just far enough to expose the barcode for scanning.

How to Find Sales

There are several ways to find out when and where the next library sale is held in your area. The easiest thing to do is to ask your local librarian when you're out scouting. Many libraries print a flyer they keep handy at the checkout counter to give away to the public. Libraries that hold several sales per year often publish a schedule with the dates and times of each sale.

One of the best ways to learn about sales near and far is to subscribe to Book Sale Finder's weekly eMail newsletter. (See *http://www.booksalefinder.com.*) They'll notify you of upcoming sales being held within a certain number of miles from your home.

Check the Book Sale Finder website for additional listings of sales outside your subscribed mileage limit in your weekly notice. There you'll find announcements for large and small book sales being held nationwide. They are one of the most reliable sources of information about library book sales available.

The more widely advertised the sale, the more competitors show up. You can give yourself an edge by getting on the mailing lists of smaller libraries because, often, they don't advertise much. Fewer competitors attend smaller sales, leaving the field wide open for you.

Contact the libraries by phone, eMail, and personal visits. Find out who organizes the library sales and make sure that that person knows who you are. The sale organizer will ensure you know when each sale is held. You also want that person to think of you when there are surplus books available. One of my very best deals was buying thousands of surplus library books. I would have never gotten it if I weren't on a first name basis with a regional manager. Be persistent and get a contact name for every library in your area.

If one of your contacts gets promoted, get him or her to introduce you to the replacement person. If your contact leaves the library for any reason without telling you, introduce yourself to the new person as soon as possible.

Don't forget to regularly check the website for individual libraries and the website for county library systems for upcoming sale announcements. Often those sales are smaller and don't make it to Book Sale Finder so there is less competition.

What to Expect

Going to a popular library sale is a little like preparing for military maneuvers. Leaving the sale with a respectable amount of valuable books depends on how well you arm yourself with competitive knowledge and the proper equipment. Consider this book your field guide for your training and preparation.

The first order of business when attending a library sale is to enjoy yourself! These events can be a hoot even though you have a profit motive. You'll encounter the most interesting and dynamic people you'll ever meet. Try to get to know them. Engage them in lively conversations. A few of the booksellers you meet may become valuable allies. Most of all, have a good time. If you can't have fun at one of these shindigs I suggest you check your pulse.

Many sales offer a "members-only" buying period when, you guessed it, only members of that particular library can shop. Member's-only sales are usually called "preview" sales and can occur from a day earlier than the main sale, to just an hour prior to when the doors open. There's normally a fee to become a member ranging from $25 to $100 per year.

As a bookseller your objective is to find as many salable books as possible and minimize the amount of deadwood you cart home. As a rule, library sales are orderly affairs even though the energy level can run quite high. They're attended by casual readers and professional booksellers alike.

For smaller sales, plan to arrive at least half an hour early to ensure you're one of the first in line. If you really want an edge get there a full hour early. For larger sales plan to arrive two or three hours early. For mega sales many people camp out overnight to ensure they're part of the first wave to hit the floor.

As previously mentioned, the energy at a library sale can run quite high. There's lots of hustle and bustle as buyers jockey for the best books. If you've ever attended the grand opening of a Wal-Mart Super Center or been part of the first wave of shoppers at a major sale on Black Friday (the first shopping day after Thanksgiving) you understand what I mean.

When the library doors open, briskly *walk* to the area containing the types of books you're seeking and start scanning. Don't be shy, because most of the time there are plenty of other booksellers scanning right along side of you. The vast majority of book buyers who frequent library sales are nice folks and are out having fun just like you. Be courteous to your fellow shoppers and enjoy the treasure hunt.

What to Bring

Having the proper equipment is just as important as implementing the proper strategy at a sale. The right tool makes any job easier. Successfully navigating a well-attended book sale is no different. Unless you're an antiquarian bookseller with a fantastic memory and a stack of cheat sheets, don't forget your scanner. In the post-1972 bookselling market there are simply too many titles to memorize and your scanner is the meat and potatoes of your business.

You can always tell the seasoned scouters from the beginners at a book sale because the beginners are the ones dragging around heavy boxes or lugging arm-loads of books everywhere they go. The pros bring a collapsible shopping cart with wheels to hold their books and navigate the floor with ease. Shopping carts can be purchased at your local Fred Meyer, Kmart, Target, or Wal-Mart Super Center stores. You can also run a Google search on "grocery cart" to find many different models.

I settled on a Jumbo Shopping Cart from Stacks and Stacks (pictured on the following page) for under $50. I bought the optional lining and flap that covers the top. It holds up to 100 books and contains an auxiliary basket under the handle (not illustrated) where I store drinks and snacks so I can work right through lunch when I go to mega sales. Visit them at *http://www.stacksandstacks.com* for a wide selection.

Be careful about the weather. Most carts don't come with covers or liners. Either buy the optional liner with a cover or keep a plastic sheet in your cart in case you have to transport your purchases from the booksale facility to your car in the rain.

Wear a comfortable pair of walking shoes because you're going to be on your feet several hours. Women should not wear high heels or pumps. Blue jeans and a shirt or blouse appropriate for the climate is the best attire. You may find yourself crawling around on the floor sifting through boxes of books beneath tables. A pair of roller blader's knee pads is helpful in those situations.

A sturdy shopping cart is essential equipment for book sales. This model can hold up to 100 books if carefully packed. Note the handy basket on the back to hold snacks and supplies. The cart is shown with and without a protective liner.

Women should leave purses safely locked in the trunk of their car or at home because it's difficult to scan quickly with a purse dangling from your arm or falling off your shoulder. Smart women use a fanny pack, backpack, or travel purse that's designed to be worn securely across the body diagonally. Backpacks also work well for men.

At a typical well-attended booksale with 3,000 or more books you'll bring home 25 to 50 books in about two hours and worth an average of $8 to $15 each, which will sell for an average of $200 to $750 online. You'll pay around $2 to $3 per book. You'll take home more books from larger sales and spend more time finding them. Smaller sales yield somewhat less.

Volunteering

Library sale organizers are frequently short of help and you may develop important contacts by offering to help set up the next sale. One way you can connect with library sale organizers is to approach the person in charge of the next sale you attend after you're done making your purchases, and ask if you can volunteer for the next sale. Most likely, your inquiry will be met with enthusiastic acceptance.

As a volunteer you may be allowed to make a certain number of purchases prior to the sale. But don't push the issue. Ask once, in a low key manner, and no more. If the answer is "no," then it's no. Making valuable contacts is far more important than picking up a few books.

The way to solidify your relationship with sale organizers is to do everything in your power to make the sale a huge success. Your reward will come soon enough, and in the least expected way. At a minimum you'll know where to find the best books when the sale starts, and get a jump on the crowd. Even if you don't receive any direct financial benefit, you're helping the community and that's always a good thing.

Friends of the Library Shelves

Libraries receive a daily influx of books donated by individuals and businesses for various reasons. Consequently, libraries often find themselves with more copies of a particular title than they can absorb. As a way of reducing surplus inventory library volunteers maintain ongoing "Friends of the Library" bookshelves where the public can purchase books for as little as 50¢ each.

Not all libraries have an ongoing sale, but most do. Use a directory search service such as *http://www.yellowpages.com* or *http://www.usdirectory.com* to find all the public libraries within a 50 mile radius of your home. Then go to *http://www.mapquest.com* and use the multiple location feature to build one or more routes containing up to ten stops each. These routes are your scouting territories.

If you're going to be a full-time bookseller, build routes in the shape of a big circle. You'll find it's the most efficient use of your time and gasoline. A round trip can cover as many as 100 miles and you'll always end up right back at your front door. If you're a part-time bookseller, your regular scouting territory will most likely be locations along the route you take home from work, because your scouting is confined to evenings and weekends. Many part-time booksellers operate their business that way.

The number of books you find at each location depends on factors such as the amount of competition you get from other scouters, the frequency with which the bookshelves are restocked, the time of day you visit each location, your scanning criteria, and your knowledge of book values, just to name a few.

The more you visit your regular scouting locations, the more efficient you become. You'll find you're able to travel between stops faster as you learn short cuts and traffic patterns.

The more you visit your regular scouting locations, the more efficient you become. You'll find you're able to travel between stops faster as you learn short cuts and traffic patterns. You'll also spend less time at each location because you'll become familiar with the stock. Learn to skip over books you've previously scanned and zero in on fresh inventory to save time. In addition, you'll build relationships with the staff who maintain the sale. You'll learn when the shelves are normally restocked and time your visits to arrive before your competition.

You'll normally find five to ten books at each location. Sometimes it'll be more, sometimes less. Don't be discouraged if you walk out of a location with no books at all; just hustle over to your next stop in search of greener pastures. My best score was 156 books from a single library in about two hours. My worst: zero in the same amount of time.

New Bookstores

I first read about this idea on a bookseller forum and was immediately intrigued. Scouting in new bookstores like Barnes & Noble and Borders may sound like sacrilege, but traditional new bookstores can be a good source of brand spanking new books that sell like hotcakes on the Internet for about two or three times your cost.

Most new bookstores have a bargain table where the books are heavily discounted. Usually those tables exist because the store is overstocked on a particular title. That's where you'll find your opportunity.

Since there's a fairly decent size Barnes & Noble less than two miles from my home, I started dropping in on a regular basis to scan the discounted books. On more than one occasion an employee couldn't resist asking what I was doing. Usually, I simply reply that I'm looking for books that aren't in my book database. It's true. I just don't mention I intend to sell them. Most people just assume I'm a collector of some sort.

I suggest you avoid wasting time scanning the coffee table books published by Barnes & Noble themselves. They normally dominate the "bargain books" section of most of the stores and almost never can be resold profitably.

Books I've bought in new bookstores that paid handsomely are *Fashion: The Collection of the Kyoto Costume Institute,* by Akiko Fukai (sold for $54, paid $18); *Battles of the Bible: A Military History of Ancient Israel,* by Chaim Herzog and Mordechai Gichon (sold for $29.95, paid $7.18); and *Letters to a Young Poet/the Possibility of Being,* by Rainer Maria Rilke (sold for $30, paid $6.80).

Sometimes you'll find multiple copies of books, but be careful! Often the entire chain is dropping a title and all the stores have them on sale. If you buy too many of them, and other dealers are doing the same thing, the online price can sink pretty fast.

For example, I bought six hardcover editions of *The Millionaire Next Door,* by Thomas J. Stanley and William D. Danko for $6.80 each. I sold two of them for an average of $14.87 a piece. Then the bottom nearly fell out and I sold the remaining four at an average of $8.65 each—a break-even after expenses. It wasn't long after I sold my last copy that the price fell below $5. The last time I checked, new copies were selling for less than $1.50 and there were more than 100 of them available for sale online.

The books you find in new bookstores are in pristine condition. You won't always find great deals, but they occasionally surface. To get them you must be on the lookout. Stick with books with a low numerical sales ranking, usually under 10,000. Books ranked that low sell off in a matter of days. The rapid turnover of low ranking books mitigates most of your risk if you price them competitively.

You can increase your margins by making sure the new bookstores have your state sales tax exempt certificate on file. (Refer to Chapter 10 for a thorough explanation.) There's no sense paying a 7 to 10 percent sales tax when you plan to resell the book online.

Don't bother trying to explain to the cashier why you don't want to pay sales tax. Ninety percent of the time they don't have a clue. Not because they aren't intelligent, but because what you're doing is so unusual they've probably never been trained to handle such requests. Present your tax certificate to the store manager before making your first purchase. Let the manager educate the cashier about how to handle tax exempt certificates.

You may save yourself an additional 10 percent of the purchase price by joining their book club. Most major bookstore chains have one. It'll cost you $50 or so per year, but the membership pays for itself in discounts if you buy $500 or more in books annually. That should be pretty easy if you're making regular stops. You may even save that amount monthly if you're fortunate enough to find a good store.

Online Buyback Program

A truly novel approach to finding inventory is to let the books come to you just like traditional brick and mortar stores handle a lot of their acquisitions. If you own a traditional retail used bookstore, customers routinely bring you books to trade for store credit. A store employee quickly eyeballs the inventory and makes a value judgment about which ones to keep or reject. Scouting is practically unnecessary because inventory of all kinds literally walks through the front door.

You can do the same thing by offering to buy books direct from the consumer through an online buyback program. The creative people at *http://www.buybak.com* have built a website you can use to purchase inventory from anyone, anywhere, and never step outside your home. What's nice about their system is that it eliminates the guesswork from the process by automatically checking online pricing and making an offer to the seller based on your customized purchasing criteria.

The challenge, of course, is driving traffic to your page and convincing ordinary mortals to punch in ISBNs so your website can do its high tech magic. That's easier said than done, and although the concept is great, the execution may prove challenging. However, if you give people a reason to visit your site in sufficient numbers, you just might hit a home run. Contact the folks at BuyBak for pricing details.

Prospecting Online

You can save yourself time and gasoline by searching the Internet for inventory. There are all kinds of variations on this technique. Here I'm going to discuss two of the most promising. Later, I'll discuss a third technique for which I coined the term "book arbitrage." If you want further ideas for online prospecting try picking up a copy of BookThink's *How to Buy Inventory Online* at *http://www.bookthink.com.* You may also want to look at their online book buying software *Book Hunt* while you're there.

Craigslist

One online scouting technique is to use Craigslist to find lots of books in bulk. Go to *http://www.craigslist.org* and find your state, then the city nearest to you. Look over the category list and find "books" or "books for sale." Click the link and start browsing the ads.

Many booksellers find salable books on Craigslist all the time. You may occasionally be pleasantly surprised at what you come across. You'll see a lot of ads from college kids trying to unload outdated textbooks. If you're going to deal in textbooks make sure the ones you buy are current (meaning they're still being used for classes) or you'll only find yourself buying cord after cord of deadwood.

Spending hours searching through Craigslist can be time consuming and often not worth the effort. You can shortcut the time and effort it takes to hunt through the site by signing up for their RSS feed. RSS stands for "Really Simple Syndication." Wikipedia defines RSS as:

> ". . . a family of Web feed formats used to publish frequently updated works—such as blog entries, news headlines, audio, and video—in a standardized format."[3]

To learn more, go to *http://www.craigslist.org/about/rss* for a *really simple explanation.* (Sorry, I couldn't help myself.)

The reason RSS is so helpful is that you tell it to monitor certain classifications like "Books For Sale," and it'll send you a notification whenever new listings are posted. Thus, you're actually notified of potential inventory instead having to hunt for it.

Getting setup with an RSS on Craigslist isn't difficult. First you'll need an RSS reader. Try the Google Reader because it's simple to use and works with most websites. To download the Google Reader you need a Google account. Browse to *http://www.google.com/account* and sign-in. If you don't have a Google account you can sign-up for one for free at the above link. Once you have an account, you can download and set up the Google Reader.

There are other readers available and in time you might want to try a few different ones before settling on one you think best suits your needs. Once you're signed up with Google, whenever a new listing for books for sale is posted, you get notified. All you do is follow the link provided and you'll be led straight to the newest offerings.

eBay

If you're enamored with the American Wild West, or if wildcatting for oil in Texas sounds exciting to you, then you'll love prospecting on eBay. Book hunting on eBay is similar to Craigslist. Entire books have been written about buying and selling on eBay so I won't cover it here. If you want to give eBay a whirl visit your local brick and mortar bookstore and browse the business, entrepreneur, or Internet marketing sections for plenty of titles with the nitty-gritty details.

Unlike Amazon, AbeBooks, and Alibris (all of which are covered below), eBay is primarily an auction site as opposed to a fixed price site. Sellers have the option of creating fixed price stores, but it's generally accepted that eBay's claim to fame is being the premier auction site for buying and selling merchandise of all kinds. You may want to use eBay primarily for buying large lots of books. To find them go to *http://www.ebay.com* and logon to your account. If you don't have a free eBay account, now may be a good time to open one. Search on the words "book lot" and chances are you'll come up with about 30,000 results. Obviously, there are many books for sale on eBay.

However, many eBay advertisers have pretty strange ideas about what constitutes a "lot" of books. For example, when I did my search today I found the following:

- Lot of 2 Bread Machine Cookbooks
- *Skiing* Magazine lot of 2
- Lot of 6 *Scooby Doo* Scholastic Books
- Handmade Lot of 4 New Bamboo Leaf Bookmarks

Needless to say one must be careful when buying from eBay, but many people find pretty remarkable deals there. Diligently search the website on a daily basis for the types of books you want and carefully screen the results to ensure you're getting a fair deal. BookThink's Book Hunt software is ideal for this.

Auction websites aren't my favorite place to buy and sell for a number of reasons, including the complex fee structure, feedback system changes, problems collecting from fraudulent bidders, and often being sent misrepresented merchandise. Despite these negatives, eBay supports a huge following and a marketplace that big simply cannot be ignored.

Remote Scouters

At the time of this writing there was at least one service advertised on *http://www.booksalefinder.com* that claimed to scout on your behalf and buy books in accordance with a set of predetermined criteria, effectively guaranteeing the resale value of the stock. To me this sounded too good too be true, so for the purpose of research for this book I gave them a try.

I placed a $90 order for which I was promised a shipment containing 20 to 25 books with a resale value of $130 to $150, all with sales rankings below 500,000, and all promised to be in "Very Good" condition or better. Even with the slimmer margins I figured it might be worth my while to add to my inventory without having to pound the pavement.

After waiting nearly two months my books arrived, and as I expected, I was sorely disappointed. The box contained worthless book club editions, books missing dust jackets, and books with stains and other damage. The people running the operation clearly don't understand the difference between "Good" and "Very Good" books. Half the shipment was unlistable and the remaining books were listed for less than half of what I paid. Not a major loss for sure, but certainly a disappointing end to what seemed to be a promising source of supply. Needless to say, I never placed a second order. I suggest you avoid these types of arrangements.

Storage Unit Auctions

People rent storage units for many different reasons. They sometimes need temporary space to store belongings between moves, or they've outgrown their home and need auxiliary storage space. A little-known secret is that when tenants default on the rent the storage company seizes the contents of the unit and auctions it off to the highest bidder.

If you've never been to a storage unit auction you're missing out on a fun activity. Arrive at least 30 to 45 minutes early and mingle with the other bidders. Auctions are fun in general, but storage unit auctions are especially fun because of the "mystery" aspect. You never know what a unit contains until the auctioneer cuts the lock and rolls up the door. Bidders are allowed just a few short minutes to visually inspect the contents from the doorway before the auction begins.

Literally anything can be stored in the unit. Once I actually purchased a fully furnished three-bedroom apartment complete with three closets packed with men's and women's clothing for only $100! I've seen units stacked from floor to ceiling with boxes packed with books, DVDs, and CDs sold to the highest bidder for less than $300. It seems businesses use storage units too, and when they go out of business the units are often abandoned.

You don't want to show up unprepared, so the first thing you'll need is a powerful flashlight to see into the unit during the brief preview given minutes before the auction. You're looking for evidence that the unit contains media you can resell. For example, stacks of Gutenberg bibles are a dead giveaway!

If there's bulky furniture in the foreground of the unit get down on the ground and shine your flashlight underneath to get a glimpse of what's hidden behind. To protect your knees, bring along a set of knee pads. Storage units are dusty places so a dust mask and work gloves are good ideas. Bring a sturdy lock to secure the unit in case you're the winning bidder. You can temporarily lock your unit and continue bidding on others throughout the day. You'll need cash to pay for your purchases because storage companies generally don't take checks or credit cards. Finally, bring your TAXID certificate or you'll pay sales tax (see Chapter 10 for a full explanation about TAXID certificates).

The bidding can be fast and furious. During the preview make sure you quickly determine the maximum you're willing to spend for the unit and never go over that amount once you've decided. When the bidding starts, position yourself so you can see who you're bidding against. The first reason is that you want to look your competition in the eye so they know you're determined to win the bid and discourage them. The second reason is to ensure an unscrupulous auctioneer doesn't have you bidding against a fire extinguisher or trash can to goose a higher price out of you.

Winning bidders are usually given 24-hours to clear out the unit or start paying rent. When I was heavy into these auctions I simply rented a U-Haul for the day because my purchases were generally bulky. But you're after media products; therefore, a pick-up truck should suffice. If you don't own a pick-up, there's always U-Haul.

Unfortunately, units you're savvy enough to win most likely contain a great many items you don't want. You may unload unwanted merchandise by making a deal with one of the losing bidders to take it off your hands. Let them know that all you want are the media items and perhaps a few personal items and that you're willing to sell them the rest at a greatly reduced price. If the unit you buy contains furniture, clothes, office equipment, or other items of value to a retailer, you may get your media for nothing. Plus you won't have to clean out the storage unit.

Thrift Stores

Thrift stores are great because they receive a steady stream of fresh donations on a daily basis just like libraries. Visit the three closest stores to your home daily. Get to know the stock clerks and find out their restocking schedules. One way to build rapport with thrift store personnel is to donate something to each store on a regular basis. You can donate lots of books you'd otherwise discard as deadwood. But you can actually donate just about anything that's in good working order. You'll find most thrift store employees are happy to help you when you're pleasant to them.

If the thrifts in your area are large chains like Goodwill or the Salvation Army, each store may carry a list of all the stores in your area. Ask for a copy and use MapQuest or Google Maps to plot one or more routes just like you did for the library sales. Once you've established a routine you can knock out 20 to 40 books in the first couple of hours of scouting. Things get a little tougher after that because your competition has already hit the stores you visit later in the day.

To find all the thrifts in your area go to YellowPages.com at *http://www .yellowpages.com* and search the keywords "thrift" and "thrift stores" to find every thrift store in your entire city, town, or county. Next try Goodwill, Salvation Army, Deseret, and any other thrift stores you know by name. You'll be pleasantly surprised at how many opportunities there are to buy good inventory within a 50 mile radius of your home.

You may increase your profit margins by donating your deadwood to the thrift and receive a 20-percent discount on the books you purchase. Also, if you make a mistake with any of your purchases you can always return the unwanted books for store credit. Check the policies of your local stores to see if these two techniques work in your area.

Unfortunately, many of the larger thrift chains are setting up their own Internet bookselling operations. The Salvation Army is widely known to sell online. Goodwill stores are now getting into the act. Each state is different, and if the major thrifts in your state haven't started selling online, you can still find fantastic bargains.

Used Bookstores

Traditional brick and mortar used bookstores can be great sources of new inventory. Smaller stores that carry 25,000 or fewer books usually yield the best bargains. Owners of smaller stores tend to be averse to selling online. In addition, the time commitment to running a store precludes them from selling online in a serious way.

Larger stores carrying more than 25,000 books are better staffed and generally have someone dedicated at least part-time to Internet sales. Even if larger stores don't already sell online their pricers tend to mark up the merchandise to the high side. Even so, price imperfections still occur which make this method of scouting worthwhile.

Price Imperfections

Just what do I mean by price imperfections? It's quite simple. A price imperfection is when the bookstore prices a book below what you can sell it for on the Internet. Most bookstores price their inventory according to a formula taught to the employees. Not all bookstores price the same, but a common pricing formula is to charge one half the original retail price. Therefore, books that originally sold for $30 are marked $15, $25 books are marked $12.50 and so on.

Price imperfections occur because bookstore owners simply aren't aware of the value of their books on the Internet. If you scout in used bookstores, chances are you'll walk out with books you can sell for a $10, $20, $50 or more profit. Consequently, don't worry about the high prices you see at used bookstores. If you have enough trade credit you can buy a respectable amount of inventory at a substantial discount because, after applying your credits, the cost of the books is reduced.

Trade Credit

You can reduce the cost of used bookstore purchases by up to 25 percent off the marked prices with trade credits. You build trade credit by trading books you can't sell on the Internet to local bookstores. Generally, credits can be used just like cash for up to 25 percent of the original retail price of the books you buy. Aggressively using trade credit can bring the cost of your books down to 30 percent to 35 percent of retail. At that price level nice profits can be made leveraging price imperfections. A few stores allow you to use trade credit to pay for 100 percent of your purchases. Those terms are usually the best, and you want to treat the people at those locations like royalty.

Don't make the mistake of thinking you can haul useless junk to bookstores and expect them to give you credit to use for valuable books. The trade must be fair for both parties. If the policy of a particular store doesn't allow enough profit margin to trade profitably, find other stores where you can.

There are plenty of books selling for next to nothing on the Internet but that sell for good money in used bookstores. Those types of books are deadwood as far as you're concerned, but to bookstore owners they're money in the bank. During your normal scouting routine you'll pick up plenty of deadwood due to purchasing mistakes. Much of your deadwood can be traded for credits with which you can buy books that sell like hotcakes on the Internet.

A large number of stores specialize in a particular genre or category of books. For example, one store may like military history, other stores prefer children's books, and others want fine art books. Take the trade credit technique a step further and truly maximize the value of your scouting efforts by learning what type of books store owners prefer to carry.

While you're out scouting at your normal haunts, think about the needs of the store where you trade and look for books you know they'll want even though they may be rejected by your scanner. You'll receive a credit equal to 25 percent of retail which you can apply toward the 50 percent off retail store price, making your purchase only 25 percent of retail plus the cost of your books. If you're lucky you'll find a store that allows you to pay for your purchases with 100 percent of your trade credit and no additional cash out of your pocket. Your only cost is the dollar or two you paid for the books you traded.

At one store where I trade the owner normally gives me a 50-percent to 100-percent profit in trade credit on all the books I bring to him because I've gotten so good at picking out books he likes to carry. He gives me a further discount off the marked prices of books I buy and allows me to use 100 percent of my credit to pay for them.

Obviously, I love the arrangement because I get an instant profit on a large number of books that meet his criteria. He loves the arrangement because he gets as many as three of my books for every one of his I take. Trade credits can be a lucrative arrangement for both parties if you can establish a solid relationship with used bookstore owners in your area.

Going Out of Business Sales

Failing bookstores are an unfortunate reality of business. When such a tragic event occurs, the store generally holds a going out of business sale. Typical prices are $1 for paperbacks and $2 for hardcovers. That's just a guideline, and stores in your area may have a different pricing structure altogether.

Always be on the lookout in your local newspaper, booksellers' network groups, and *http://www.booksalefinder.com* for folding businesses. If you get wind of one before it becomes public, try to work out special presale arrangements and negotiate a bulk purchase of their inventory. If you're unable to make such arrangements, you'll want to approach the sale the same way you approach a library sale. Come prepared with the right equipment such as your cart, your supplies, and your wits.

Well-attended going out of business sales are little more than controlled chaos. Don't be surprised to find wall-to-wall people all politely elbowing each other to jockey for the best books. The store is often cramped, with barely enough room to navigate the aisles.

A lot of bookstore owners realize that a large percent of buyers attending the sale are Internet dealers. Thus they've taken a page from library sale organizers and are starting to hold an exclusive presale to those willing to pay a fee prior to the free public sale. Many booksellers grumble about paying a $20 to $100 entrance fee for the privilege of attending the presale of a faltering business. Personally, I welcome the fees, because a hefty entrance fee is an effective barrier to all but the most serious sellers, and that decreases competition.

Going Out of Business Case Study

I went to a local going out of business sale where there were about 50,000 books up for grabs. They had a presale day and charged $20 admission to anyone wanting to attend. Hardcovers were $2 and paperbacks $1. I gladly paid the fee because I knew it would thin the herd quite a bit. To my astonishment there were absolutely no members of the general public at the presale and there were only two, count 'em, TWO other dealers present and only ONE of them had a scanner. I was in book scouter's heaven!

I bought 125 books in about three hours for an average of $1.50 each, which I listed for over $1,500. I say bring on the fees. I would have happily paid $100 for such an opportunity. In fact, I *have* paid $100 just to get into a sale one hour earlier than the general public. That day I bought 75 books worth nearly $1,200 at $1 each in that extra hour. I went on to buy another 40 books over the next two hours after the doors were opened to the general public and the masses descended upon the sale.

Bulk Purchases

Operating a brick and mortar store is a tough business. The vast majority of small mom and pop stores are more a labor of love than a profitable enterprise. For the most part those owners operate their stores because of a deep appreciation for books and for the industry. Smaller stores occasionally experience cash flow problems and could use an infusion of capital.

You can help them by offering to purchase a large quantity of books at a substantially reduced price. Your purchases give them needed liquidity while rapidly increasing your inventory at favorable prices.

This is not the kind of arrangement a store owner is willing to make with just anyone walking in off the street. The relationship must be cultivated with mutual trust and respect.

Financial negotiations are a delicate balance between art and science. Under the right circumstances, people do amazing things to help a friend. Just remember that the benefits go both ways and all parties concerned must be satisfied with the relationship.

Bulk Purchase Case Study

Once I was scanning in a bookstore where this particular owner also lists about 25 percent of his books on the Internet. Therefore, he only offered a 10 percent discount off the marked price of Internet books, and they weren't eligible for purchase using store credit. I had already negotiated a 50-percent store credit on my trades plus a further 20-percent cash discount on non-Internet books, making my effective discount 60 percent.

For example, a book that sells used for $10 is priced at $5. I'd then receive an additional 20 percent discount, or $1, making my cost for the book only $4. He was adamant that his Internet books weren't eligible for further discounts beyond the 10 percent posted at the counter. All Internet books were identified by a special price tag on the spine.

I spent several days scanning his inventory and pulling books that met my scouting criteria. I was the first person who had ever come into his store day after day and bought stacks of books. While I worked I made small talk with him whenever he wasn't busy. I learned where he was from and that he was very proud of his wife and children. He talked to me in surprisingly intimate detail about his business, his customers, his employees, and so on. He turned out to be an interesting guy and I genuinely liked him. He even revealed his overhead expenses and the fact he needed $120 per day in sales to make his rent.

Armed with that information, I made sure I didn't stop scanning each day until I spent at least $100 to $125. After several days he *voluntarily* came to me and whispered in a hushed tone, so other customers wouldn't hear him, "What will it take to get you to buy my Internet books?" I told him I needed to think it over since I'd already determined that the prices on his Internet books were a bit too steep for me to resell profitably.

I returned the next day and gently reminded him of the economics of selling on the Internet. I pointed out he was already paying 15 percent to Amazon and Alibris and when I sold the books that expense would fall onto me. I asked for an additional 20-percent discount to make buying his Internet books mildly profitable for me. He thought about it for about ten minutes, then accepted my offer for a 30-percent cash discount off his Internet books.

I reset my scanner to factor in the additional discounts and I began concentrating on his listed books. Buy signals started popping up with acceptable regularity, and I spent two more days in his store buying books with higher profit margins (and higher purchase prices). I eventually purchased more than 250 books at an average cost of $4. I listed those books for an average sale price of $19 and most of them were sold within eight months.

A week prior to walking into his store I was a complete stranger to this man and his dealings with me were strictly by the book. By being a quantity buyer, paying cash every single day for my purchases, and befriending him, he decided on his own to cut me a better deal to encourage me to increase my volume and, presumably, help him with a temporary cash flow situation.

This was a win/win. He sold more books in a shorter period than he thought he would and I got a nice bump in total inventory. Gaining his friendship and knowing my numbers are what made it happen. I've cemented similar friendships with a number of store owners and now I have exclusive purchasing arrangements with them whenever an infusion of liquidity is needed.

A Few More Words about Professional Contacts

Your most profitable transactions will come from referrals by people you meet in the course of everyday business. That's why it's important to guard your reputation with pit bull tenacity. Treat everyone you meet with dignity and respect. Above all, conduct yourself with the highest level of integrity at all times.

Get to know the people responsible for maintaining the book section of each venue you visit. For example, do you know the names of the Friends of the Library personnel who stock the library shelves at each stop on your route? You should. Do your best to visit when those people are restocking the shelves. Ask their names and chat it up a bit. Tell them what a great job they're doing. Ask how you can best help keep their bookshelf displays looking neat and orderly—and it doesn't hurt to occasionally point out you've straightened things up a bit. That one act alone wins big points for sure.

Who stocks the bookshelves at the thrift stores you frequent? What are their names? Find out and greet them every time you shop. You can even try inviting them to lunch on occasion. Those people can be invaluable for cluing you into changes in pricing policies, stocking schedules, and upcoming sales. This information can give you a competitive advantage over your colleagues when you get it first.

Does this type of networking pay off? You bet it does. There's a certain public library I visited once every two weeks where my personal contacts paid off big time. At this particular location they had a difficult time selling significant numbers of books; at least until I showed up. As it happened, this location was so far out of the way that few booksellers bothered to visit.

On my first trip to this library I was dumbfounded when I snagged 153 books in less than two hours. The library personnel were so excited they even opened up the storage room and let me scan there too. They told me they had a lot of books in their off-site storage facility (somebody's garage) and wanted me to return in a few days to take those off their hands after they'd restocked the shelves. A few days later I returned and bought another 65 books.

I made it a point to visit that location every two weeks like clockwork. I also made sure I always visited on the same day when the library volunteer was there stocking shelves so I could exchange pleasantries with her. I even helped stock the shelves on occasion. Furthermore, I introduced myself to the branch manager. He expressed his gratitude to me for buying so many books. It seems the local community was getting upset with him because they felt their donations weren't being distributed to the public more aggressively and he was under a lot of pressure from his management to move the books out. Given the circumstances, I made my visits regular and productive by buying as many books as possible.

After a year of bi-weekly visits, I received a phone call from the branch manager. One of their procurement employees overbought a batch of *New York Times* bestsellers and the entire county library system was overstocked by several thousand mixed-title books. He asked me if I might be interested in buying any of them. I agreed to meet with him along with a second branch manager to inspect a few sample boxes of books. At the meeting I scanned several boxes and found almost all of them had a sales ranking below 10,000 and most of them had been published within the last 18 months.

Realizing what a bonanza I found, I asked what they wanted for the lot. Incredibly, they only wanted 50¢ per book. I ended up buying nearly 2,000 of their overstocks. Due to the excellent sales ranking, more than 90 percent of them sold within 60 days at prices ranging from $5 to $12 each. Had I not carefully cultivated my relationship with the decision makers in that organization, I'm convinced I would have never received that phone call. Nor would I have been offered such a fantastic buying opportunity.

I have other examples of librarians and used bookstore owners referring me to private collectors. I also have examples of librarians referring me to other library branch managers to cull their overstocks. In each of these instances I've earned thousands of extra dollars in sales I would not have otherwise gotten.

Another group of contacts that should be cultivated are store owners who don't sell books as their primary business. For example, antique stores can be a great source for rare books. Ask them to refer you whenever they meet someone who wants to sell a large number of books. Sit down with a copy of your local yellow pages directory. Go through the directory and make a list of all the various business that are *not* bookstores, but may sell books as a sideline or who may be a good source of referrals.

I've gotten referrals from bookstores, librarians, antique store owners, private individuals, members of networking groups, real estate agents, estate sale organizers, and local eBay sellers, to name a few. How many more can you put on your list?

Advanced Book Sourcing

Up until this point the techniques and sources for books I've shared with you are the same ones I used when I started my business. They worked great for more than three years. The problem was I wanted to grow my business larger than what can be accomplished by one person scouting alone in traditional book sourcing locations.

As my inventory approached 10,000 unique titles I found I was unable to grow further because I was selling nearly as many books each month as I could buy. In a good month I could buy up to 1,800 unique titles. In that same month I would sell 1,500 books. If I was unable to scout at least 20 days out of the month (five days a week), I would actually see a net *decrease* in my inventory. I was stuck at 10,000 titles, give or take a couple of hundred books. What I needed was a way to grow my inventory in greater amounts than what I was selling each month.

What follows are the techniques I used to achieve above average growth for my business. These are advanced strategies that are far beyond the scope of this book. I give them a brief mention to give you an idea of what's possible if you're willing to go the distance. If you are interested in making the "big score," visit *http://www.internetbookselling.com* regularly for news about the publication of my follow-up book *Advanced Internet Bookselling Techniques: How to Take Your Online Bookselling Business to the Next Level,* where I explain in great detail how I used the following methods to grow my business beyond my wildest dreams.

Acquisitions

Buying out another online bookseller is not for beginners. The stakes are high, the risk is great, but the reward is steady monthly income year after year if you can pull it off.

The lead that brought me my first acquisition came from a tiny online classified ad in the "Books for Sale" section at *http://www.booksalefinder.com.* The ad offered 4,300 books for sale that were already listed online. The seller needed to raise cash for personal reasons and wanted a serious buyer. I was looking for something a little bigger than what was in the ad, but I decided to contact the seller anyway because I was curious about the details of the offer.

As it turned out, the seller had a warehouse packed with another 27,000 unsorted books which she agreed to include in the deal for a nominal increase in the sales price. After signing a letter of intent, I hopped on a plane and flew to Ohio where I inspected the books and closed the deal. I shipped nearly 32,000 books back to Arizona and ultimately listed about 8,500 of them. The rest I donated to charity and took a nice tax deduction.

Despite my lack of experience the transaction turned out to be profitable, due more to luck than skill. If I were doing the deal today, I would get a better price and list close to 20,000 books to make the transaction even more profitable. Hindsight is always 20/20.

Nevertheless, my experience with that purchase gave me the knowledge I needed to do large transactions on a regular basis and laid the foundation for even more advanced techniques.

Book Arbitrage

Essentially, an arbitrage is when you buy a commodity in one market and simultaneously sell it in another market, generating a profit in the price difference between the two markets. For example, simultaneously selling a book on Alibris and buying it from Amazon. Arbitrage is a technique most frequently used in the stock market, but I started tinkering with the concept using books as my commodity.

There's no question that price spreads exist between the various marketplaces. If pricing were perfect, arbitrage opportunities wouldn't exist—but rarely does the market remain perfect for long, if at all. Therefore, savvy booksellers occasionally spot bargains where others fail to look.

To play this game effectively, become a subject matter expert in the genre you arbitrage. It's difficult to turn a quick profit if you're unsure of the value of your item. You'll need to know the sales history of the item and you'll need an automated means of initiating the purchase of the target item, once it's been sold on the competing marketplace.

I've had a few nice successes as well as colossal bombs playing with arbitrage. This is definitely not an activity for beginners, but it's there if and when you're ready.

Book Fairs

If you're interested in the antiquarian book market you might want to start attending book fairs held around the country each year. Don't plan to purchase anything during your first couple of visits. Instead, focus on getting to know the key vendors. Inspect their inventory. Learn the history behind the books. You'll find attending the fair is a tremendous experience all by itself.

Your chance of succeeding as an antiquarian bookseller is far greater if you choose one or two genres in which to become an expert. For example, you can specialize in history, science fiction, collectible biographies, or literature. You can be specific in your choice too, such as narrowing your specialty down to American history, mystery writers, French biographies, or British literature. Learn the different points of interest that make the most sought after books in your chosen realm of expertise valuable. Learn where the best places are to find them. Become the go-to guy or gal on the subject.

One good place to start your education is at the annual Antiquarian Book Conference held in Colorado each year. You'll discover a wealth of resources and meet many knowledgeable collectors.

Books Wanted Advertising

As with all advertising you're going to have to spend money, but usually not a lot. The effectiveness of this technique depends on how good of a copywriter you are and the overall availability of books in your area. I've advertised on Craigslist with reasonable results. The types of responses I got were usually college students trying to unload used textbooks—most of which I turned down. I would always have them first eMail me the ISBNs of the books so I could look them up on Amazon and determine their market value. I saved myself quite a bit of running around by insisting on those eMails. If the prospect refused to provide the ISBNs, I simply moved on.

Other places to advertise are your local freebie papers (like *Penny Saver*), supermarket bulletin boards, and the entire range of your local newspapers, although newspapers can be a bit pricey. If I were you, I'd reserve newspaper advertising for higher end collections when you're ready and can afford the expense. This is definitely an advanced technique.

Local Auctions

You may find many valuable books auctioned off for pennies on the dollar at local auction houses. Look in the yellow pages under "Auctions," "Auction Houses," and "Auctioneers." Another good place to look is in your local newspaper under the same categories.

This is a specialized field where good connections with the local auctioneers win out over just showing up. Often the auctioneers have prearranged agreements with buyers to take all the books up for sale before the auction, or to buy all books left over after an auction. It's not often you'll walk in off the street and win a bid for a boatload of great books, but it can and does happen.

Postal Service Auctions

Have you ever had the experience of having a package lost in the mail? There are numerous reasons why packages fail to reach the intended recipient:

- The package bursts open and the contents become separated from the outside address.
- The recipient fails to respond to the notice placed on their door and the post office is unable to return the package to the sender because the return address is illegible.
- The recipient's address is illegible and there's no return address on the package.

No matter what the reason, when a package can't be delivered to the intended recipient the post office has no choice but to auction off the contents to the highest bidder. Auctions are held throughout the year at Mail Recovery Centers located around the country. You never know what is being offered at any given auction. Merchandise can include jewelry, clothing, art, and gift items. Many auctions contain large quantities of books that never reached the intended recipient.

There can be significant expenses involved in participating in postal auctions, especially if you don't happen to live near one of the recovery centers. Bulk books can be purchased at the Atlanta auction, but picked up in St. Paul, Minnesota. If you're not a big player, then multiple air fares, hotels, meals, and rental car expenses can erode potential profits.

Visit *http://www.usps.com/auctions* to get the latest schedule of auctions dates. To be placed on the USPS auction mailing list contact the Mail Recovery Centers below:

Atlanta Mail Recovery Center
5345 Fulton Industrial Boulevard SW
Atlanta, GA 30378-2400

St. Paul Mail Recovery Center
443 Fillmore Avenue East
St. Paul, MN 55107-9607

Don't bother trying to find a phone number or eMail address for either of the Mail Recovery Centers. For whatever reason, they just don't want to be contacted that way. You must send them snail mail and ask to be placed on their list.

Just because you don't live near the Atlanta or St. Paul Mail Recovery Centers doesn't mean you can't participate in auctions. Lost, damaged, or unclaimed goods are sold via auction or sealed bids at respective local district sites. Contact the local postal facility in your area to obtain information on any local or district sales.

Publishers

You can open accounts with the major book publishers and receive discounts of 35 percent to 40 percent off retail. This makes sense if you have your own website and are able to drive a reasonable number of buyers to it at a reasonable cost. However, don't expect to compete with larger third-party sellers or even Amazon itself since those competitors heavily discount their listings and in many cases profitably sell books for less than you can buy them wholesale.

Until you become a large player you won't command the kinds of quantity discounts available to large sellers. Also, you can forget about going head-to-head with Amazon on their own website selling new books because the commissions and fees collected by Amazon automatically puts you at a competitive disadvantage. New book sales are best left to more experienced sellers who are well capitalized or have a niche unrecognized or undesired by larger players.

Remainders

Remainders are books that publishers have in the warehouse that have run their course commercially. They're left over after sales have dropped off and the publisher has moved on to the next project. These left-overs are called "remainders" and they're sold to wholesalers for pennies on the dollar, who then sell them to retailers like us either directly, by mail, or at trade shows. Remainders are identified by a black mark on the bottom or top edge of the book so they can't be returned to publishers for refunds.

I attended my first remainder event at the Atlanta Spring Book Show in March 2007. The Spring Book Show brings together the leading remainder book distributors to showcase their wares and sponsor training sessions on selling remaindered books. I was mesmerized by the seemingly endless aisles of books; tens of thousands of them. I spent three days in classes and a day and a half doing nothing but scanning the inventory of as many vendors as I could. They must have thought I was pretty funny.

Nevertheless, I purchased more than 1,100 books composed of more than 200 unique titles. Despite my inexperience, I recouped my original investment in less than four months and the "remaining" stock pulled in steady sales for eight more months. During that year I refined my purchasing algorithms and developed software to wring maximum value from remainder purchases, all of which is spelled out in my advanced book.

Treasury Department Auctions

The U.S. Treasury Department seizes large quantities of goods from individuals and businesses who've failed to comply with federal tax and licensing requirements. Eventually, those goods are auctioned off to the general public to the highest bidder.

A wide variety of items are sold including cars, boats, airplanes, real estate, electronics, industrial goods, jewelry, computer equipment, apparel, household goods—and books. Items may be new or used and are sold in lots ranging from single items to wholesale quantities.

More than 300 public auctions are held each year. You can listen to a recorded message of upcoming auctions 24-hours a day by calling the Public Auction Line at (703) 273-7373. Customer service representatives are available from 8:00 a.m. to 5:00 p.m. Eastern Time to answer specific questions. For a fee you can also subscribe to a listing service to alert you of pending sales.

For more information visit *http://www.treasury.gov/auctions* to learn how to get specific dates and times of auctions in your area.

Wholesale Distributors

One of the most common questions I'm asked is, "Where can I buy books wholesale?" Beginners think I have a "secret" list of book wholesalers I use to make a fortune on the Internet. In reality, no such list exists. Every book wholesaler and distributor in the country can be found by doing a few simple Google searches.

If you don't believe me, try it for yourself. Logon to *http://www.google.com* and enter the following phrases in the Search box:

> "book wholesalers"
> "book distributors"
> "book wholesalers & distributors"

Come up with a few combinations of your own and you'll find hundreds of thousands of links to people who'll gladly sell you books at wholesale prices. Discounts vary dramatically so you want to compare prices between the various vendors.

Two of the biggest and best distributors are Ingram Book Group and Baker & Taylor. Both vendors supply brick and mortar as well as Internet bookstores with new books, DVDs, and CDs. You can visit Ingram at *http://www.ingrambook .com* and Baker & Taylor at *http://www.btol.com*. Each distributor has a lengthy application process before you can start buying from them. Once you're set up, you'll have access to more than one million band new books.

You can buy *New York Times* bestsellers up to 40 percent off retail. However, only the big players get the best discounts and they actually sell the same books for what you buy them for as a small bookseller. Selling new books on the Internet is definitely a game for advanced sellers.

Build a Solid Foundation of Diamonds

All of the information presented in this chapter may seem a bit overwhelming. Don't sweat it too much, and realize that everything will fall into place in due course. Keep in mind that the business model discussed here is designed to take you from bunting the ball to swinging for the fences in about a year. Be patient and learn how to bunt before trying to score a home run.

What I mean is, collect all the low hanging fruit you can find on a daily basis. Over the course of your day you'll begin to uncover the occasional diamond. Add your diamonds to your inventory and sooner or later they'll sell and shower you with incredible profits. I'm talking about buying books for a dollar or two and selling them for $75, $100, $200 and more. Over time you'll learn how to spot diamonds with more regularity. And you'll find that the value of your inventory grows more from skillful buying than happenstance.

Your high turnover inventory constantly changes, but your diamonds accumulate and slowly sell off, one or two here, one or two there. One day you'll wake up and find that a large percentage of your inventory consists of diamonds that sell with amazing regularity. You'll also discover that your overall average sale price has increased far above the average selling price of your bread-and-butter transactions. That's the magic of building a foundation of diamonds.

CHAPTER 4

How and Where to Sell Books

Internet bookselling is no different than most traditional businesses; you find a need the public is willing to pay for and you fill it. You don't find a product and then try to get people to buy it. The customer comes first in all aspects of your business—first, foremost, and always.

Listing Books

Knowing how and where to buy books is not enough to make a go in this business. To be a successful Internet bookseller, it's essential you learn how to properly list books for sale in the various marketplaces.

You're going to spend a great deal of time listing inventory. Hopefully, you'll develop the habit of listing every single day, even if it's just a few books. Consistently listing on a daily basis smoothes out your sales curve and provides steady income. Don't fall into the feast or famine mode of letting your books accumulate and only listing when you have a stack sitting in the corner, or wherever you keep them.

Describing Your Books

Bookselling comes with its own unique vocabulary that can be complex if you get carried away. In this book I'm only going to discuss the basic terms you need to learn to get your business up and running fast. Getting a firm grasp of bookselling terminology helps you write more accurate and authoritative descriptions of your listings. Accurate and authoritative descriptions boost sales, as you'll see below.

For a more comprehensive glossary of bookselling terminology visit the Independent Online Booksellers Association (IOBA) at *http://www.ioba.org/terms .html*. The IOBA offers a number of benefits for aspiring Internet booksellers, but they're strict about whom they accept into their fold. Take a moment to visit their website for membership information. For the sake of convenience the IOBA has graciously allowed me to reproduce their glossary in the Appendix for easy reference when you're away from your computer.

Each marketplace uses slightly different terminology for describing books. However, the terminology used by the IOBA follows the more traditional approach and should be learned until it's second nature. Amazon implemented its own simplified terminology that loosely follows traditional vernacular. But Amazon's sheer size makes its descriptive style a strong competing standard. For that reason I adopted the practice of using the Amazon terminology with a mixture of traditional terminology where the traditional terms more clearly describe the condition of the book being listed.

The populist terminology used by Amazon sellers appears on the Amazon website at *http://www.amazon.com/gp/help/customer/ display.html?nodeId=1161242* as follows:

- *New:* Unused, unread books direct from the publisher or authorized distributor in perfect condition.

- *Like New:* An apparently unread copy in perfect condition. Dust cover is intact, with no nicks or tears. Spine has no signs of creasing. Pages are clean and are not marred by notes or folds of any kind. Book may contain a remainder mark on an outside edge, but this should be noted in the listing comments uploaded to Amazon's website.

- *Very Good:* A copy that has been read, but remains in excellent condition. Pages are intact and are not marred by notes or highlighting. The spine remains undamaged.

- *Good:* A copy that has been read, but remains in clean condition. All pages are intact, and the cover is intact (including dust cover, if applicable). The spine may show signs of wear. Pages can include limited notes and highlighting, and the copy can include "From the library of" labels.

- *Acceptable:* A readable copy. All pages are intact, and the cover is intact (the dust cover may be missing). Pages can include considerable notes—in pen or highlighter—but the notes cannot obscure the text.

- *Unacceptable:* Moldy, badly stained, or unclean copies are not acceptable, nor are copies with missing pages or obscured text. Books that are distributed for promotional use only are prohibited. This includes advance reading copies (ARCs) and uncorrected proof copies.

Stay away from "Unacceptable" books since you're prohibited from listing them anyway. Meaning, don't be a smarty pants and "upgrade" unacceptable books to "Acceptable" and list them. For that matter, don't waste your time listing books that fall into the "Acceptable" condition either. No matter how well you describe an "Acceptable" book, you're going to receive a disproportionate amount of negative feedback relative to the additional sales obtained from that category. It's simply not worth the hassle, with one exception, which I'll discuss in a moment.

Traditional terminology used by antiquarian booksellers can be found on the IOBA website at *http://www.ioba.org/desc.html*. But to save you a little bit of trouble here it is:

- *As New; Fine; Mint:* Without faults or defects.

- *Near Fine:* A book approaching FINE (or AS NEW or MINT), but with a couple of very minor defects or faults, which must be noted.

  [*NOTE:* From here on, there may be "+ (Plus)" or "– (Minus)" in a grade, which will mean that it is above the grade noted, but not quite to the next higher grade for "+," and that it is below the grade noted, but not quite to the next lower grade for "–", i.e., Very Good + (or Plus)/Very Good – (or Minus). Which means the book is better than Very Good and the dust jacket grade is less than Very Good.]

- *Very Good:* A book showing some signs of wear. Any defects or faults must be noted.

- *Good:* The average used book that is totally complete (as issued) and intact. Any defects must be noted.

- *Fair:* A worn book that has complete text pages (including those with maps or plates), but may lack endpapers, half-title page, etc. Any defects or faults must be noted.

- *Poor; Reading Copy:* A book that is sufficiently worn that its only merit is the complete text, which must be legible. Any missing maps or plates must be noted. May be soiled, scuffed, stained, or spotted, and may have loose joints, hinges, pages, etc.

Again, stay away from books in "Poor" or "Reading Copy" condition. The resulting customer service headaches aren't worth the few extra sales. However, as with everything in life, there are exceptions to the rule.

For example, if you decide to wade into the antiquarian market, there are books so rare the only condition you can find them in is "Poor," or "Reading Copy." The decision on whether to buy and sell them are judgments you'll make after developing the necessary expertise to play in that market. For now, steer clear of items that are less than "Good" or "Fair" quality.

Whichever terminology you adopt, always disclose all defects in your listing descriptions. A complete list of defects can be found in Appendix 1. Common defects include, but are not limited to, ex-library books, remainder marks, book club editions, page tanning, folded page corners, foxing, cover or board dings, dust jacket tears, stains, smudges, a book plate, previous owner signature or inscription, underlining, highlighting, and writing of any kind on the interior pages. In short, anything that detracts from the "newness" of the book should be disclosed. All of the above defects are thoroughly explained in Appendix 1.

Sample Book Descriptions

When you come right down to it, there are as many ways to describe a book as there are booksellers. However, so long as you disclose all known defects and accurately describe any relevant details about the book, you'll be on solid ground.

Sophisticated antiquarian sellers learn the traditional language for book descriptions and use it until it becomes second nature. Sellers of common books adopt the more populist language of Amazon and are perfectly happy.

Below you'll find a few sample listing descriptions that represent various styles of the sellers. Over time you'll develop your own style that reflects the market you serve. Let me caution you not to copy another seller's verbiage and use it as your own. That's cheating, and it's against marketplace rules. If a seller sees listings that are identical to his or her own, that seller has every right to report the offender to the marketplace seller support department. If that happens, you may get your account cancelled, and that puts you out of business.

Practice writing descriptions of various types of books and develop your own way of speaking to your customers. Just be honest in your listings and back up your claims with a solid grasp of book terminology and you'll serve your customers well.

First let's look at a few downright awful book descriptions. I give these descriptions without identifying the seller as an illustration of what I consider bad practices:

Example #1 – Like New: "Some Highlighting, but otherwise perfect condition."

What is "perfect condition" *except* for the highlighting? Go figure, but I would never describe a book in perfect condition with such a major defect staring the customer in the face. A perfect book is *new*. All marketplaces require new books to be unused and unread.

Example #2 – Very Good: "Very good condition, but has some underlining and notes in pencil."

Not quite as egregious as the first example, but it still violates most marketplace policies. While Amazon bars books from being listed as Very Good that have notes or highlighting, the IOBA only says "Any defects or faults must be noted." I suggest you err on the side of caution and not list books with writing of any kind as Very Good. At best they can be listed as "Good," but if the writing or highlighting is extensive (on more than five percent of the pages), they should be listed as "Acceptable," or not at all.

Example #3 – Very Good: "typical used book"

Aside from the lack of punctuation, just how "typical" is "typical"? If the above sentence were followed with more detail, it would be alright. However, this description leaves the customer devoid of any information that helps the buying decision. Honestly, I love sellers who list books this way because they severely reduce their competitiveness.

Although I don't have firm statistics, I can attest to the fact that a respectable percentage of my sales are at prices higher than my competitors—sometimes significantly higher. I attribute those sales primarily to the detailed descriptions I give every one of my books.

Now let's see a couple of good descriptions. Once again, the descriptions appear without identifying the seller:

Example #4 – Good: "The bottom corner is bent or has a small crease on a few pages. A handful of pages have a scraped spot on the bottom edge. The jacket has minor shelf-wear. No writing or underlining."

This example is not bad. Defects are clearly disclosed in reasonable detail. Notice how the average customer isn't confused with technical book jargon. This is an easy description to read and understand for the average person.

Example #5 – Good: "1912 Harcourt Publishers hardcover with no dust jacket, dark green cloth boards, gold foil lettering and artwork. The spine is lightly sunned and board edges are moderately bumped. Interior pages are free from underlining, note-taking, and highlighting."

This is an excellent description. It's always a good idea to insert the publication date and the name of the publisher, especially for pre-ISBN books, because those are typically the ones most collectors want. Having the information readily available saves you the trouble of answering an excessive number of eMails from interested buyers.

Also, notice how defects are clearly disclosed in reasonable detail. There is a bit of technical book jargon, but only where appropriate and only when it is clearly understood. Appendix 1 contains a complete list of technical terms with full explanations. This is how the small bookseller should describe books. If you've already been selling for awhile, go back to older listings and rewrite them to fit this model. If you're just starting out, spare yourself that hassle and develop a clear writing style early in your business so you won't have to do any retrofitting.

A Few Tips and Caveats

Large scale sellers work from a completely different paradigm and such detailed descriptions are not always possible, or even desirable. The inherent difficulty for large scale sellers to consistently match the quality of small bookseller's descriptions give the small seller a competitive advantage in the post-1972 market that can't be matched by size.

The examples I've given above help you leverage the size advantage small sellers enjoy over larger competitors. It's been my experience that better descriptions equate to higher sales. Use your advantage to the maximum extent possible.

Book Research

If you purchase bulk quantities of books at estate sales, yard sales and bag day at book sales, you're going to wind up with a number of books without a barcode or ISBN. These "pre-ISBN" books can be quite valuable and should be properly researched before relegating them to the donation heap. Most pre-ISBN books take considerably longer to sell than post-1972 titles. Many sellers have dubbed slow selling titles "long tail books" as a spin on the title of Chris Anderson's excellent book, *The Long Tail*. I recommend you pick up a copy for yourself. It contains excellent insight on the concept of "selling less of more."[1]

You'll find most of your long tail books by researching pre-ISBN titles, so learning proper research techniques is important. The data uncovered while researching isn't going to necessarily provide definitive information about demand and value. Your research produces raw data about the number of available copies for sale, and how other sellers priced them. It's up to you to turn raw data into useful information.

More market-oriented information can be obtained by consulting a service that provides historic sales data such as that provided on the Alibris website or with eBay's "Completed Items" search screen of closed auctions.

The easiest way to begin your research is with Amazon's "Advanced Search" feature. For some inexplicable reason Amazon has chosen to bury it under a myriad of page links. You can find the feature at *http://www.amazon.com/b/?node=241582011*.

(If the link printed in this book stops working try browsing to Amazon's home page, click "Help" and use the help search box to search for "Advanced Search." Scroll down the results page until you find "Advanced Search, Read More." Click the "Read More" link and you'll magically find yourself at the Advanced Search page. I recommend you bookmark the page because you're going to use it a lot.)

Once you're at the Advanced Search page the only information required to do a thorough search is the author's name, title of the book, the type of binding it has (hardcover, paperback, and so on), followed by "During" under the "Pub. Date" box, and then the year the book was published. This search finds all the website pages (known as "catalog pages"), currently on Amazon that match the parameters of your book.

If you get hits from your search, scroll through the results until you find a catalog page that matches the title, author, and publication date of your book. When multiple catalog pages match your book, choose the one carrying the most listings and use the ASIN (Amazon Standard Identification Number) of that page to list your book and price it accordingly.

If the catalog page or pages returned from the Amazon search don't have any copies of your book listed, use a book search service that scans all the major marketplace venues and Internet bookstores to find books similar to yours. There are quite a few book search services on the Internet from which to choose. My favorite tool is Addall.com, but below you'll find a partial list of the most popular services. A more complete list can be found in the "Resources" area of *http://www.internetbookselling.com*:

- http://www.addall.com
- http://www.bookfinder.com
- http://www.chambal.com

Once you receive the search results from Addall.com, scroll through the pages and find the book or books that match the one you have and price your copy accordingly. Use the "refine search" feature at the bottom of your screen to narrow your results or to sort results a number of different ways. If the Amazon Advanced Search feature and the Addall.com search fail to produce any matching results try one or two other book search services.

If you still come up empty-handed, then you may have just hit the jackpot because it might mean there are no other copies of your book available for sale anywhere on the Internet and your book has the potential to be quite valuable. However, more research is required before you begin celebrating.

Your next step is to Google the title and author and read what others have written about it. You may find the book in plentiful supply on several private websites even though none are listed on the major marketplaces. That has happened to me a number of times. If that's the case your best option is to select a price that represents the median of the available copies. This is to strike a balance between maximizing profit and ensuring the book sells in a reasonable amount of time. Then list your copy as you normally would using the price derived from the Google search.

Googling a title can provide additional insight into how popular it is with collectors and researchers. Lots of mentions about the book, or many references to it in professional or scholarly publications may also be an indicator of value.

If there are no copies for sale on private websites, carefully read any "buzz" you find on the Internet using Google searches. You may get a few hints about the value of your book from articles and blog posts. Before assigning a price, take a closer look at the "points" (see below) of your book to further determine its value.

Although I've said that antiquarian book collecting is beyond the scope of this book, it's inevitable that you'll occasionally run across books that are more valuable than most post-1972 titles. To help prepare you for that eventuality I'll briefly discuss what to look for. However, I strongly encourage you to buy the references mentioned throughout this book, in the Appendix, and on my website for in-depth treatment of the subject.

Issue Points

Understanding issue points for a particular book can mean the difference between getting stuck with a penny book and picking up an extremely valuable book for a song. Bill McBride defines issue points this way in his handy guide, *Points of Issue*:

> "A *point of issue* occurs when a change is made in a book during the production of the first printing of the first edition without that change being noted as a change elsewhere in the book. Thus, some copies of the first printing exist without the change and some with it."[2]

Most collectors want to buy books as close to the original first *edition*, first *printing*, and first *state* as possible. In simpler terms, issue points help collectors identify books that are in the original condition when they were first published.

Therefore, knowing the issue points of collectible books is critical to identifying the most valuable books in your market.

Since this book doesn't address collectibles, you'll want to pick up a few reference books on the topic. Bill McBride's handy reference guide fits nicely in a shirt pocket or purse.

Identifying First Editions

Quite often the edition of a book can greatly increase its value. Usually the first edition, first printing of a collectable book holds the greatest value because it's the edition closest to the author's original work. "First, firsts" are often printed in limited quantities, making them scarce and hard to find in excellent condition. For example, first editions, first printings of Ernest Hemingway and J. K. Rowling are highly coveted and valuable.

Identifying first editions can be tricky. There are almost as many ways to identify first editions as there are publishers who produce the books. The easiest way is to check the copyright page and see if it's a "stated" first edition, because it actually states "First Edition." Sometimes it'll state "First Edition. First Printing." That makes it easy. Should all of life be so simple.

But all of life isn't quite so simple, and the most common way publishers use to identify a first edition is to use a number line. The number line is a string of numbers that help identify the edition of a book that has multiple editions. Most number lines look like this:

10 9 8 7 6 5 4 3 2 1

The number one at the end of the number line indicates the book is a first edition, but not necessarily a first printing. The rest of the numbers will be used in the future to identify the current edition of the book.

Publishers often do multiple print runs without changing the number line because the contents of the book remain unchanged. In many cases the publisher adds something like "4th Printing" or "4th Printing, 2003" on the copyright page even though the number line stays the same. That's why you see long lists of printings with different years after each printing number, and those numbers can top 100 if you're looking at a runaway bestseller.

Once a revised edition is produced the only indication given that you're holding a second edition is that the number one is missing from the number line and it'll look like this:

10 9 8 7 6 5 4 3 2

The two, then three, and so on are erased when subsequent editions are published. Sometimes, for each lower number that's erased from the right of the number line, the next consecutive higher number is added to the far left of the line to identify future editions. For example:

11 10 9 8 7 6 5 4 3 2

Sound confusing? Oftentimes it is. The older the book the more frequently you find that it uses a cryptic identification method, or it may not have any indication of which edition it is at all. In that case you rely on the publication date or a first edition reference book like *Zempel and Verkler, First Editions* to tell you if your copy of Adam Smith's economic treatise is a first.

Go further back in history and many books don't even have a publication date! Now those can be a real pain in the posterior to research. For undated books, learn the points of issue of the title to accurately determine its age. Otherwise, you're forced to list undated books with terms like "No Date", "n.d.", "ca 1850", or "cir 1850" as an approximate date.

Finally, knowing who the main reprint publishers were around the time the book was produced can help determine if it's a first edition. For example, if a book is published by A.L. Burt, or Dover, it's unlikely to be a first.

There are entire books written specifically to help book collectors identify first editions. I've already mentioned *Zempel and Verkler*, but also read *American First Editions*, by Merle Johnson and *First Printings of American Authors*, by Mathew J. Bruccoli.

Inspecting Your Books

After spending the day scouting you'll take your books home for inspection and listing. The first thing to do is find a comfortable chair and arrange six boxes on the floor in front of you. We'll call them your receiving boxes because they'll receive the inspected books when you're done with them. Label each box for a specific condition of book:

1. New.
2. Like New.
3. Very Good.
4. Good.
5. Ex-Library.
6. Writing (books with note taking, underlining, or highlighting).

Next, to help you with the listing process, you'll need an assortment of the small-sized Post-Its on which to write notes about defects. For example, I write the letter "C" to indicate a cocked spine. I'll write "Sig" to indicate a previous owner signature, or the letter "T" to identify page tanning.

For a comprehensive list of "Book Defect Notes," go to the "Resources" area of my website for an up-to-date copy of my list. The website is free, and contains many useful hints and suggestions for running your business.

Begin your inspection by sorting books by size and stacking them on your work table or desk. Tackle the largest books first so you can place them in the bottom of your receiving box for easy stacking after they've been inspected. List larger books that don't fit a Priority Mail envelope together as a group for easy shelving. When you're ready to start listing, use the following steps to inspect each one of your books:

Step 1: Fan through each page of the book looking for writing of any kind, including note-taking, underlining, or highlighting on the interior pages. If anything is found, you immediately know the book goes into the "Writing" box and that the best condition you can possibly give it is "Good."

Step 2: Fan through the book a second time looking for water stains or pages that look like they've ever been wet, or have severely damaged corners, dirt, smudges, or any other kind of damage beyond normal wear-and-tear you'd find on a typical used book. If anything is found, go through your supply of Post-It Notes and stick the appropriate one on the front of the book for each defect. As you get better at inspecting books steps 1 and 2 can be combined.

Step 3: Next look at each individual page of the first five pages for a previous owner name, signature, inscription, address label, name plate, autograph, or other identifying marks. Check the last few pages of the book too. If anything is found, place the appropriate Post-It Note on the front of the book.

Step 4: Now examine the edges of the book for writing (including rubber stamps), stains, and smudges. If anything is found, place the appropriate Post-It Note on the front of the book for each defect found.

Step 5: Finally, examine the dust jacket or covers (front and back) for tears, fading, stains, writing, or any other kind of damage beyond normal wear-and-tear for a used book. If anything is found, place the appropriate Post-It Note on the front of the book for each defect.

Step 6: Ex-Library books have the term "DISCARDED," "WITHDRAWN" or other identifying marks, such as the library name stamped on the edges and interior pages. Often, there's a check-out pocket glued to the inside back of one of the boards. Sometimes the pocket is removed leaving tell-tale damage to the back endpaper or the inside back of the top or bottom boards or cover. Ex-Library books should always be placed in the "Ex-Library" box with all its defects identified with Post-It Notes.

Step 7: After all defects have been identified, decide in which of the six boxes it should be placed. Please see the "Describing Your Books" section for guidance on making this determination.

As you examine each book you may find you're putting a lot of Post-It Notes on one with many defects. If that happens you might want to reconsider listing that book unless it's extremely rare and buyers are willing to pay top dollar despite the awful condition. Otherwise, chuck it and move on.

Before continuing, I'd like to elaborate on listing books and digital media as "New." It's dishonest to list anything as "New" unless it actually is. Don't be a wise guy and think you can list books as new that were bought from a thrift store. Merchandise that can rightfully be listed as new comes from distributors, wholesalers, retail stores that sell new books, or straight from publishers.

You can list as "New" books, DVDs, CDs, and VHS tapes that have been purchased from thrifts and other places, if the item is still in its original shrink wrap and unused. Otherwise, you're defrauding your buyer.

Improperly listing items is sure to generate negative feedback. You'll also be forced to refund an excessive number of orders and, hopefully, you'll get your account closed by the marketplaces.

One final point I want to make is that many buyers decide whether to continue doing business on certain venues based on their purchasing experiences with third-party sellers. Improperly grading and describing books can result in unhappy customers who don't return, hurting the marketplace and all third-party sellers. Consumer fraud is serious business, so please keep your operation above board.

You won't be allowed to list certain books on Amazon under any circumstances, such as an "Advance Reading Copy" (ARC) or "Uncorrected Proof" titles. These books are sent to book reviewers and editors prior to publication to generate "buzz" about the author and are not intended for resale. Critics review the books and donate them to charity when they're done, and that's how they end up in your hands. You'll often buy them without even knowing you purchased an ARC or Uncorrected Proof, because you didn't see the warning notice printed on the cover.

Having said that, a couple of marketplaces actually allow you to sell ARCs and Uncorrected Proofs, but if you sell them on Amazon they'll close your account. If you handle them at all, be careful you don't sell them on venues where they're prohibited. I hesitate to name any venues that allow them because policies change all the time. It's best if you check with the marketplace venues you use to confirm that it's okay.

Amazon also prohibits third-party sellers from listing books originating in countries outside the United States as "New." The reason Amazon gives is:

> "Media products originating from other countries that are sold on our international sites are generally ineligible for selling on the Amazon.com site in 'New' condition. These restrictions help to distinguish products that are subject to copyright restrictions and likely limited to distribution in native markets."[3]

For example, if you live in the United States and you try to list a book published in Great Britain on Amazon.com with a condition of "New," Amazon blocks your listing. However, you are allowed to sell it as a used book. You can also sell it as a new book on Amazon.co.uk as long as you have an international account.

These restrictions are good examples of why it's so important to sell on multiple marketplace venues. In all three examples cited above, those books are eligible for resale on other marketplaces, so it doesn't hurt to buy those kinds of titles when you find them in the field.

Preparing to List

Once the inspection process is complete, organizing your books into groups of like condition helps to speed up listing them online. I've had sellers tell me they tripled their listing speed using this method.

Decide on which of the six boxes of books to list first; "New," "Like New," "Very Good," "Good," "Ex-Library," or books with writing. Let's start with "Good," since you'll most likely have more of these types of books than any other. You can have one box, or you may have a dozen boxes. It doesn't matter. What matters is that all the books be in "Good" condition. You'll need a desk or work table in close proximity to your listing computer for easy handling of the books.

The next thing you do is create three rows of books with two stacks in each row on your desk or work table. On the first row place all books with dust jackets that have no defects beyond normal wear and tear for a used book in a stack on the right. In the stack on the left place all books with dust jackets that have one or more Post-It Notes. These are the books with one or more defects that must be disclosed.

Now do the same thing with books with no dust jackets, except you'll place those two stacks of books on the second row. The right stack is for books with no defects beyond your standard "no dust jacket" category. And the stack on the left is for books with additional defects that must be disclosed.

Finally, arrange your paperback books in the same manner, except your two stacks are on the third row. Books with no defects go on the right and books with one or more defects on the left. Keep stacking them up until you either run out of books or workspace.

One final bit of organizing I do is to group barcoded books, ISBN-only books, and pre-ISBN books together within the stacks. Grouping your books this way helps to get them online in the minimum time possible. Now you're ready to list.

Here are my books, neatly organized and ready to list. Barcoded books are separated from ISBN-only and research books. You can further segregate by hardcover and paperback. Grouping your books speeds up the listing process.

Putting Books Online

You want to enter your inventory as quickly and efficiently as possible. One way to speed things along is to purchase an inexpensive hand-held scanner that attaches to your computer through a standard USB connection. Simply scan the barcode found on the back of most books to instantly populate the data entry form of your inventory management system software.

Having an industrial-strength inventory management software program gives you a distinct competitive advantage over sellers who don't have one. Computerizing your inventory allows quick and easy data entry for listing new books online by pulling all the basic information needed for the listing such as the ISBN, title, current price, and weight from one of the marketplaces. All you supply is the condition and description of the book.

Most inventory management software allows you to store a series of basic descriptions from which to pick and choose. You'll want to select the description that fits the book you're currently listing and customize it with the specific defects, if any, of the book in hand. Customizing the description can involve anything from cobbling together a series of one-liners, to as easy as selecting from a group of canned descriptions containing the exact list of defects in your book.

Here are several basic book descriptions I use when there are no significant defects to disclose. It simply describes normal wear-and-tear most buyers expect to find when purchasing a used book. In reality, the descriptions are a bit harsher than the quality of the actual books I sell. Therefore, buyers are pleasantly surprised to discover a better product than anticipated when it arrives. This strategy probably costs me a few sales, but it does wonders for feedback. Having excellent feedback results in additional sales, so overall I consider it a wash.

GOOD – Clean

"Hardcover with moderate shelf-wear, rubbing, fraying, tears, fading, chipping, and bumping to dust jacket cover, board edges, corners, and spine. Binding is tight and square. Interior pages are free from underlining, note taking, and/or highlighting. Book is in stock and ready to ship same or next business day. Select Expedited shipping and receive your book within 3–5 business days. Buy with confidence! Please leave feedback after your purchase. It helps other buyers know we are a responsible and reliable seller. Thank you!"

VERY GOOD – Clean

"Hardcover with clean dust jacket and minor shelf-wear on edges and corners. Binding is tight and square. Interior pages are clean and free from writing and/or highlighting. Book is in stock and ready to ship same or next business day. Select Expedited shipping and receive your book within 3–5 business days. Buy with confidence! Please leave feedback after your purchase. It helps other buyers know we are a responsible and reliable seller. Thank you!"

NEW

"New item that's in stock and ready to ship same or next business day. Select Expedited shipping and receive your book within 3–5 business days. Buy with confidence! Please leave feedback after your purchase. It helps other buyers know we are a responsible and reliable seller. Thank you!"

Here are a few one-liners I use to build book descriptions from scratch. All I do is cut and paste the description into one of the basic descriptions shown above for each defect shown on the Post-It Notes attached to the book.

Curled Front Cover: The front cover is curled from the book being read.

Edge Writing: There is writing on one or more edges of the book.

Remainder Mark: There is a remainder mark on the edge of the book.

Signature: There is a signature, name plate, rubber stamp, or inscription from the previous owner written in the book.

Tanned: The interior pages have tanned with age.

The one-liners are stored in a file on my computer, organized in alphabetical order. The bold text tells you what defect is being described. After a little practice, it's easy to find the wording needed to custom describe any book you list online in less than a minute.

Pricing Made Easy

The method of Internet bookselling described in this book is tailored toward post-1972 books. That's a far cry from antiquarian book collecting where an entire range of factors influence the value of books such as rarity, condition, scarcity, points, whether the book is flat-signed or inscribed (a flat-signed book is the author signature only with no inscription to the recipient), edition, printing, value, and so on.

In *Among The Gently Mad,* Nicholas A. Basbanes says of the complexities of assigning value to antiquarian books, "Easily the most frequently used, and therefore the most frequently misused words in book collecting are *rarity, scarcity,* and *value.*"[4]

For the business model suggested in this book, pricing is relatively straight-forward. Post-1972 books are plentiful and easy to price since market prices are already established. You know the price range because your scanner wouldn't have identified the pick as a salable item if it hadn't first met your scouting criteria. How you actually price your books during the listing process depends on where you want your books to land on the pricing continuum in conjunction with your overall perception of the market in general, and how fast you think the book may sell.

Frequently, you'll be advised by some authors and inexperienced sellers to beat competitor listings by a penny. Only the desperate and the foolish follow that policy. It's a sure way to get involved in a "race to the bottom" as your competition tries to beat your lowest price by a penny and trigger a vicious bidding war.

For example, let's assume you scanned a copy of *Modern Political Thought: Readings from Machiavelli to Nietzsche,* by David Wootton. At the time of this writing the lowest price for the book in Good condition listed on Amazon is $17 with a sales ranking of 65,000. Thinking you want to capture the next sale you list your copy for $16.99 to undercut the competition. The problem is the competition is thinking the same thing, and using his or her automatic repricer, responds by immediately undercutting your price by a penny and relists the book at $16.98. Not to be undersold, your repricer now relists your copy for $16.97, and the race is on!

Generally, the same holds true when matching the lowest price book in the same condition because half the time a less savvy beginner undercuts you even though you don't play the game. Let's say instead of beating the competition by a penny you simply match prices. Yet the competition sees your price match and still undercuts you by a penny. You see the lower price and match it again, and again, and again. This madness goes back and forth until the price of the book drops to a penny and neither one of you make any money. I ask you, just how dumb is that strategy?

Avoid Price Wars

I suggest a more sensible, not to mention far more profitable, pricing strategy. Instead of matching or beating the lowest price in the same condition as your book, try pricing a penny below the second lowest price in the same condition as your book. Let's see how that works.

Take the David Wootton book example from above and price it according to the new pricing rules. The lowest priced book in the same condition is $17 (as of today's writing). The next higher price is $25.95, so to avoid the race to the bottom you price your book at $25.94.

If you closely monitor your sales history you'll discover your higher priced listings often sell before your lower priced competitors, if you consistently write excellent book descriptions and have above average feedback. *Many buyers pay more for properly described books because of the increased confidence in the integrity of the seller who takes the time to give an accurate and detailed description, as well as demonstrates a proven track record with plenty of excellent feedback.*

Another approach is to list your book at the average of the three lowest prices. Using an average price forces you to rely on the strength of your listing description and excellent feedback. If a book sits on your shelf too long you can always lower the price to make it move.

Where to Sell Your Books

Now that you know how and where to buy books, you need to know how and where to sell them for a profit. Does this mean learning Internet coding languages like HTML, Java, and PHP to develop a website, and then market your site to find customers? No. Fortunately, it's easier than that.

You'll sell your books on Internet marketplaces. Essentially, the big Internet players have already built the websites and do all the marketing. All you do is supply the product as an independent third-party bookseller and ship the order when it sells.

There are a couple of dozen marketplace venues worth noting. Most list all media categories such as books, DVDs, CDs, and VHS tapes while others specialize in just books, games, or software. As your inventory grows, get it listed on as many venues as possible to generate sales from many different markets. Don't make the mistake of building your business so it's locked-in to just one marketplace.

The following is a list of the biggest marketplaces available to third-party sellers. I don't list fees because they are subject to change so frequently it's best you logon to the marketplace website for their most current pricing.

AbeBooks.com

Founded in 1995 by two couples from Victoria, British Columbia, AbeBooks specializes in books and doesn't accept listings for other types of media. "Abe" stands for Advanced Book Exchange and the marketplace is usually referred to as ABE on the blogs.

AbeBooks was acquired by Amazon in 2008, but is independently operated as a wholly owned subsidiary. They have headquarters in Victoria, British Columbia, Canada with offices in Dusseldorf, Germany. AbeBooks reports having more than 110 million new, used, rare, and out-of-print books offered for sale through their marketplace by "thousands" of third-party sellers.

Website: *http://www.abebooks.com*

Alibris.com

Launched in November 1998, Alibris has grown into one of the largest independently owned and operated marketplaces. It also claims to be the first successful online bookseller service. Initially, Alibris (first named Interloc) was available to professional booksellers only. As the Internet bloomed into an economic power-house, Alibris was born and opened its doors to third-party sellers.

With claims of more than 100 million used, new, and out-of-print books offered to consumers, libraries, and retailers, Alibris has become an important part of the selling strategy of serious Internet booksellers. They also claim to host thousands of independent sellers worldwide. In addition to a monthly fee, expect to pay a percentage of each sale.

Website: *http://www.alibris.com*

Amazon.com

Clearly recognized as the leading marketplace venue in the world, third-party sellers can expect 50 to 80 percent of their sales revenue from Amazon-generated traffic. Based in Seattle, Washington, Amazon opened its doors to the public in July 1995 and refers to itself as having "Earth's Biggest Selection." In fact, you can sell just about anything on Amazon.

Amazon has affiliate websites around the globe including *http://www.amazon .co.uk* (United Kingdom), *http://www.amazon.de* (Germany), *http://www.amazon .co.jp* (Japan), *http://www.amazon.fr* (France), and *http://www.amazon.ca* (Canada). Basic accounts don't pay a monthly fee, but they do pay a flat "per book" charge for each item sold, a closing fee, plus a percentage of the sale price in commissions. ProMerchant accounts pay a monthly fee, a closing fee, and a percentage of each sale in commissions, but no flat per book charge per sale.

I could spend a lot of time discussing the advantages and disadvantages of selling on Amazon, but I won't for the simple fact that Amazon owns the lion's share of the Internet bookselling space and to make decent money, you simply must be an Amazon Pro Merchant—period. For maximum sales potential, Amazon is the best possible place to focus your bookselling business.

Website: *http://www.amazon.com*

AntiqBook

This site is based in the Netherlands and caters to the European antiquarian market. Even though the antiquarian market is small, AntiqBook supports about 900 sellers representing more than 9.5 million books. It'll take time before you're ready for the antiquarian market, especially the international antiquarian market. However, I included Antiqbook anyway for reference purposes.

Their system offers third-party sellers two different payment options. Your first choice is to pay a modest tiered monthly fee based on your number of active listings. Your second choice is to pay 15-percent commission on each sale. Please see their website for complete details.

Website: *http://www.antiqbook.com*

Barnes & Noble

Barnes & Noble has been flirting with third-party booksellers for a long time. It appears they've gotten serious about competing head-to-head with Amazon and developed a first class website. Third-party books can be accessed by clicking a text link from the B&N catalog page.

To become an Authorized Seller on the B&N website you submit an application to be approved by the Seller Relations team. Check their website for current fees.

Website: *http://www.barnesandnoble.com*

Biblio

Small but effective, Biblio is where discriminating buyers and sellers go for used, rare, and out-of-print books and textbooks. The Biblio folks estimate more than 50 million books are listed on their website offered by more than 5,500 small Internet booksellers. Located in Asheville, North Carolina, Biblio charges low fees and makes third-party seller support a top priority.

Website: *http://www.biblio.com*

Bibliophile Bookbase

Customers contact independent sellers through Bibliophile Bookbase for availability, postage, and payment options of listed items. This Switzerland-based marketplace went online in 1999 as a multi-lingual, multi-dealer book listing service. At last report it offers more than four million items for sale. Presently, there are no fees for listing your inventory although that can change in the future.

Website: *http://www.bibliophile.net*

ChooseBooks

Presently supporting more than 10,000 small Internet booksellers, ChooseBooks is reputed to have more than seven million used, rare, antiquarian, and out-of-print items listed for sale on their site "from both sides of the Atlantic."[5] ChooseBooks.com merged with ZVAB to establish an international bookselling site with Spanish, German, French, English, and other language books.

You can have them process your credit card payments, or you can process your own. If they do the processing there are additional fees. There is no monthly fee to sell on ChooseBooks, and the per sale commission is reasonable. Check their website for current rates.

Website: *http://www.choosebooks.com*

eBay

The granddaddy of eCommerce websites, eBay boasts more Internet traffic than any other marketplace. The folks at eBay state it succinctly on their website where they say:

> "With a presence in 39 markets, including the U.S., and approximately 84 million active users worldwide, eBay has changed the face of Internet commerce. In 2007, the total value of sold items on eBay's trading platforms was nearly $60 billion. This means that eBay users worldwide trade more than $1,900 worth of goods on the site every second."[6]

The eBay website offers a number of different selling formats that are so different from one another they're discussed separately below. If you become an eBayer choose the format that best suits the needs of your business. Each format has its own set of fees and rules so carefully consult eBay's website for complete information.

Website: *http://www.ebay.com*

eBay Auctions

Having the reputation as the world's largest online auction marketplace is eBay's claim to fame. You pay an upfront fee to list your items for a set time limit. Potential buyers bid up the price right up to the moment the auction expires and the sale is awarded to the highest bidder. If there are no bidders you can opt to relist the item for another fee and start the process over again. You may also feature a "Buy It Now" price as part of your auction for quick sales or for listing multiple quantities of the same item.

In general, selling individual books is not a good idea. Often, an eBay auction is a better venue for selling bulk lots of books that don't sell well on bookselling marketplace sites, or selling collections of books all of a certain category, such as by author, genre, or other unique aspect that makes the collection valuable.

However, there are exceptions to every rule. Individual pre-ISBN collectible books do quite well through eBay auctions. I suspect that's true because they benefit from a more detailed description, multiple photographs, and the ability to use targeted keywords in the listing title.

eBay Classified Ads

With so much visitor traffic it makes sense eBay would attempt to extend its revenue base by offering classified ads to sellers. You're able to connect with many interested buyers and not just the highest bidder for your inventory. You choose which supported categories will carry your ad, which you can optionally renew every 30 days until cancelled or the item is sold.

Buyers work directly with sellers. Links from classified ads to seller websites are permissible. Potential buyers incur no obligation by contacting sellers.

eBay Fixed Price Listings

This format lists your items at a set price for immediate purchase and bypasses the bidding process entirely. There are actually two Fixed Price formats: 1) "Buy It Now" Fixed Price listing with no bidding allowed, but with the additional option of including a "Best Offer" link to allow buyers to negotiate their own price, and 2) "Auction-Style Buy It Now" letting buyers choose to make an immediate purchase or compete in the auction listing.

eBay Stores

You can list all your items for sale in a central shopping destination with a flexible and customizable eBay Store. Your store can also use the "Best Offer" and "Store Inventory" features to generate additional traffic and increase sales of your items. Store merchandise appears in the main search results when there are 30 or fewer Auction-style and Fixed Price results.

eCampus

The mission for the folks at eCampus.com is to be the "fastest and most convenient"[7] way for college students to get textbooks. They also allow students and professional independent booksellers to sell textbooks. The website was born in 1999 and continues to set standards in the textbook marketplace. There are no start-up fees, and no per-listing fees for third-party sellers. Instead, you pay a small commission on each sale.

Website: *http://www.ecampus.com*

Gemm

If you sell a lot of vinyl records, LPs, CDs, VHS, cassette tapes, and DVDs, then get connected with Gemm. They claim to host more than 30 million items offered by "1,000s of Sellers Worldwide."[8] If they don't have a category for what you're selling you can eMail them and request that a new category be added to the website. Presently, there are no listing fees or monthly fees, but there's a sliding scale commission fee schedule for sold items.

Website: *http://www.gemm.com*

Half.com

The formidable Half.com was once considered a contender to rival Amazon and was bought by eBay for (as rumor has it) just that purpose. However, it seems eBay's heart wasn't into the effort and promptly announced plans to shut the site down and absorb the seller base into their auction market.

Thanks to a deafening outcry by sellers and threats of mass defection to competing marketplaces, eBay thought twice about dispensing with Half.com and reversed itself. Today, Half.com remains free of monthly fees and maintains a modest commission fee structure on closed sales, which makes it a great place to sell.

Website: *http://www.half.ebay.com*

Play.com

Best known as a gaming and entertainment website, Play.com has grown into a full-fledged eCommerce marketplace where you can sell books, electronics, computers, and many other items. Independent sellers are called "PlayTraders" and can set up one of two types of accounts.

The basic account has no monthly fee, but each sale comes with a transaction fee. The pro account comes with a monthly fee, but no transaction fee. Each type of account is charged a percentage commission on each sale. There are additional fees if you want your revenue electronically transferred to your bank account.

Website: *http://www.play.com*

TextbooksRus

This is another website that specializes in buying and selling textbooks by students and professional booksellers alike. There are no monthly fees or per book fee on sales. There is only a straightforward commission on gross sales—very simple indeed.

Although billed as a textbook website you can list any type of book for sale. Students do read more than just texts (much to the chagrin of their parents I'm sure). The simple fee structure makes this website a great place to start your business also.

Website: *http://www.textbooksRus.com*

TextbookX

In addition to textbooks, you can list other books, games, and movies on this website too. Your inventory is listed right alongside all new and used items, giving your listings exposure to a large number of potential customers.

Your seller account membership is free and there are no listing or monthly fees when posting your items for sale to millions of buyers. However, there is a per book fee plus a sales commission on each sale.

Website: *http://www.textbookx.com*

TomFolio

TomFolio.com describes itself on its website as a provider of "used and rare books, periodicals, and paper ephemera," comprised of "an international co-op of independent dealers."[9] Member companies can actually purchase a voting share of stock in the co-op and help shape the direction of the organization.

The co-op is operated by ABookCoOp (catchy name, huh?), established in 1999 in Wisconsin by a small group of independent booksellers. The bylaws of the co-op state that membership is limited to retail businesses that maintain their own physical inventory.

In correspondence with a representative of ABookCoOp I was told that the stipulation that sellers maintain their own inventory was not to be interpreted as requiring that they operate a brick and mortar retail store. The purpose of the restriction is to discourage drop-shippers from joining. Drop-shippers are sellers who don't actually stock the books they advertise. They simply mark-up the listings of other sellers and "drop" orders in their laps for shipping when a sale occurs. The practice of drop-shipping is generally frowned upon by most marketplaces.

Website: *http://www.tomfolio.com*

ValoreBooks

The folks at ValoreBooks.com claim on their website to be the #1 marketplace for students to buy books from more than 10,000 small Internet booksellers with more than 100 million books listed. Professional booksellers and students alike can buy and sell textbooks on the site.

Although the site is textbook-centric, it does advertise the ability to buy "best-sellers" and a quick check of the website indicates just about any kind of book with an ISBN can be bought and sold.

Website: *http://www.valorebooks.com*

Your Own Website

In the future you may want to consider creating your own website. It's not a project for the beginning bookseller and is best left until after you have at least a year of experience under your belt. However, when the time is right you can sell directly to buyers and avoid up to 18 percent in marketplace commissions on sales.

Don't get me wrong, I'm not against the marketplaces charging commissions on sales. They certainly earn those commissions by providing a market for your inventory. You'll understand what I mean when you bear the cost of marketing and driving traffic to your own website. Actually, you can get along perfectly well without your own website, especially if you have no plans to grow into a large business.

If you insist on going it alone, the easiest way is to rent a template from one of the services that provide bookseller websites. They're relatively easy to setup and the monthly maintenance fees are reasonable.

Chrislands

You can get a professionally designed website template from Chrislands that includes an integrated shopping cart. They host and maintain the site, provide all the required software, and perform the integration of your Amazon inventory into your independent website bookstore. You also get a choice of customer payment methods including PayPal or credit cards if you have a merchant account. All you do is customize the site with the "look and feel" you desire and promote the site.

Chrislands is actually owned by AbeBooks (and ostensibly by Amazon) and can therefore boast of tight integration with the FillZ inventory management software system.

Website: *http://www.chrislands.com*

White Oak Books

Originally a travel agency called White Oak Travel Services, it eventually morphed into White Oak Books (WOB) and became an Internet website provider for booksellers. Their templates offer a number of unique feature functions to make website creation easy. The setup fees are among the lowest and the monthly maintenance fee is quite reasonable.

White Oak Books uses Amazon payments to process orders and incur Amazon fees whenever you make a sale. Those fees are mitigated a little by affiliate commissions you earn from Amazon for sending payment processing business their way.

Website: *http://www.whiteoakbooks.com*

Yahoo! Stores

While a bit pricier and more complex to set up, Yahoo! Merchant Solutions offers a more sophisticated approach to creating your website for the more ambitious. Easy site design, integrated shopping cart, a marketing component, product promotion, payment processing, inventory management, reports and statistics, web hosting, and offline application integration are just a few of the perks available.

Website: *http://smallbusiness.yahoo.com/ecommerce*

The Importance of Multi-Venue Listings

From the beginning, plan to list your inventory on multiple marketplace venues. Initially, I listened to bad advice and set my business up with Amazon as my only marketplace. The software I chose focused on Amazon as my only access to customers. It's true that Amazon provides the lion's share of sales, but it's a huge mistake to put all your eggs in one basket.

Listing your inventory with multiple marketplaces provides a number of benefits that are just too important to ignore. For example:

- Listing your inventory on the next two largest venues after Amazon increases your revenue 10 to 20 percent due to the increased exposure.

- You diversify your market risk by having multiple portals to customers should you lose one of your accounts (it happens!).

- Some items, such as higher priced antiquarian books sell faster and for higher prices on venues that specialize in the antiquarian market.

For all the above reasons and more, plan to maximize your marketplace exposure by working with as many venues as you can handle. The above reasons are also why a number of popular inventory management software programs did not make the list discussed in "Tools of the Trade." In the end, the conversion headaches from migrating from a single venue product to a multi-venue product just aren't worth the effort.

Where to List Your Books First

The reality of Internet bookselling is that Amazon is the 800-pound gorilla on the block. If you don't sell on Amazon you aren't a player, unless you specialize in the high-end antiquarian market. Expensive collectibles have a market all their own. I assume you're a typical small independent bookseller. Therefore, the first place to list your books is on Amazon as a ProMerchant seller.

Currently, you'll pay $39.99 per month to be a ProMerchant, but it's well worth the money. Many beginners opt to sign up for Amazon's basic account, which doesn't carry the monthly fee. What they fail to realize is that with the basic account, you pay an additional $1 per book for each sale as a processing fee, on top of all the other fees.

If you're selling less than 40 books per month you can save a little money. However, selling fewer than 40 books every 30 days is a hobby, not a business. If you're looking for a hobby, you're reading the wrong book. If you want a profit-making business, then take my advice and immediately establish your ProMerchant account, and bypass the hassle of converting later on.

After signing up with Amazon as a ProMerchant, list your books on all marketplaces that don't charge a monthly fee. There are eight marketplaces on which you can sell books for free. All of them can be managed by the Art of Books or FillZ inventory management systems. The free marketplace venues are:

- BarnesAndNoble.com
- Biblio.com
- eCampus.com
- Gemm.com
- Half.com
- TextbookRus.com
- TextbookX.com
- Valore.com

Ignoring free sites is leaving money on the table. Undoubtedly, new venues will pop-up after this book goes to print, and some will go bust. When you hear about these things, please post a comment on the readers forum at *http://www .internetbookselling.com* so I can update the next edition of this book.

It's possible to earn a living by selling on Amazon alone and throwing all your eggs into one basket. But I don't believe that's a wise strategy. A one-marketplace approach leaves you at the mercy of a single vendor while simultaneously costing your business additional sales every single day.

Once your inventory reaches 1,000 books and you're consistently adding 200 to 300 new listings each month, it's time to think about selling on the remaining fee-based marketplaces. Start with the most popular of the smaller marketplaces, Alibris, and then expand to AbeBooks. Continue expanding to the rest of the marketplaces as you can afford to pay the monthly premiums from existing sales. When adding new marketplaces to your distribution channels, each one should generate enough *profit*, not *revenue*, equal to three times the monthly fee to cost justify itself.

Inventory Allocation Across Marketplaces

One problem with selling on multiple venues is "double sales." A double sale occurs when a book sells on more than one marketplace and you only have one copy of the book. Your inventory management software monitors each marketplace and removes books sold on one venue from all other venues to avoid double sales.

That's all fine and dandy except that there are inherent processing delays from when the sale occurs, when the order is detected, when the delete request for a sold book is sent to other marketplaces, and how fast other marketplaces process delete requests.

Under normal circumstances, everything functions smoothly and double sales are avoided. Nevertheless, there are occasions when a customer places an order for your book on a different marketplace than the one where the first sale was made and—BAM!—you've got a double sale, and you can only fill one of them. That means the second order has to be refunded. If you refund too many orders you can jeopardize your selling privileges on one or more marketplaces.

You can minimize the number of double sales by listing your fastest selling books only on Amazon. Your slower selling inventory can be listed on Amazon as well as all of the remaining marketplaces. The deciding factor on which books to list on which venue is the Amazon sales rank.

We discussed Amazon sales rank previously and we'll look even more closely at it later, but for now, I'll just say this: because books with lower sales ranks sell faster, restrict listings of books with a sales rank of 300,000 or lower exclusively to Amazon to reduce the chance of selling the same book twice. Books with a sales rank above 300,000 can be listed on all marketplaces. Double sales won't be completely eliminated, but they'll be manageable.

CHAPTER 5

How to Find and Sell Digital and Analog Media

Although the primary theme of this book is Internet bookselling, large profits can be made with CDs, DVDs, Audio Books, and yes Virginia, vintage VHS tapes. These additional media are plentiful and can represent an important part of your overall profits. Throughout this book I've mentioned disks and tapes almost in passing. In this chapter, we'll cover them in more depth.

When you scout you'll find many disks and tapes in the same outlets where you buy books. Prices vary, but you can expect to pay a low of 10¢ to a high of $10 each. Don't be afraid to pay up if the item is worth it. Remember the Danny Kaye video I mentioned earlier? Even though the video cost me 25¢, it sold for $229. I would have gladly paid $50 for the opportunity to own it.

Every bookseller has his or her own strategy when it comes to acquiring and offering disks and tapes. In reality, merchandising disks and tapes isn't any different than merchandising books. However, there are a few special skills to master to do it successfully. In this chapter, I'll share tips and techniques that have worked well for me. I've sold thousands of dollars' worth of disks and tapes, and now I'll show you how you can too.

Physical electronic media is identified with a Universal Product Code (UPC) just like books are identified with an ISBN. Most disks and tapes have a UPC barcode printed on the package the same way ISBN barcodes are printed on dust jackets and the backs of paperback book covers. Scouting for electronic media doesn't involve any more effort or specialized knowledge than scouting for books. Just scan the barcode and let your look-up tool tell you if the item has value.

Keep in mind that disk and tape Amazon sales rank values don't directly correlate with book sales rank values. A book with a sales rank of 25,000 is not the same as a CD or DVD with a sales rank of 25,000. A reasonable rule of thumb is to multiply CD and DVD sales rankings by a factor of five to give yourself a general idea of what the sales rank might be if the item were a book. For VHS tapes, multiply the sales rank by eight to arrive at a rough equivalent sales rank of a book.

For example, suppose you scan a CD and the sales rank is 10,000. Using a multiplier of five, your CD is roughly equivalent to a book with a sales rank of 50,000. Scan a VHS tape with a 100,000 rank, multiply it by eight, and you have a tape that may be roughly equivalent to an 800,000 sales rank book. These are rough estimates I use in my business based on my sales data and what I've learned from other booksellers. They are by no means scientific, but rather a rough guideline for you to use if you choose.

Buying a CD or a DVD is riskier than buying a book for resale because even a damaged book can be read in most cases, and many buyers overlook quite a few imperfections if the book is desired badly enough. The same is not true of digital media. If a DVD or CD is severely scratched, the damage may interfere with the ability of the disk to play at all and no matter how badly a buyer may want it, the item is useless and, therefore, has no value whatsoever.

You can mitigate some of the risk with buying digital media by going down to your favorite electronics store and picking up a bottle of CD/DVD cleaner and scratch repair solution. It might be possible to repair minor scratches and turn an otherwise unsalable CD or DVD into a moneymaker. While you're there pick up a 100-count package of CD jewel cases as well as a 100-count package of DVD boxes. You can get each for about 20¢ to 30¢ apiece when purchased in bulk.

Having a supply of blank cases on hand is important because many of the CDs and DVDs you find in the field play perfectly fine but the cases are in poor shape. All you do is transfer the CD or DVD and artwork to a new case, and you increase the resale value of most items. Afterward, you can juice up your online listing description with something like this:

> "Artwork and jewel case in perfect condition. No cracks, scratches, or other noticeable damage."

In short, for an average of 25¢ it might be possible to tack a dollar or two onto the price of the item and give yourself bragging rights about how spiffy your product looks. There is nothing unethical about this practice since the CD jewel case or DVD box has no intrinsic value. Most buyers prefer an undamaged case for maximum future protection of their purchase.

Some sellers even pop for the expense of a resurfacing kit. Unless you plan to specialize in electronic media, don't spend a great deal of money on the kit. High quality resurfacing kits can easily cost north of $700. You can pick up an inexpensive scratch repair system like SkipDoctor for under $50.[1] It may not be the best, but for the home-based business it should suffice.

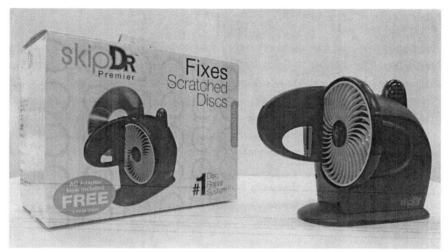

An inexpensive scratch repair kit like Skip Dr. comes in handy if you sell a lot of digital media.

Finally, keep your disks and tapes on a bookshelf by themselves instead of mixed in with your books. The sharp edges of the plastic cases may scratch book covers and dust jackets. Also, the small size of DVDs and CDs promote cocking (a slanted spine) and warping, especially with tall books that lean over because there's nothing pressing against them along the top edge to support the weight. And stocking your media on a separate bookcase makes it easier to access and store because most items are a uniform size and shape.

DVD Sales

Without question, DVDs have been the most profitable digital media I've sold. They're not as plentiful as books, but they fetch higher average prices than common books and you can usually buy them for $2 to $5 each and sell them for $8 to $20 each. You'll find that the most consistently profitable area of DVD sales is television series because they often go for top dollar, especially if the program is still airing. The most popular series command the highest prices for complete seasons. Individual movies seem to go in the opposite direction.

Prices for the most popular films plummet quickly after being released on DVD. Unless you can lay your hands on used or new copies soon after being released on DVD, they'll usually scan at penny prices by the time you find them in thrift stores and libraries.

When buying DVDs, always open the case and verify that the disk is present. You have no idea how many times I've bought empty DVD cases because I was so excited about finding a hot title I failed to open the case and verify that the disk was there.

In addition, get into the habit early on of inspecting each disk for scratches before buying instead of waiting until you get home. Inspecting DVDs in the store before taking them to the cash register not only saves money when you avoid buying damaged goods, it forces you to verify that the disk is actually in the box.

While you're at it, verify the title of the disk against the booklet or insert and make sure they match. Popping open the case and confirming there's a DVD inside isn't enough. Take a good look and satisfy yourself the correct DVD is present and in good shape.

In some stores DVD disks are removed from the case by management to prevent theft. Just take the empty case to the register and the cashier will retrieve the DVD from behind the counter. You'll have an opportunity to examine the disk at that time.

I rarely play a DVD before listing it online unless I am personally interested in the subject matter. There just isn't enough time in a day to play each DVD prior to selling it. Nevertheless, customers rarely contact me to demand a refund, because each DVD is inspected before it's purchased. It's inspected a second time prior to listing, and finally, it's inspected a third time after it's been sold. If serious defects are discovered during any one of the three inspections, the DVD is rejected. Only rejects just prior to shipment require a refund, and that doesn't happen often.

You may hear a lot of talk from other sellers about region codes on DVDs. So let's cover region codes now with this explanation from Wikipedia:

> "DVD video discs may be encoded with a region code restricting the area of the world in which they can be played. Discs without region codes are called all region or region 0 discs.

> "The commercial DVD player specification requires that a player to be sold in a given place not play discs encoded for a different region (region 0 discs are not restricted). The purpose of this is to allow motion picture studios to control aspects of a release, including content, release date, and, especially, price, according to the region."[2]

In plain English, many DVDs contain a special code that only allows them to be used on machines in the country in which the DVD is released. The reason for this is because movie studios want control over movies released for home use to avoid conflict with theatrical and private distribution in other countries.

For example, they don't want DVDs sold in the U.S. to end up in Europe when the same movie is being released in European theaters. If the U.S. version of the DVD fails to play on European equipment, then studio profits are protected at the box office.

None of my customers have ever reported a problem with region codes. I suggest you don't lose any sleep over it. You may want to check higher priced items just to be on the safe side. Otherwise, the cost to refund a DVD that won't play on a customers' DVD player is far less than the cost and hassle of checking each and every DVD for its region code. For those of you who want more information go to *http://en.wikipedia.org/wiki/DVD_region_code* and get all the skinny on region codes you want.

Recent DVDs I've sold are *Platinum 4 Disc DVD Set (Exercise Video Set)* for $200; *Israel: A Nation Is Born* for $96; *Now and Then, Here and There* for $59; and *Charlton Heston Presents the Bible* for $58. I paid an average of $3.19 for each DVD. You may notice that these DVDs, like more valuable books, are all nonfiction titles. Content-driven media tends to sell better than pure entertainment-driven media.

CD Sales

Ninety percent of the time we're talking about music CDs, but quite a few audio books are on CD. Many people like to listen to audio books in the car instead of the endless commercials played on music radio stations. Back in the day we used to call them "books on tape." But "books on CD" doesn't seem to have quite the same ring to it, so "Audio Books" has replaced the term, or at least become more widely used since the term has actually been around a long time.

Just like when you buy DVDs, always open the jewel case and inspect the CD before taking it to the cash register. Look for excessive scratches or even cracked or broken disks. I actually opened a jewel case once and discovered that the CD was broken completely in half.

Don't forget to verify the title of the disk against the booklet or insert. You always want to confirm that the correct CD is present and in good shape.

Testing CDs is a bit easier than testing DVDs. My objection to testing every DVD is basically a lack of time. There simply aren't enough hours in the day to watch every movie prior to listing and selling them online.

CDs are a bit different. There are far more multi-tasking opportunities available that allow you do listen to a large number of CDs without impacting your schedule much. For example, you can listen to CDs as you drive between scouting locations, or even while driving around town taking care of personal errands. CDs also make excellent background music while performing chores around the house. Try listening to CDs while listing or answering customer correspondence.

Combined with the inspection process described earlier, your confidence in the quality of the disk is greatly enhanced. You can easily claim to potential customers in your online listing description that the CD "plays great."

Personally, I prefer to limit my CD purchases to unopened packages that can be listed as new products. When the item is unopened, listening to the disk to ensure its quality becomes moot because it's brand new. Besides, new disks fetch higher prices than used ones. That doesn't mean you never buy used CDs. You should, but only the few that hold exceptional resale value.

You'll find your best deals at yard sales where CDs are typically priced extremely low. Another technique you can use to give yourself a leg-up on your competition is to get into the habit of asking the owners if there are more CDs (or DVDs) in the house they might like to sell. Often, one of the owners will go into the house and return with an armload of additional items that weren't on display when you arrived.

Recent CDs I've sold are *Undiscovered [Soundtrack]* for $40, *Golden Oldies Jukebox CD* for $34, *I Would Die 4 U* for $20, and *Reload* for $13. I paid an average of $1.69 for each CD.

VHS Sales

Everyone knows VHS technology is obsolete, yet there are many vintage and unopened VHS tapes fetching high prices. However, dealing with VHS is fraught with pitfalls, so caution is the watchword. I don't actively pursue VHS tapes, but I pick them up when I happen across good ones during my normal scouting activities.

The first way I identify good VHS tapes is by looking for unopened shrink-wrapped tapes I can sell as new. Normally when you scan tapes they turn up as penny items online, but the new copies still hold value. So I only look for the new ones and I occasionally find one I can sell for $8 or more.

Testing used VHS tapes is just as problematic as testing DVDs. There just isn't enough time in a day. Besides, tapes can wear in such a way that even if you test them there's no guarantee they'll play on your customer's machine. If you've ever owned more than one VCR chances are you've experienced popping a tape in one machine and having it play horribly, only to pop it into another machine and discover it plays just fine. Your chances of getting a finicky tape diminish if you stick with unopened packages.

VHS still sells. Especially obscure titles not available on DVD. VHS yields the best return when purchased in bulk at estate sales and auctions.

The second way to acquire VHS tapes is to buy them as part of a bulk purchase of books and research them as a secondary part of the deal. This type of arrangement is particularly appealing when the batch of tapes contains a number of older, unique titles having subject matter of specific interest. The remaining factor that may make a bulk purchase interesting is if it contains a number of brand new, unopened, shrink-wrapped titles you acquire for about 10¢ on the dollar. With such a low acquisition cost, I only need to sell a handful to break even, and any sale after that is gravy.

The best places to find bulk lots of VHS tapes (or CDs, or DVDs for that matter) accessible to the small independent bookseller are yard sales, estate sales, bag day after public library sales, and private collections. Make reasonable offers and they'll call you back for more when additional stock becomes available.

VHS tapes I've sold are *An Evening With Danny Kaye* for $229 (as I mentioned earlier), *Celebrating Haydn with Sir Peter Ustinov* for $125, and a second copy of Sir Peter for $100, just to name a few. I paid an average of 75¢ for each tape.

Cassette Tape Sales

Books on tape used to be all the rage. Now we have books on CD because audio cassettes have gone the way of the 8-track. (You do remember 8-track tapes, don't you?) However, unlike 8-tracks there are still cassette players in use that play cassette tapes quite well. Therefore, some cassettes have become quite collectible.

You'll have the most success with tape *sets* that aren't available in any other format. I don't think I've ever sold an individual cassette tape, so I stopped buying them unless it was for my own use.

Why does old technology like cassette tapes sell? I can't speak for anyone else, but I personally still use cassettes in my car because I can buy them so cheaply. I buy audio books all day long for as little as 10¢ while I scout so I have something to listen to while driving if I'm not previewing CDs prior to listing. I prefer listening to audio books rather than sitting through endless boring commercials on the radio.

After I'm done with the tapes I buy for personal use I donate them to Goodwill. They in turn give me a 20-percent discount off my next purchase in exchange for the donation. I've bought as many as 60 books from a single Goodwill store paying an average of $2.99 per book. My little cassette donation entitles me to a $35.88 discount. Not bad for only investing a dime!

As mentioned previously, cassettes sell slowly. In addition, I'm selective about the cassettes I buy. I can report one cassette sale worth noting and that's *The Antagonists* for $43, for which I paid 75¢. I've sold a number of other cassette tape sets at lower prices.

Game Sales

Hopefully, you've realized by now that selling digital media of all kinds is pretty uniform. Games are no exception. As always, when you get a hit on your scanner, open the box to confirm the disk is present. Furthermore, ensure that the title printed on the disk itself matches the artwork on the case, and examine the back of the disk for excessive scratches.

One additional point to remember about buying games is to make sure all the disks are present. Read the printing on the case and see if it tells you how many disks come with the game. If the box indicates there are more than one disk inside, count the disks to make sure you have them all. If the instruction manual is in the box make sure you play that fact up in the online listing description. Finally, many games come with an activation code. Make sure the code is included in the package or the game is useless to the customer and you'll only end up refunding the purchase.

I have a bookseller friend who has sold "vintage" computer games on 3½" floppy disks for good money. Don't overlook what is typically considered outdated computer technology. The current generation of young people has probably never seen the original Donkey Kong or Pac Man games. Some of them would be fasci-nated to see what started it all. However, I suspect the bulk of the vintage computer game purchasers are adults desiring to experience a bit of nostalgia.

Game disks are notorious for not playing well on a customer's equipment. That's why you must be doubly careful when buying games. Some machines are unforgiving when it comes to scratches. If you find yourself selling a lot of game disks, then a resurfacing kit is especially important.

Games I recently sold include *Star Wars Battlefront II [Xbox]* for $39.95, *Star Wars Knights of the Old Republic II [Xbox]* for $17.70, and *Fable: The lost Chapters [Xbox]* for 11.69. I paid an average of $4 for each game.

Software Sales

Dealing with software is fraught with pitfalls. In my naiveté during the early days I purchased popular software programs thinking I was going to make a decent profit when in fact those programs still sit on my shelves to this day. Almost no one buys old software. Yet you can find old versions of most popular software titles listed online in almost every marketplace; especially the more well-known office productivity titles. I've never sold one. So I stopped buying them. There may be people out there who do alright with this category of media. I'm not one of them.

My success with software has always been with relatively new releases of specialized programs that address a specific educational need. Knowing the publication date is crucial in this market. Buying an out-of-date program gets you nowhere. Nevertheless, I've had success selling software on the Internet. A couple of my best sellers have been *Delmar's Heart & Lung Sounds* for $21 and *Digital Texturing and Painting* for $26. I paid an average of $3 for each program.

Enjoy Being "In The Know"

On a personal note, I've greatly expanded my own movie library because I know all the best places in town to buy inexpensive DVDs. I'm out there shopping every single day and invariably run across terrific deals. I purchased the entire *Matrix* trilogy on DVD for pennies on the dollar. I've also purchased many of my all-time favorites on DVD at a fraction of the cost, including a black-and-white version of *It's A Wonderful Life* with James Stewart.

If you're a music lover you'll have the privilege of sampling a wide variety of music from every genre imaginable without spending a fortune. If you love audio books, whether they're on cassette tape or CD, you'll find hundreds of them on subjects of all kinds for as little as 10¢ each. I'm an audio book lover and buy several each week. My favorites are kept handy for repeated listening. For example, I recently bought a $200 cassette tape set on small business tax reduction strategies for $3.99 in a thrift store.

Buying high quality entertainment media at bargain basement prices is one of the perks of this business I absolutely love. I started collecting so many titles I started hurting my profits. Therefore, I made a rule that I'd only keep for personal use items that scanned below my minimum price floor because they're unprofitable to sell online. Everything else had to be listed online and if I acquired something I really wanted to keep, I'd purchase it from the company from my personal checking account at the online price.

It may sound silly to treat purchases that way, but it's imperative that you draw a line between your personal and business lives. Treat your bookselling as a business at all times and not only will your profits improve, you'll keep the tax man at bay too.

CHAPTER 6

Fulfillment

Getting orders into the hands of your customers is called fulfillment. An efficient fulfillment process that keeps costs low while providing world-class customer service to buyers boosts your feedback rating, and ultimately, sales.

A large part of your business reputation is built on how you handle fulfillment. Processing orders in a timely and professional manner is crucial to establishing positive relationships with customers. Paying attention to the little things reaps big rewards in the long run.

Order Processing

The first step in fulfilling orders is getting order information from the marketplace. How you do that depends on the technology built into your operation. The simplest and least expensive method is to wait for the marketplace to send you an eMail indicating that you received an order.

Some marketplaces include all the information needed within the eMail to fill the order, including the name of the item ordered, the customer's shipping address, eMail address, amount of the purchase, shipping allowance, commissions charged, and the net amount you'll receive into your bank account.

All marketplaces used to use eMail to alert sellers of pending orders. However, due to privacy concerns most have eliminated sensitive customer data from the eMail and you have to logon to your seller account to access transaction information. More marketplaces are expected to follow suit. For marketplaces that still provide customer information in eMail form, all you do is print the eMail, clip the buyer name and address to paste on your outgoing package, and use the rest of the eMail as a packing slip.

For Amazon and other marketplaces that no longer provide customer information in eMails, you logon to your seller account and print a pick list and packing slip online. The pick list is a list of all the orders you received that day. A packing slip is included with each individual order. Furthermore, you'll need to cut and paste customer information into your postage software (more about that later) to print the mailing label.

If you use an inventory management software program as explained in Chapter 8 and Chapter 9, integrated with an online postage service, you can bypass all these manual steps and let your software do the heavy lifting. Your inventory management system prints the pick list, packing slips, and postage.

If money is tight, you can go the manual route and print packing slips from the marketplace website. But automating the front-end of the fulfillment process saves far more in time and effort than what you pay for the software and services. The time saved can be better spent scouting, listing, or fulfilling even more orders with the same effort.

On the subject of money, the savings you get from electronic delivery confirmation alone eventually pays the cost of your equipment and monthly subscription. Delivery confirmation should be on all of your packages.

Pulling Inventory

Your Pick List is the first thing your inventory management system spits out. Otherwise, you print your Pick List from your online seller account on each venue. Your Pick List is the list of orders to be filled that day. At a minimum it'll consist of the item "SKU," title or description, quantity, and the name of the customer.

SKU stands for "Stock Keeping Unit." A SKU is a unique identifier you assign to a book to help you find it on your bookshelf after it sells. When your inventory is small, having a SKU system isn't that big of a deal. As you grow, a SKU system is essential for easy retrieval of sold books.

If you're using one of the SKU systems suggested in this book, pulling sold items from your shelves is a snap, because the Pick List is sorted by SKU. All you do is roll your book cart down the isle between bookshelves and pull each sold item one-by-one. Since the list is sorted by SKU there is no backtracking, and pulling items is quick and painless.

Preparing for Shipment

Before packing your books for shipment, clean them up a bit to ensure that your customer has a good experience when the package is opened. Before beginning your cleaning operation, lay a small cloth towel down on your work table to provide cushion between the table and your book. Next you'll need a small hand

My cleaning supplies are ridiculously simple. They consist of a bottle of Goo Gone, a damp cloth, a dry cloth, and a smooth rag I call my "chemical cloth" for applying Goo Gone, a 320 sandpaper block, and a white eraser.

towel that remains dry, a smooth cloth such as an old t-shirt cut into strips to apply Goo Gone or Bestine, and a dampened face cloth.

Start by checking the front endpaper for the price bookstores often write in pencil in the upper right corner of the page. The last thing you want is to upset your customer with the fact you paid $1 for a book he or she just bought for $50. Use a white eraser because they do the best job of completely removing any trace of pencil marks. Colored erasers leave streaks on the page so avoid them. White erasers can be found in any office supply store.

You may also find small price tags stuck to the front endpaper. Carefully peel away the tag and ensure you do as little damage to the page as possible. That includes dinging the page with your fingernail while trying to wedge it under the corner of the tag.

Frequently, you can gently remove the price tag without damaging the page, leaving only a tiny bit of glue residue behind. In those cases use your dry towel to gently brush over the sticky area. This causes lint from the towel to cling to the residue and greatly reduce stickiness. Then use your white eraser to remove the remaining glue residue from the page.

In cases where you encounter a stubborn price tag that begins to damage the page as it's removed, take care to avoid tearing completely through the paper. So long as you only remove a layer of paper and don't go all the way through you can repair the damage as shown below. If there's any glue residue left, carefully remove it using the dry towel and white eraser technique. Be extra careful because the paper is thinner due to the top layer of the page being peeled off with the label. Most likely there is little to no remaining residue because it'll have been peeled away with the top layer of paper. What's left is a patch of the endpaper that doesn't match the surrounding area.

To mask the damaged spot take a number 320 sand paper block and gently sand the spot as well as the immediate surrounding area until the damage is nearly indistinguishable from the rest of the page. Lightly run your fingers over the sanded area to see if it feels smooth to the touch. If it's still rough, hit it with the sandpaper again.

Practice this technique on a few penny books before trying it on a book you've sold. It's not a difficult skill to learn, but it does take a few tries to get it right. Also, never use sand paper if the front endpaper is colored stock. You'll sand off the color and ruin the page. If the endpaper is colored you're limited to peeling the label, using the dry cloth, and *lightly* erasing the residue.

If more than minor traces of your work are left contact your customer and explain the damage. Offer a discount and 80 percent of the time the customer won't care. Otherwise, you refund the order and relist the book with the damage disclosed in the listing description.

Give the edges of the book a quick inspection for minor smudges. This imperfection can often be removed by lightly sanding the edges with a number 320 sand paper block. This technique is not meant to remove water stains, ink stains or large areas that have been smudged. It's strictly for minor smudges that can be easily removed with light sanding to give the edges a brighter appearance.

Don't try to sand a deckle-edge book (books that have uneven sheets on the lead edge). You'll ruin its appearance and diminish the book's value. If a deckle edge book is heavily stained, it's best to disclose the damage in your listing description or consider not selling the book at all.

Finally, your attention should be turned to the dust jacket if working with a hardcover book, or the outer covers if working with a paperback. Be especially careful when working with hardcover books. Dust jackets are made from a variety of paper textures and can be ruined easily if you use the wrong cleaning solutions. For the sake of this discussion, the term "cover" is used when referring to either a dust jack or paperback book cover.

If you're working with standard glossy coated cover stock and there are no labels, price tags, or stray ink marks you want removed, use your damp cloth to first wipe down the front cover. Once you've used the damp cloth, *immediately* wipe the cover down with the dry cloth to remove all traces of water. Repeat the

This is a deckle-edge book. Notice the uneven pages on the lead edge.

process for the spine and back cover. Never leave water in contact with the book, not even for a minute or two. Always dry it off to avoid damaging the book.

Many times you'll encounter labels or price tags on the covers and spine. If you find they don't easily peel off, there's a safer way to remove them. Labels and price tags are nothing more than paper with an adhesive backing. Removing them is ridiculously simple. All you do is rub the paper off with your damp cloth. That's right, just rub it off! Once the paper is gone the only thing left is the glue. Spray your chemical cloth with a cleaning solution like Bestine or Goo Gone and wipe away the glue. If the area being cleaned is close to the edges of the book, take a sheet of glossy paper and slip it between the front or back endpaper and the cover so the chemical doesn't bleed onto the interior pages and stain them.

When the glue has been removed it doesn't hurt to wipe down the rest of the covers and spine with your cleaning solution to brighten them up and make the book look as new as possible. Remove any traces of chemicals with your dry towel so it doesn't feel slippery to the touch.

The damp cloth and chemical cloth combination doesn't work on certain types of covers. Covers made from flat or matte paper without a glossy finish or rough paper dust jackets are severely damaged using this technique. Your only choice is to wipe down the covers with a dry cloth and lightly use your white eraser to remove minor pencil marks or minor smudges. To avoid accidentally damaging non-glossy finished covers, you might want to use a separate dry, clean cloth.

Joyce Godsey encourages booksellers to approach book repair with common sense and caution in her book, *Book Repair for Booksellers: A guide for booksellers offering practical advice on book repair:*

> "One can easily turn a good book into scrap paper. It is assumed you have researched the damaged book and found it not valuable enough to demand repair by a professional. It is more work for a conservator to correct a bad repair than to just start from scratch. If the book has great monetary or sentimental value, it is probably best left 'as is' or restored by a professional."[1]

Packing and Shipping

Presentation is everything, and when your customer receives a package from you, ensure that it gives a good impression of your business. You don't want to send out poorly packaged books and risk damage to the contents. Neither should you send out packages that look like they were put together by a two-year-old. When your customer receives a package from you it should radiate professionalism, care, and attention to detail.

Bubble Mailers

As a home-based business most of your books will be shipped in bubble mailers because they're inexpensive, easy to store, and easy to handle. The majority of your books will weigh two pounds or less, so bubble mailers work well. Heavier and expensive books should be boxed with a few extra precautions, which we'll discuss in a moment. For now, we'll address the bread-and-butter books you'll sell on a daily basis.

Always properly size the book to the mailer. Don't try to save a few pennies by squeezing a book into a smaller mailer. The added tension on the package makes it more susceptible to breakage. The corners of the book may also be damaged.

When you ship merchandise in bubble mailers, make sure the edges of the folded flap line up with the body of the mailer to avoid a sloppy appearance. As you press down the self-sticking flap make sure it's smooth and doesn't contain bubbles. Use a short strip of packing tape on the flap for additional reinforcement.

Center your shipping label on the side opposite the flap to give a nice appearance to the package. Smooth out the label with your hand to get rid of bubbles underneath. Some booksellers recommend taping over the shipping label as added protection. Most shipping labels are thermal labels, and I don't recommend you

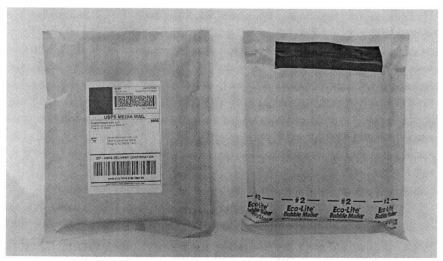

Here's an average size book inserted into a #2 bubble mailer. The black tape shows you how I seal the package.

tape over them. That's because a chemical reaction is created between the tape resin and direct thermographic paper. The reaction fades the name and address on the label. I've had packages returned to me with the shipping label almost entirely blank, thereby making the package undeliverable.

In the following illustrations I use 2" black electrical tape instead of transparent shipping tape so that you can clearly see how the mailer is sealed.

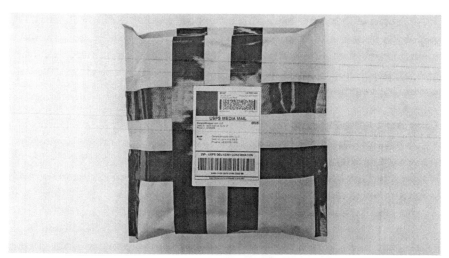

Here's a large book bubble wrapped and inserted into a #6 bubble mailer. Again, the black tape shows you how I seal the package.

For heavy or large books I use a #6 Kraft bubble mailer. But first, I wrap the book in bubble wrap for added protection. After sealing the envelope I tape down the edges so there's no gap to get caught in post office machinery. Then I run two strips of tape completely around the length and width of the mailer for additional strength. If necessary, I'll run a third strip of tape in each direction just to be safe.

You can find bubble mailers locally or on the Internet. When buying locally expect to pay two or three times what you'll pay when buying online. For that reason you only want to buy shipping supplies locally in an emergency, like when you forget to reorder and you accidently run out.

Boxes

Boxes provide superior protection for their contents. When using flexible depth boxes you can standardize on fewer sizes thereby making your shipping operation simpler to manage. For example, I use Multi-D boxes from Packaging Control Corporation. Multi-D boxes only come in three sizes and can accommodate 99 percent of your needs.

Packaging Control has a cool animation on their website at *http://www.multi-d .net* that demonstrates how the boxes work. Make sure you have your speakers turned on to get the full effect.

The downside to boxes is the cost and added difficulty in packing. Boxes can cost anywhere from 50 to 150 percent more than comparable sized bubble mailers. For example, shipping small books in a bubble mailer can cost as little as $0.14 each. Mailing the same size books in a box can easily top $0.40 each depending on your shipping costs from the manufacturer.

In addition, boxes are more difficult to handle when packing. After you've used boxes for a few dozen packages you'll start to get the hang of it. But when you're hiring help at minimum wage the training issues can be more significant than you might think. Remarkably, some people are utterly helpless when it comes to wielding a tape gun and never get the hang of it.

Take a Flexible Approach

While the advantages of boxes are indisputable, the most rational approach is to use a combination of bubble mailers for lighter, less damage-prone books. For heavier items use boxes for the added protection. This approach limits the need to stock shipping supplies to size #0, #2, and #6 bubble mailers and all three sizes of a flex box like Multi-D.

You need the #0 mailers for mass market paperbacks, DVDs, CDs, and small light-weight hardcovers. Size #2 is what you'll use to ship the majority of your books and #6 mailers are for books too large to box. The Multi-D boxes handle everything else.

Media Mail

Ninety percent of your shipments will use Media Mail because it's the least expensive method available to small sellers in most cases. Bound Printed Matter (BPM) can be less expensive for shipments traveling shorter distances, but BPM isn't available as an electronic shipping option unless you're using a Manifest System.

A Manifest System automatically weighs your packages, chooses the best method of shipping, and prints your mailing labels. It's very expensive and for it to pay off economically, you should ship a minimum of 1,000 packages per week.

Media Mail used to be called "book rate" postage. Over time the term "media" came to include books, DVDs, CDs, VHS, cassette tapes, and software. Therefore, the USPS replaced "book rate" with "Media Mail." Every package sent via Media Mail can be searched by postal officials and returned to the sender if the contents aren't on the list of approved items.

If you're using an electronic shipping system to print your labels, always use Delivery Confirmation (DC) on your packages no matter what the price of the contents. Electronic DC is less than a third the cost of buying it at the Post Office counter, and it'll easily pay for itself by avoiding refunds due to fraudulent non-delivery claims made to the marketplaces.

Priority Mail

Don't overpay for Priority Mail (PM) shipments. Many beginning booksellers accept Priority Mail orders when they shouldn't and significantly hurt their profits.

How can it be a mistake to accept Priority Mail orders? Isn't it best to give buyers the option to select expedited shipping to increase the chance of getting the sale? Of course, but you don't want to lose money in the process. The best way to ship most books via USPS Priority Mail is in a flat rate envelope. I won't name rates because by the time you read this the post office will most likely have raised rates—again. In fact, they may have raised rates several times since I wrote this chapter.

The idea is to only offer expedited shipping for books that fit into a Priority Mail envelope and can be mailed for a flat rate. If you stick to this rule, your mailing costs are usually be covered by the shipping credit. The shipping credit is the money you receive from the marketplace to cover postage and handling. Best of all, the envelope is free; courtesy of USPS.

This is an easy rule to follow. Just keep around a sample flat rate Priority Mail envelope as you're inspecting and listing, and ensure that oversized books fit into the envelope before choosing expedited shipping. Otherwise, you can eat up any potential profit with additional postage costs.

For expensive items don't be afraid to pop for a Priority Mail box. You'll pay about double the price of a flat rate Priority Mail envelope, but it's good customer service.

There is a seventy pound limit for Priority Mail shipments, and the contents must fit in the envelope or box without structural reinforcement. However, there is a bit of a fudge factor on the reinforcement restriction. Here's a direct quote from the USPS Domestic Mail Manual (DMM):

> "Any amount of material may be mailed in a USPS-produced Priority Mail flat-rate box or flat-rate envelope. When sealing a flat-rate box or flat-rate envelope, the container flaps must close along the normal folds. Tape may be applied to the flaps and seams to reinforce the container; provided the design of the container is not enlarged by opening the sides and the container is not reconstructed in any way."[2]

Early in my business a postal employee challenged me because I had taped a bulging Priority Mail envelope to keep it from bursting open during shipment. She ultimately accepted the package with the attitude that she was doing me a favor. Not being wise to the actual postal regulations concerning package reinforcement, I sheepishly accepted her act of generosity and counted my blessings.

Later that evening I related my experience on one of the bookselling forums and a fellow bookseller came to my rescue with the above quote from the DMM. Needless to say I was elated to learn I hadn't overstepped my bounds after all.

This is a flat-rate Priority Mail envelope. Make sure the book fits this envelope before offering expedited shipping.

I continued packing my orders as usual and the next time that postal employee complained about one of my packages I politely pointed to the DMM reference quoted above and squelched the objection.

Before inserting your book into the package, bubble wrap it to protect the corners and edges from bumps during shipment. The bubble wrap also protects against moisture from rain or spills. When seeing if the book will fit the envelope, make sure to take the bulk of the bubble wrap into consideration.

International Shipping

Most beginning booksellers have a complete meltdown at the prospect of shipping internationally, but the panic attack is completely unwarranted. In fact, international shipments, like Priority Mail shipments, can boost your bottom line, depending on how promptly marketplaces increase shipping credits after postal rate hikes.

Priority Mail and Priority Mail International use the same envelope. International mail used to be shipped in a Global Priority Mail (GPM) envelope. The GPMs had a distinct red border along the bottom edge for easy identification. Domestic priority mail went into a flat-rate Priority Mail envelope (DPM). The DPMs were distinguished with a dark blue border along the bottom. One day the post office realized they could save money by combining domestic priority shipping and international shipping envelopes. This made life easier for booksellers too because there was now only one envelope to worry about.

Don't be afraid to ship internationally. You pack and ship international orders the same way you pack and ship domestic Priority Mail orders with the added responsibility of filling out a simple customs form. You pick up the forms for free from your local post office. The postal clerk will gladly show you how to fill one out, and after a few times you'll do it in your sleep.

If you use a service like Endicia Dazzle, the required forms are printed automatically and you won't even have to stand in line at the post office to have them round dated by a postal clerk. Just drop your packages off at the window, exchange a few pleasantries with the postal employees, and be on your way.

Be careful to ensure that all listings created for international shipping fit into the Priority Mail International envelope just like your domestic Priority Mail. If not, you'll have to ship the item in a Priority Mail box at a cost three to five times more expensive. Also, there is a four pound limit for flat rate Priority Mail International envelopes.

For example, at the time of this writing a flat-rate Priority Mail International envelope costs $12.95 to mail just about anywhere in the world. A book that's a mere one-eighth of an inch too large to fit into the envelope costs an astonishing $35 to mail, depending on where it's going. The rule of thumb is, if it doesn't fit, don't ship.

Of course, there are always exceptions to every rule. For example, you may find that First Class International mail is sometimes less costly for shipping to Canada and Mexico. When shipping internationally, always double check your shipping method to ensure you're getting the best rate.

Shipping Expensive Books

Until now the method of bookselling I've described pertains to bread-and-butter books you'll sell every single day; but occasionally, you're going to run across a real diamond that sells for hundreds of dollars. The first time you sell a diamond you may naturally be nervous about how to best protect yourself from fraud. Believe it or not, there are actually people who buy expensive books only to return an inferior one for a refund—leaving the seller holding the bag. When you sell your first diamond you can resist the urge to panic because I'm going to show you right here how to handle large transactions.

I sold my first diamond for $175 years ago and nearly went into cardiac arrest contemplating the prospect of being defrauded or of having the book disappear in the bowels of the U.S. postal system, never to be seen again. I immediately jumped onto the bookselling forums and asked for help and was lucky enough to get a great deal of good advice on handling large transactions.

First of all, set a ceiling on books you're willing to ship without insurance. Some booksellers insure all books over $50. Others insure anything over $75 or $100. Others still substitute delivery confirmation for insurance. It all depends on your personal level of risk tolerance.

I don't advocate relying on delivery confirmation in lieu of insurance for expensive items. Delivery confirmation only proves the package arrived at a particular address. Unless you incur the added expense of having the recipient sign for the package you can't prove who actually received it. There's a debate over the financial merits of paying for insurance versus paying for signature confirmation.

Personally, I prefer insuring the retail value of any book over $75. If you don't insure the retail value most insurance only covers the actual cost of the lost item. That bites if you pay $2 for a book that sells for $200 and it gets lost in the mail. You'll only recover $2—the insurance alone costs more than that! Because of the limited coverage and major hassle to collect, avoid USPS insurance. I always use Endicia to insure my packages.

Marketplaces change their reimbursement policies all the time. It used to be true that if you had delivery confirmation and a package was lost the marketplace wouldn't charge your account if the customer filed a claim for an order that was never received. Nowadays, sellers are finding themselves increasingly liable even though they have delivery confirmation.

The actual decision making process on who's liable and who's not is often a closely guarded secret, or at a minimum subject to a bizarre form of fuzzy logic. The only sure way to protect yourself is with insurance for the full retail value of the item.

After establishing your ceiling, there are other steps to take. For example, consider placing a small dot with a pen somewhere in the book that only you know about. The dot should be so small that it would never be noticed unless someone knew exactly where to look. I always put multiple dots in the book, the exact number of which I've never publicly revealed, in case a so-called clever scammer looks for pen dots to duplicate in an inferior copy to send back to me for a fraudulent refund. Before I started using this technique I suspect I was defrauded twice with the "switcheroo." However, two losses out of tens of thousands of books sold make the risk pretty miniscule.

Expensive books should be shipped via Priority Mail with delivery confirmation so the package can be tracked. For books that sell for $200 or more you might also request a signed return receipt so you know who took delivery of the package.

If the book fits in a USPS Flat-Rate Priority Mail envelope, wrap the book in bubble wrap with the packing slip facing outward so the destination address can be easily read should the package burst open.

After wrapping the book in bubble wrap, shore up the bundle by using a strip of packing tape around the width of the book and a strip around the length. Slide the bundle into the PM envelope, seal the flap, then tape the flap with packing tape as shown in the illustration on the next page. A single strip of tape along the seams of the envelope wouldn't hurt either. Affix your shipping label in the appropriate spot and you're good to go.

If the book won't fit into a Flat-Rate Priority Mail envelope you'll need to ship it in a Flat-Rate Priority Mail box. Wrap the book in bubble wrap and tape the bundle as explained above.

Next assemble your PM box and add a layer of bubble wrap in the bottom of the box. Insert the book standing on the bottom edge, just as if you were placing it on a bookshelf, resting on the layer of wrap, and fill the space on all four sides of the book with more bubble wrap, effectively suspending the book in mid-air away from all outer edges.

Top off the package by covering the top edge of the book with more wrap, seal the box, and tape the seams at the two ends with packing tape. Affix your shipping label in the appropriate spot and once again you're good to go.

Bubble wrapping expensive books and securing the wrap with packing tape keeps it safe, dry, and secure.

If you're going to ship oversize books internationally, keep in mind the increased cost of shipping in a box instead of a flat-rate envelope. That's okay if you're selling an expensive book, especially if you've increased your price by the amount of additional shipping it costs to send the book overseas in a box.

Recycled Shipping Materials

Some beginning booksellers use recycled material almost exclusively to save money. So long as you do a good job of packing you shouldn't get any complaints. Just make sure you use lots of tape. You can protect your books with recycled bubble wrapping and use recycled brown paper for an envelope.

If money is tight you can almost certainly get your packing material for free if you're creative. Recycled cardboard that can be used for constructing shipping boxes is readily available from supermarkets, convenience stores, and thrift stores, and can be obtained at no cost. You'll need to practice a bit before you get the hang of it.

There are lots of websites that demonstrate how to make cardboard boxes. Try doing a Google search on "how to make cardboard boxes" or "how to make a cardboard box." You'll get hundreds of thousands of hits explaining how to do it.

Repricing

To remain competitive in the marketplace you must periodically adjust the prices of your books either up or down relative to your competition. This is called repricing. Regular repricing keeps your inventory competitive in the marketplace. Your repricing strategy can be as simple as matching the lowest price in the same or better condition once a month or as sophisticated as a complex nested rule structure executed hourly to maximize revenue and inventory turnover. The strategy you adopt depends entirely on the goals you set for your business and often on your technical ability to write scripts.

Repricing can be done manually or using an automated tool. When your inventory is small, manual repricing is not a problem. You simply log onto your marketplace account, compare the prices of your inventory with competitors, and change your prices accordingly right there within your account.

With manual repricing you have total control over raising or lowering prices to reflect changing market conditions. Your judgment and intimate familiarity with your inventory aid your decisions about specific price points for a given item. You have the advantage of always knowing exactly where a product sits price-wise relative to your competitors.

The downside to manual repricing is that it takes an incredible amount of time. Manual repricing is best suited for smaller inventories when the bookseller has more time than money and even less programming acumen. Furthermore, to be truly effective, repricing must be consistent. If you only reprice your inventory whenever the opportunity presents itself you'll get inconsistent results.

You can gain a certain amount of consistency by scheduling a reminder to yourself to reprice at regular intervals. Schedule the reminder to pop up on your screen at the appropriate time. This is easy to do with Outlook. You can also subscribe to a free reminder service to send you eMails to jog your memory.

With larger inventories an automated repricer is a must. Automated repricing gives you many of the benefits of manual repricing except for perhaps being more intimately familiar with the prices of your books. However, putting your pricing on automatic pilot offers consistency of execution as well as adherence to a clearly defined pricing strategy that's not subject to the vagaries of manual decision making. To truly maximize the profit potential of your inventory you must implement an automated repricing strategy.

Despite the many benefits of automated repricing, it does have its downside. When two automated repricers get locked into a price war it triggers the dreaded "race to the bottom." Fighting it out with another seller's cyber robot is a no-win game because it unnecessarily drives prices down to pennies.

Two types of sellers destroy prices. The first type is the large outfit that acquires books by the ton, paying little or nothing for them, and charges pennies for books that should sell for dollars. The big guys can make a profit on the shipping because of the bulk mail discounts they get from the post office.

The second group of destructive sellers is beginners desperate for sales who undercut you in a bid to move their books to the top of the queue. Please don't play that game either. It's not necessary. You can earn a comfortable living charging reasonable prices for your books without resorting to cutthroat price competition.

Another thing that's good to know about automated repricing tools is that they come in two flavors. Most tools are controlled by a series of checkboxes you use to select a set of rules to reprice your inventory. Those types of tools are fine if you don't have programming experience. Ultimately, you want a tool powered by a scripting language like JavaScript, VBScript, Pearl, or something similar. When you program your script, instead of merely checking off a bunch of checkboxes, you have the ability to build any desired level of sophistication into your repricing strategy.

Here's a three-step repricing strategy for you to consider that helps to maximize your earnings while preserving the price levels of your inventory. By carefully pricing your inventory on a daily, weekly, and monthly basis you can avoid price wars, profit erosion, and racing to the bottom.

Daily Pricing Strategy

Daily repricing is for raising your prices in those instances where a higher priced book sells over *yours*. Yes, it'll happen to you, too. However, you can leverage the moment by increasing your prices to match the next higher price.

It's been my experience that one to three percent of my prices are raised with daily repricing. That means I raise prices on the equivalent of nearly 100 percent of my inventory every 90 days. That extra profit goes straight to the bottom line with no additional sourcing and listing effort since the repricing process is totally automated. If you don't reprice daily for the sole purpose of increasing prices due to leapfrog purchases, you're leaving money on the table.

Don't place a limit on the amount of upward price movement your repricer makes. Artificial limitations on price increases are one of the weaknesses of standard "checkbox" types of repricing tools. Most of them force you to set a limit on the maximum amount of price movement the repricer is allowed to make on a percentage basis.

For example, if prices go up or down by more than 25 percent, the repricer takes no action. But what if the next highest competitor is double your price and your repricing tool only makes a 25-percent adjustment? You leave 75 percent of the potential extra profit on the table if the item sells. That's one of the reasons why a tool powered by a scripting language is superior to a checkbox approach.

Checkboxes lock you in to a set percentage or hard coded amount. With a script, you have unlimited freedom to dictate your rules.

Weekly Pricing Strategy

Your objective with weekly pricing is to remain competitive with small downward price adjustments by your competitors. The unfortunate reality of Internet bookselling is that prices tend to erode over time more often than they improve. The ebb and flow of price fluctuations can be up or down on a given day, but overall most long-term prices trend downward with daily peaks and valleys. Your daily repricing strategy is meant to capitalize on the upward price movements whenever they occur. However, your weekly strategy is meant to reflect minor downward trends to stay competitive with the market when your primary stock consists of bread-and-butter items. (Antiquarian prices have a life cycle of their own and are beyond the scope of this book.)

Making negative price adjustments on a weekly basis slows the downward price spiral of your inventory and helps maintain a higher average selling price. Higher average selling prices mean less work for more money. Your scripting tool should easily schedule your weekly strategy to run in the background like clockwork.

Monthly Pricing Strategy

Infrequent repricing and strict controls on negative price adjustments tend to cause your inventory to become uncompetitive over a period of time. Therefore, you need to occasionally bring it back into alignment with the overall market to keep sales rolling in. Experiment with running a single repricing once per month with a higher negative price adjustment threshold to correct the imbalance. If you normally run your repricer with a maximum of 3-percent negative price adjustment, run the repricer once per month with a 50-percent negative price adjustment. Almost immediately, you'll see a spike in sales before volume settles back down into your normal range.

Don't make your monthly negative adjustment in conjunction with a monthly sale or you'll give away the store. Execute the two strategies separately to maintain the integrity of your average sale price. If the price of a book is dropping like a rock you could see significant price erosion each month. However, the idea is to remain competitive and sell the book quickly before it erodes too far to be profitable.

Beware of Predators

There are predatory sellers out there who look for unsophisticated sellers using an automated repricing tool. They try to trick your repricer into drastically lowering your prices so they can scoop up your valuable inventory for pennies on the dollar, only to resell it at higher prices. Always protect yourself by establishing a limit within your script on how far you allow your prices to decrease over any given time.

Further protect yourself by periodically changing your price adjustment threshold to foil would-be predators watching your inventory. Always, always, always have a price floor below which you won't sell an item. Never publicly reveal your thresholds or floors on open forums or you'll only invite trouble from lurking predators.

Purging Dead Listings

No matter how hard you try to make good purchasing decisions you're bound to pick up a few duds along the way. It's inevitable. Many of the duds are outright mistakes—books that should have never been purchased in the first place. Most of the time your duds were actually good buys at the time of purchase, but price competition ran them down to penny status. At that point they simply become dead listings.

As the weeks, months, and years roll by the dead listings accumulate and eventually choke the profitability out of your business because of the carrying costs for inventory that never sells. Carrying costs are the monthly expenses you pay to store your inventory. If you work from home your carrying costs are reduced to little more than the opportunity cost on the capital spent to purchase the books. Opportunity costs exist when you have money tied up in inventory that could earn interest elsewhere. Keep your carrying costs down by learning how to jettison dead listings before they become a financial burden.

The only time you have to worry about dead listings is after you've completely maxed out your storage capacity. Up until that point keeping low priced books on the shelf doesn't represent a serious carrying expense, especially if you work out of your home.

You can sell many dead listings ahead of lower priced competitors by adopting the practice of writing excellent descriptions. Maintain a price floor low enough to attract bargain hunters while high enough to ensure a profitable sale.

However, the day of reckoning comes sooner or later and you'll reach the absolute maximum number of books you can store. When that day arrives you have three choices:

1. Obtain more space.
2. Purge your inventory.
3. Hold a sale.

Obtaining more space is obvious and I won't spend time on it other than to say you don't want to invest money renting storage or warehouse space unless your entire inventory consists of steady selling items with less than 5 percent to 10 percent of deadwood. That's when you're truly maxed out and renting space might make financial sense.

Your second choice is to reduce inventory by purging dead listings from your shelves. Start purging items that have been around the longest and are selling for the lowest prices. Once you've removed those items and you feel you still need more space, start removing the lowest priced items with a sales rank above a certain ceiling, like 1.5 million. Your particular inventory may call for a higher or lower ceiling. Ideally, what you want is a steady turnover of stock to keep your capital investment to a minimum because you're using the same dollars over and over to reinvest into more inventory. Whatever inventory level is needed to achieve your financial goals is where you want to be.

Your remaining choice is to hold a sale. Since you're going to purge inventory anyway, you might as well get paid for the privilege. You do that before purging deadwood by marking down the listings that have been on the shelf the longest. Match the lowest selling price in the same or better condition, with an absolute floor of $1. You'll get a spurt of sales at fireside prices, but those are sales you wouldn't have otherwise received. This works especially well for home-based operations with low overhead. After sales taper off to previous levels, your sale has run its course and you can proceed with purging deadwood from your shelves.

Customer Service

World-class customer service goes a long way toward establishing your name as a honest and reliable seller. It's critically important I drill that point into your head, so I'm going to spend a little more time talking about it.

The Two Rules of Customer Service

I'm about to proclaim two of the few clichés you'll read in this book. Speaking as one who has spent years in the Internet bookselling trenches, I wouldn't include them if they weren't worth taking to heart and practicing. Hopefully, I can offer you a different perspective on how to apply them to your business.

You'll run into all types of people in this business. Most bless and enrich your life, while others try to make your life miserable. Luckily, the former group is larger than the latter by many orders of magnitude. Nevertheless, make it a practice to treat your customers as if they all belong to the former group. It won't always be easy at first, but soon world-class customer service becomes a habit, and you'll develop company policies and procedures that make it a snap.

Rule #1: The Customer Is Always Right!

Okay, okay. You've heard this one a thousand times. But it's absolutely true. You'll be wise to apply it in your everyday interactions with your customers.

I once worked in the Information Technology department of a large bank in Southern California as the Vice President of Technical Support. I traveled to another state to negotiate a contract with a medium size software vendor. This particular contract represented a significant amount of revenue for the vendor and a successful outcome would put a nice feather in my cap back at the office.

I was looking forward to ironing out the final details of the contract and returning home, but almost immediately, there were snags. To do business with this vendor the bank needed certain customizations to the software or it would not be a good fit for us. However, the vendor resisted any requests for software enhancements on our behalf, even though we were willing to pay for them. Each request was met with excuses of lack of staff or time. They wanted us to buy the product off the shelf with minimal customization.

For two days I struggled with the software company's sales representatives. Finally, in exasperation I exclaimed to one of the sales people, "You guys should know that the customer is always right!" Without hesitation, and with a completely straight face, one of the negotiators for the software vendor replied, "But the customer isn't always right." With an equally straight face I calmly replied, "You're right, I'm wrong, and we're done." I got up, walked out of the negotiations, and inked a multi-million dollar deal with their biggest competitor less than three weeks later.

I use that experience in my bookselling business daily. Customers make what I sometimes consider odd, outlandish, unreasonable, and frivolous demands every single day. I go out of my way to accommodate them. I don't want to give customers a reason to buy from a competitor or to leave me negative feedback (more about feedback later). That's because ultimately, the customer *is* always right. The customer is the reason you're able to make payroll. The customer pays the bills. Without the customer, you have no business. That makes the customer right, all the time.

Does that mean you allow customers to take advantage or defraud you? Of course not, but you'll be amazed at how easy it is to get into the habit of accommodating your customers. You'll find that for the most part, it only costs you a little more time.

Rule #2: If the Customer Is Ever Wrong, Consult Rule #1

What if a customer is being totally unreasonable? Then ask yourself, "Is this a profitable sale?" If the answer is yes, accommodate him or her and smile while you're doing it. What if the customer requires constant attention and hand-holding? Give the customer all the attention he or she wants and hold hands, but try to get the customer to give you more business. As long as the customer is doing profitable business with you he or she *deserves* to be treated well.

You should even accommodate a customer who is "wrong." For example, you'll occasionally get a customer who claims his or her book never arrived, yet the post office tracking website says the package was delivered. Is the customer trying to defraud you? It's possible, but not likely. Besides, the track record of the post office, while excellent, is not perfect. Do you take the hit? The customer only cares about receiving his or her purchase. Many booksellers simply refund the purchase price. I don't always do that. I refer the customer to the marketplace venue's guarantee policy after asking the customer to take a few preliminary steps.

Another exception is when a buyer is clearly attempting to defraud you. For example, you sell a brand new book or shrink-wrapped CD or DVD and the buyer claims the book contains writing or highlighting, or that the disk is scratched. I won't cave-in to a fraudulent buyer and I'll fight tooth-and-nail, right down to the bitter end.

On Amazon buyers are protected through the A-Z Guarantee program to force sellers to grant a refund. On Half.com it's the Buyer Protection program. Other marketplaces have their own procedure for buyers to seek redress for orders they believe are not what was represented. Sending a polite note to the customer explaining how the guarantee program works is all that's needed. When you're contacted by a customer complaining that an order hasn't been received, look-up the tracking number on the USPS tracking web page and confirm delivery was made to the address. If USPS indicates the package successfully arrived, send the following eMail to the customer:

Dear Customer,

Thank you for your message.

According to the USPS online tracking system, your package was delivered on _____ . If you are unaware of its arrival please check with other members of your family and perhaps your immediate neighbors in case another person received the package and forgot to tell you.

You may track the status of your package by accessing the USPS website at: http://www.usps.com/ and entering your tracking number where it says "Track & Confirm." Your tracking number is _____ .

I appreciate your business and I hope to be of service to you again in the near future.

Joe

While polite, the above response makes it clear the customer has the responsibility to at least make sure the order hasn't been received by another member of the household or by a neighbor. Notice the generic wording of the form, making it easy for you to simply drop in the delivery date and tracking number. Nothing else needs to be changed.

Most customers inform me a few days later that the order was found. If the customer contacts me again indicating the order hasn't turned up, I decide whether to refund the order, or ask the customer to file a claim with the marketplace. Here's an example of how I ask the customer to file a claim with Amazon:

> Dear Customer,
>
> Thank you for your message. I did some additional research on your order today and determined that your package must be lost in the mail.
>
> Unfortunately, I don't have a replacement to send you. I recommend you file an A-Z Claim with Amazon. The A-Z guarantee program protects buyers in situations like this. When you file your claim just explain that the Post Office failed to deliver your package. Amazon will contact me; I'll support your claim by providing the tracking number of your shipment and my shipping details and Amazon will use the package insurance to refund your purchase price.
>
> If you have any questions about how this process works please do not hesitate to contact me for additional assistance. Rest assured your money is not lost and I'm truly sorry this transaction did not go smoothly for you.
>
> Sometimes the Post Office will deliver a package weeks or even months late, so your item may show up some time in the future. If that happens, please let me know, but feel free to keep it as my gift to you as compensation for any inconvenience this situation may have caused.
>
> I appreciate your business and I hope to be of service to you again in the near future.
>
> Joe

Notice that no changes are required to this eMail message. Just click "reply" to the customer, copy and past the message from your word processor, and send it on its way.

When a customer files an A-Z claim, Amazon makes a decision on who's responsible for paying the claim. First Amazon contacts you via eMail to inform you that a claim has been filed. You're given the opportunity to "state your case" and explain why you're not responsible for the loss. All you do is provide Amazon the date the order was shipped and the tracking number. Summarize for the Amazon folks any correspondence between you and the buyer. As long as you've shipped the order on time and can provide a tracking number, you shouldn't be held responsible for the loss. Amazon has never held me responsible whenever I've done those two things.

If a marketplace venue doesn't offer a buyer guarantee, then immediately refund the purchase price. If it's an expensive item, it should be insured prior to shipment.

International orders cannot be tracked; therefore, if the customer claims the order hasn't been received within the allotted time promised by the marketplace, issue a refund. For expensive items you can file an insurance claim to recover the majority of your loss.

Don't let the lack of tracking ability deter you from pursuing international business. You'll have few problems with international orders. If you avoid them you'll leave a considerable amount of money on the table.

Correspondence

If you look at my Amazon feedback you'll see that the vast majority of the negative comments and ratings I received over the years are due to being slow to respond to customer inquiries. When people take the time to write you an eMail expressing concern about an order, they expect a prompt reply. By prompt I'm talking about a *maximum* of 24-hours. Take longer than that and you're not offering world-class customer service and your feedback scores show it.

When it comes to customer service, the one lesson to take away is to make it a priority to beat the 24-hour deadline answering correspondence. (Even if it's to deliver bad news, i.e., you're out of the ordered item.)

Always, and I mean *always* treat your customer with dignity and respect. Your correspondence should be a model of politeness and professionalism. Often, customers leave positive comments even when they didn't like the outcome if they believe their feelings were acknowledged.

John A. Goodman reminds us in his book *Strategic Customer Service:*

> "Customers expect to be treated in certain ways, given the organiza-
> tion, the product they are buying, the amount they are spending and

their history as customers. They may or may not want the 'warm fuzzies,' . . . but they definitely want and expect genuine interest in their question, request or problem, and quick, friendly, competent delivery, whether it is the mocha without whip cream, but with a genuine smile or a solution when the organization fails to do it right the first time."[3]

Customer Feedback

When starting from scratch you obviously won't have any feedback for customers to consider when making a purchasing decision. As time goes by you'll find about 10 percent of your customers actually make the effort to leave feedback of any kind. That means for every 10 sales you make you'll only receive one feedback rating. Better make it a good one by delivering accurately described, securely packaged merchandise in a timely manner!

The scary part about early feedback is a single negative can have a devastating impact on your overall score. Imagine if after selling your first ten books you receive one positive feedback rating of 5 out of a possible 5 score. That means you have an overall feedback score of 100 percent positive. That's great. Then your next feedback score comes in as a 1 out of a possible 5. Now your overall feedback rating plummets to 50 percent positive. Ouch! Many buyers consider the feedback score of the seller before making a purchase, and at 50 percent positive, it seriously hurts your chance of landing a sale.

When you don't maintain an excellent feedback score you potentially leave money on the table. Therefore, your goal is to quickly build as much positive feedback as possible before getting your first negative. That's because positive scores soften the blow when your first negative arrives. And by the way, everybody gets negative scores eventually. It's best to take steps to prepare for them ahead of time. Having said that, if you can't maintain a one year score of 98 percent or better, something is wrong in your customer service or fulfillment department.

How to Get Excellent Feedback

You can realistically boost your feedback response rate to 20 percent or more with a few simple techniques. In fact, you have the opportunity to nudge customers into leaving positive feedback on at least five, count'em, *five* different occasions without appearing pushy or over bearing.

I want to add a caveat to the following section by saying that after Amazon implemented "charge when shipped" it severely limited the amount of sanctioned contact that sellers have with buyers. Therefore, I strongly recommend you thoroughly review Amazon's current policy regarding order acknowledgement eMail before implementing this strategy. If you run afoul of Amazon's guidelines you could receive a severe reprimand, or even have your account closed. So don't play fast and loose with the rules. In fact, it's a good idea to review the policy statements of all marketplaces on which you sell before implementing an aggressive customer contact program.

The first opportunity to urge the customer to leave positive feedback is in your online listing description. In every single listing description ask the buyer to leave feedback after receiving his or her order. Say something like, "Please leave feedback after receiving your order so other buyers know they can count on us!" Right away you've got the customer thinking positively about you, and your chance of getting positive feedback is enhanced *if* you follow through with world-class customer service.

Your second opportunity to legitimately solicit positive feedback is when the order is placed. Once the customer places an order with you he or she should receive an Order Acknowledgement eMail indicating that the order was received and that you'll be shipping it soon. Your inventory management system should perform this chore automatically.

Customers appreciate being informed that their order is in good hands and that it's receiving proper attention. The Order Acknowledgement eMail is your second opportunity to coax your customer into leaving feedback. Taking the time to acknowledge the order leaves a favorable impression. And customers are generally receptive to a casual mention that you'd appreciate positive feedback after the order arrives.

Upon shipment of the book the customer should receive an "Order Shipped" eMail to announce the package is on the way. Again, your inventory management system should automatically send the eMail on your behalf. This is the third opportunity to gently solicit positive feedback. Your request is favorably received because getting a acknowledgement eMail indicating that the package is in the mail is impressive and customers absolutely love the extra attention.

Your fourth opportunity to gain positive feedback is in the shipment itself. Always include a packing slip containing the title of the item ordered, the customer's name and address, your name and address, the description of the item as it appeared online, a short note thanking the customer for the order, and guess what? Yup, within the body of the note you ask for positive feedback.

When the package is received (in record time, right?) the customer is thrilled to leave you positive feedback. After all, you've been informative, prompt, polite, and highly professional every step of the way. By now, the customer feels that the *least* he or she can do to thank your for all your hard work is logon and leave you glowing positive feedback. Well, at least 20 percent of them will feel that way using my eMail follow-up method.

Just in case the customer doesn't immediately feel compelled to leave you positive feedback, send the customer an eMail reminder a couple of weeks after the estimated arrival of the order. This is your fifth and final attempt to coax the customer into leaving you positive feedback. Unlike the first four attempts, your communication was welcomed information the customer wanted and needed about his or her order. This last attempt is an unsolicited message and is only allowed because you have a prior relationship with the recipient.

Send *one, and only one,* follow-up message with the primary purpose of ensuring the customer is happy with the order. Within that context you may ask one final time for positive feedback. If you send more than one unsolicited request for positive feedback you could find yourself being accused of spamming and have your eMail account shutdown by your ISP or, worse, have your marketplace account permanently closed—putting you out of business.

If the customer doesn't leave you positive feedback after five attempts, consider it a lost cause and move on. To help you implement your program you can use a product like Feedback Forager to automate a lot of the process. You can find more information about Feedback Forager at *http://amazon.wolfire.com.*

One final word of caution: Amazon has recently changed its policy regarding third-party sellers contacting buyers. Consult with the current guidelines before sending eMail to customers obtained through Amazon's website. Make sure you don't violate the rules and you'll be fine.

Avoiding Negative Feedback

Actively soliciting positive feedback from customers does little good if you offer poor customer service. When it comes to getting positive feedback the best defense is a strong offense. That means delivering superior customer service at all times and avoiding negative feedback altogether.

You avoid negative feedback through frequent communication with your customers for the purpose of keeping them informed of the status of their order every step of the way. When a problem occurs notify the customer immediately and give him or her one or more alternative courses of action. For example, if a book you've listed was improperly described, send the customer an eMail and fully disclose the additional defect(s) *before* shipping the order. Wait 24-hours and if there's no response, contact the customer a second time through the marketplace from which the order originated.

Use the marketplace for the follow-up message because many customers don't accept eMail from unknown senders and your first message may have ended up in a spam folder. Most customers have the marketplace eMail address in a known-senders list (or "white list") and your message stands a better chance of getting through.

After waiting another 24-hours it's time to refund the order. Some booksellers advocate contacting the customer via snail mail as a final step. However, doing so causes you to miss the "ship by" date by a considerable length of time. Besides, sending snail mail still doesn't guarantee you won't get negative feedback.

I've found the better choice is to issue a refund and follow-up with a postcard informing the customer of the reason. It makes no sense to send another eMail because the customer either has a problem receiving your messages or is away for an extended period of time. Either way, you're constrained by the "ship by" requirements of the marketplace and you're forced to act or you could find yourself in hot water if enough customers complain.

In the end, good customer service depends on good communication and fast shipment. When you can't deliver the goods, fast refunds, prompt, courteous explanations, and settling disputes overwhelmingly in favor of customers usually save the day.

CHAPTER 7
Building Your Business

I wish I could give you a magic formula that instantly generates buckets of cash without you having to lift a finger. Unfortunately, no such magic formula exists, and you have to build your business the old fashioned way: through hard work, determination, commitment, and *cunning*.

It's been my experience that using a combination of techniques for getting sales creates a synergy greater than the sum of the individual methods themselves. What follows are the techniques I use successfully in my business on a daily basis to steadily push sales and profits higher.

What If You Have Very Little Money?

If you have more time than money, you can still start an Internet bookselling business. You'll just have to be more creative than your competition. Also, without a reasonable amount of start-up capital, you can expect your progress to be slower—especially if you can't immediately afford a scanner.

Assuming you can't afford a scanner, and you don't have adequate capital to immediately buy a significant amount of inventory, your first order of business is to get on the fast track and sell from your personal library. Those sales are pure profit because there is no acquisition cost or carrying cost to consider. Next, take all the books you can't sell on the Internet to a local bookstore and trade them for store credit. If there are stores that allow you to use 100 percent of your credit to pay for your purchase, go there first. Your second choice is to go to stores with the next most generous trade policy that accept the majority of your trades. Finally, go to stores with the largest selection of books for which you can trade.

Go back to Chapter 4 and review my recommendations on the types of books to buy. While you're in used bookstores trading deadwood, write down the title, author, and ISBN of books that look valuable. Return home and look-up the books on Addall.com to verify their value. When you get a hit, go back to the used bookstore and pick up those books with an Amazon sales ranking below 50,000. If there are a number of used bookstores in your area (maybe eight or more), buy the books with a sales rank below 10,000 first for maximum inventory turnover, then go up to 50,000 after exhausting the supply of lower ranking books.

Your second order of business is to review the garage sale strategies discussed in Chapter 4. Pay as little as possible for inventory because without a scanner you're going to bring home lots of deadwood. However, the garage sale strategy produces more profits than losses and your capital base grows if you consistently make the rounds.

You'll want to actively pursue estate sales to purchase large numbers of books at rock bottom prices. Go on the last day of the sale and make an offer of five or ten cents per book. You'll be surprised at how many takers you'll find. Most sale organizers counter your offer and negotiate with you from there. Don't be afraid to pay up to 25¢ per book if there's a lot of nonfiction included.

Always try to be fair because if the estate sale organizers feel you've taken advantage of them they won't return your calls or work with you in the future. Getting a bad reputation with estate sale organizers is a sure way to kill that portion of your business.

A Heavy Duty Scouting Plan That Works

It's not enough to know where to find books to buy. You need a systematic, step-by-step plan for harvesting them. Intellectually, most booksellers know where to find inventory, yet they still have difficulty bringing in enough books to earn a decent living. You won't have that problem because I'm going to share several methods I use to acquire more than enough inventory to meet my needs.

If you're serious about getting your business off the ground, this plan helps you ramp up your business in record time. Practiced diligently, you can buy 40 to 80 books every single day you scout, under normal circumstances. Some days you'll bring home fewer books, some days more. But a good average should be around 60 salable books.

The first thing you do is trot down to your local office supply store and buy yourself a weekly day planner. It doesn't have to be a big fancy affair. A simple "At-A-Glance" planner is just a bit smaller than an average trade paperback and works nicely. That's all I use.

Now go to *http://www.yellowpages.com* and record the name and address of every public library and thrift store within 50 miles of your home in a spreadsheet. Periodically save your work to avoid the risk of accidentally deleting it and having to start all over again!

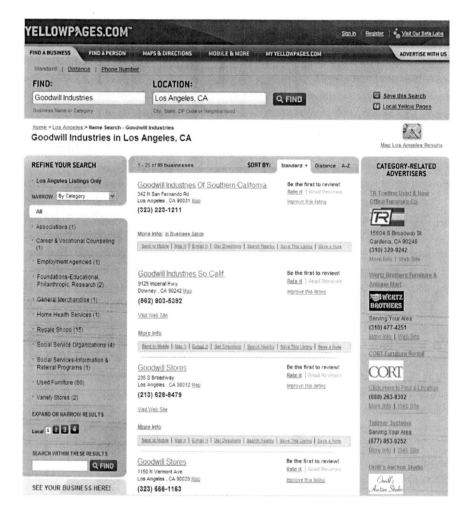

Now use *http://www.google.com/maps* to create a scouting route with eight to ten locations on each route. Use the advice in Chapter 4 and create circular routes so you end up where you started for maximum efficiency. Keep libraries and thrifts on separate routes because, in the end, recordkeeping is easier to handle when you're not mixing procurement methods. That's because libraries generally only take cash and checks, while thrift stores prefer cash or credit cards. Never pay with cash if you can help it. Always use a credit card when possible, and use checks when necessary. This way you'll always have an electronic audit trail of your activities that's downloadable for easy bookkeeping.

For the sake of argument, let's assume you're a full timer, and you look up all of the public libraries, thrift stores, and used bookstores in your area as explained in Chapter 4, and you end up with 11 routes. That's a good start because that gives you one route per day for two weeks. If you end up with fewer than 11 routes you need to widen your territory so you'll have a full two weeks of stops to make. You want two weeks of stops to allow each location to adequately restock before you visit again. Pull in all the locations you can within 50 miles of your home to get the 11 routes you need to make this work. If you end up with more, all the better.

If you're part-time, you only need half as many simply because you won't have time to hit them all consistently. Choose the locations closest to home as your territory. If those prove to be duds, you'll need to widen your circle until you find enough reliable sources that yield the quantity and quality of books you require.

After you've compiled the needed routes, open your day planner and assign a different route to each weekday of the week covering a two week span. As you become familiar with each route you may discover that particular days of the week work better for certain routes and you'll want to switch things around. For now, don't worry about fine tuning your schedule. Just make a plan and stick to it for a month or two as you get your bearings. As a full-timer, your weekday goal is to pick up 250 to 300 books per week from your routes—half that many if you're part-time.

For weekends, get on *http://www.booksalefinder.com* and keep track of library sales. Attend each one in your area every weekend. If you can fit more than one into a single weekend, go for it. Your weekend goal is to pick up 50 to 100 books. If the library sale is insufficient to reach that number, supplement your weekend scouting with your 11th route—which should consist exclusively of thrift stores because most of your competitors will be at the library sale. The weekend routes, schedules, and quotas are identical for full-time and part-time booksellers.

This is the exact scouting regimen I used the first few years of my business, and it worked beautifully. I use a slightly different model now because of my size, but sometimes I really miss the good old days.

Hit the Road for Fun and Profit

I love to travel. In fact, I've traveled a great deal of my life. When I discovered I could combine my love of travel with my bookselling business I thought I'd died and gone to heaven. The idea is called the "road trip."

One of the main reasons I love Internet bookselling is because of the total freedom it gives me. This, combined with the exhilaration of being on the wide open road is the stuff dreams are made of. Well, at least for me.

From the beginning of your business start learning where the best areas of the country are for acquiring books. Some are better than others. If you happen to live in a target rich environment, then taking road trips is more of a personal preference than necessity. If you live in an area where books are difficult to find, road trips may be just the ticket to build your inventory more quickly.

Road trips work best when your spouse or significant other is involved with your business. Even a working spouse can process orders while you're out of town. The road trip takes a member of your team to greener scouting pastures if your area is thin on inventory (assuming you're not unattached). Road trips can also supplement an already abundant territory if you're able to extract greater yields from more distant locations.

Of course this all presupposes that the remaining member of the team is involved with the business deeply enough to handle processing, packing, and shipping the orders while the traveling partner is on his or her walkabout. I know booksellers who even have their children help out with the business. It's a great way for the little tykes to learn responsibility while earning money they can spend however they choose.

There are a couple of different ways to approach your trip. You can drive to your destination and back or you can use public transportation. Each method has pros and cons. Generally, driving yourself is the more economical choice. However, if you plan to scout nationally, especially if you're dealing with higher end inventory, flying or taking the train or bus may be the most sensible option.

Using Public Transportation

Clearly, the least stressful way to take a road trip is to let someone else do the driving—or flying, whichever the case may be. Take a hint from the movie *The Accidental Tourist* and pack light.[1]

Two types of travelers fly to their scouting destinations: the antiquarian book dealer who traffics in high-end merchandise and the bulk buyer looking for tons of books from failing brick and mortar stores, Internet booksellers throwing in the towel, or salvage from thrift stores and spent library sales. If any of these business models fit your profile, the cost of a plane ticket, rental car, and hotel room won't faze you a bit. You're dealing with big numbers and travel expenses are figured into the freight.

When I pulled off my first acquisition I was scared to death when I boarded a plane. After closing the deal, I shipped more than 30,000 books back to Phoenix and I was positively mortified. But when I returned home I had more fun triaging those books than a mosquito in a nudist colony.

Your trips around the country don't have to be quite so ambitious. However, if there are no mega book sales in your area you may want to consider taking a road trip where you can pick up a couple hundred books in a single day. Two hundred books in a day represent about $2,400 worth of raw inventory. By raw I mean it hasn't been cherry picked by the seller. You'll sell at least 33 percent of that within 30 days. The majority of the remaining books sell off at a rate of about 4 to 5 percent of the outstanding physical inventory per month. One fly-out per month to places where you score that much inventory pays for your trip, and adds significantly to your inventory.

Personally, I wouldn't fly anywhere for less than 300 books of raw inventory. The trip can't cost more than $600 to pull off including transportation, lodging, and meals. If you tighten your belt you can take quite a few trips using those parameters. When purchasing your books don't forget to factor in the cost of shipping your inventory back home for listing.

Using Private Transportation

If you're not traveling too far or if you're traveling a circular multi-state route, driving your own car, van, or truck with an *enclosed* bed is frequently more economical. Personally, I prefer to rent an SUV or van for maximum storage capacity.

Once again, consider all your costs before proceeding. To make the road trip worthwhile, don't stop scouting each day until you score at least 100 books. Consider 75 of those books as part of your ongoing inventory, and the remaining 25 books to pay your daily living expenses. I've found this to be a good, practical rule of thumb because 25 books bought for about $2 each and sold for $14 yield a gross profit of $175 per day. Now, you'll usually only sell about a third of them within thirty days (this is your new listing sales rate; more about that later), so you actually end up with about $58 per day, which is enough to get by on.

You won't sleep in the best hotels or eat the best food, but you'll increase your weekly inventory by 75 to 100 more books per week than if you stayed home. That translates into an additional $1,050 to $1,400 per month in new listings sales revenue.

Local Road Trip "Surges"

Local road trip surges work well too if done with the same single-mindedness used during out-of-town trips. You get better economics and limited family separation to boot. I frequently use the local road trip to make up end-of-month gaps in my scouting consistency.

They work like this. Create five 10-to-12-location circular routes that bring you home each day. However, don't end your day until every stop on the route has been hit. Ordinarily, traffic, store yields, and scheduling keep me from completing a given route. However, when I'm on a scouting surge, nothing, and I mean *nothing*, keeps me from completing all the stops on my route. I rarely fail to hit 100 books per day when I'm in surge mode.

You'll find when you're surging that your day stretches to 10, sometimes 12 hours. You hit the first location at 9 a.m. and you may not leave your last location until 9 p.m. when stores close. It's a grueling regimen that shouldn't be kept up for long, but a week-long surge can net at least 500 books if you're determined.

Once I surged for an entire month just to prove I could do it. I was near exhaustion by the end of the ordeal, but man did that extra revenue boost my morale, bottom line, and ongoing *residual sales.* (Don't forget, residual sales are the percentage of books sold from your total inventory over an extended period of time. Stay with me because I'm going to thoroughly explain residual sales in Chapter 8.) Yeah, I know it's a shamelessly male macho display of runaway testosterone. But hey, it's a guy thing, what can I say?

You don't have to be so brutal with your scouting, but planning a week-long surge once a month, once every other month, or once a quarter can give an extra boost to your momentum (not to mention your bank account). If a week seems a little over the top for you, try it for two or three days. In the beginning every little bit helps. The sooner you hit a state of equilibrium between monthly unit sales and your ability to replace sold books, the sooner you can relax a bit.

Outsmart Competitors with These Strategies

Internet bookselling is becoming more competitive every day. Books like mine are teaching thousands of people how to earn a good living with little risk by getting involved with this fascinating business.

When I first started, finding great books to sell was like shooting fish in a barrel. But within a couple of years the gems became harder to find and I had to develop strategies to stay one step ahead of the competition. Below, I'll share my best ideas.

Double Team the Competition

Couples working as a team have a huge advantage in this business. Even a spouse working part-time can score 50 to 100 books per week. That's as many as 400-plus books per month generating gross revenues of at least $3,500. You'll see how I arrived at that figure later when we go through a little bookselling math.

My wife scouts one day per week and she normally brings home an average of 60 books. We each take a different route to cover twice as many locations. There are days when the two of us bring home nearly 250 books combined. We rarely fail to bring in at least 100 good quality books in eight hours as a team.

Avoid the Crowds

Keep track of the library sales in your area. Library sales tend to attract large numbers of people. If there are a decent number of thrift stores in your area, scout there instead of the library sale. Most of your competition track library sales too. While they're slugging it out at the sale, you'll have a near monopoly at the thrift stores.

This strategy works particularly well with a two-person business. One member of the team goes straight for the thrift stores. The second member of the team hits the library sale for the first hour only, and then takes on a second thrift store route, leaving the crowd behind. On weekdays, full-timers can visit the best locations during off-peak hours and not only avoid excessive competition, but rush hour traffic to boot.

Learn the Scouting Patterns of Your Competition

Most days when you're scouting you'll run into competitors. Ninety-nine percent of the time they'll be down-home, friendly folk, just like you and me. The other one percent should simply be avoided.

When you meet other friendly scouters, feel free to briefly exchange pleasantries about the business and maybe even share a tidbit or two of "inside baseball," depending on the frequency of your exchanges and how well your personalities click. Always try to be friendly to everyone you meet. That includes the competition. At the same time don't give away the store—literally! Don't reveal your best scouting locations, don't brag about what you earn, and don't share your operating procedures anymore than absolutely necessary.

What's absolutely necessary? It's not unusual or improper for another scouter to ask which scanning service you use. It makes no sense to try to hide that information because anyone with eyes can see your screen unless you go to extraordinary lengths to hide the display. Doing so only makes you appear aloof and snobbish. Be happy to share the obvious, but keep your trade secrets to yourself.

On the other hand, do try to collect intelligence about your competition. Where do they scout? Which locations are the most lucrative? What scanning service do they use? How reliable is it? Smile a lot, but don't say much.

Whenever you run into competition learn his or her name. Discretely make a written note of the person's name, day of the week, and time you met. Do those things whenever you encounter another scouter and pretty soon patterns emerge. People are creatures of habit. They tend to do what's comfortable and familiar, even to their own detriment. Break that mold and do the unexpected. Learn the habits of your competition and use that knowledge to your advantage.

For example, if you learn that a certain person scouts a certain store on a certain day, at a certain time, get there 30 minutes earlier and scoop up the best buys. With luck you'll be in and out before your competition arrives and they'll never be the wiser.

If it appears that someone is always 30 to 40 minutes ahead of *you*, change your routine and skip a store to get 30 to 40 minutes ahead of him or her. Keep your competition guessing about your strategy and the law of large numbers turns in your favor.

Form Alliances

Another reason to be nice to your competition is because you may want that person as your ally, especially if you're working alone and don't have a spouse or significant other at home to back you up. I'm not talking about a partnership. I'm talking about a strategic alliance.

For example, I encounter a certain competitor on a regular basis. She and I seem to work the same territory and we tend to buy the same kind of books. She's also smart and employs a number of the same strategies as me as we attempt to outfox each other. Somewhere along the line, and without any formal agreement or even acknowledgment of any sort of alliance, we started helping each other. She tells me where she's already been so I don't waste time hitting the same store and walk away empty handed. I do the same for her.

However, we never tell each other where we're going next unless we bump into each other at more than one store. We're smart enough to know we're only going to dilute our collective efforts by going head-to-head at each store, so we agree to go in opposite directions so we both achieve maximum value for our efforts.

If your relationship with a couple of competitors becomes closer you may even want to start alerting each other about planned vacations or what days of the week you each intend to take off. That way one of you can step up his or her scouting to maximize the number of books purchased while the other is away.

You can have several such informal alliances with people you encounter on a regular basis. However, if you learn that one of your strategic partners is misleading you to gain an advantage, all bets are off and it's open warfare complete with subterfuge, misinformation, and every other guerrilla scouting tactic available in your arsenal.

Incremental Profits

This section is complex and not at all intuitively obvious. However, I ask that you stick with me and consider these concepts. They're more than just theory because I've practiced them for years with great success. They're more of my private little "not so secret—secrets" that are effective because not many people put them to use on the same scale as I have.

Essentially, *incremental profits are made when you quickly "flip" books as fast as possible on razor thin margins.* Using the quick flip you turn over the same dollar investment numerous times throughout the year to create an astronomical return on investment.

My cash flow began to improve measurably after I was introduced to the concept of incremental profits by a successful Internet bookseller. I met this fellow through his brother-in-law, a chap I met on a bookselling forum. They are both booksellers, but with radically different approaches to the business.

My acquaintance prefers the antiquarian end of the business, and he's knowledgeable about many aspects of his craft. I learned and continue to learn a great deal about the antiquarian market as I take my first timid steps into that world. However, it was his brother-in-law who inspired me to develop my own version of what he described to me as "incremental profits."

My particular implementation of the concept is especially useful to the beginning Internet bookseller because it recognizes the need for immediate cash flow from the business. It's a concept so simple one almost immediately and instinctively misunderstands it. But if you embrace the idea it feeds your hungry business the cash it needs to keep itself from starving to death.

Sales Rank Terminology

To understand incremental profits you need to understand the importance of sales rank. The proper way to grasp sales ranks is to equate "higher" sales ranks with lower numbers. A lower number is considered a "better" ranked book. Conversely, "lower" sales ranks equate with higher numbers and are considered "worse" books. Thus, "better" selling books have "high" rankings which mean low numerical numbers, and worse selling books have "low" rankings which mean higher numerical numbers.

Are you confused yet? Me too. If you want a fuller explanation of how Amazon devised these mathematical contortions I suggest you pop over to FonerBooks at *http://www.fonerbooks.com/surfing.htm* for a far more academic treatment of the subject.

Personally, I'm a simple man who views the world in simple terms. I don't care to contort my mind with mental gymnastics every time I ponder my business. Therefore, I choose the less sophisticated, yet intuitively comfortable view that better-ranked books are more desirable and have lower numbers. Conversely, poorly-ranked books are less desirable and have higher numbers.

You can choose to be correct and simply reverse everything I'm about to say or you can take the easy road and travel with me. It's your choice, but my vernacular works just fine for my purposes.

Profitability vs. Cash Flow

Compared against higher ranked books with slower turnover, you naturally want to gravitate toward lower ranking inventory. That is, until you remember that the highest prices are almost always found in poorly-ranked books. Not always, but almost.

Logic tells you greater profits are found in the higher end of the sales ranking scale, say between 500,000 and 1.5 million. I've sold quite a few $100 to $400 books that had atrocious sales ranks. However, those sales are not commonplace and require patience, skillful pricing, and bit of luck to capture. Still, it does happen, with mathematical regularity.

But your *cash flow* comes from turning over your inventory as quickly and often as possible. And for that you need the lower ranked books that sell for razor-thin profits. If you're confused now, continue reading because it's only going to get a little murkier, my friend.

Do you invest in the stock market? No? Then let me introduce you to two concepts called Rate of Return (ROR) and Return on Investment (ROI). Applying those two investment terms to your business can help improve your cash flow.

From the booksellers' point of view your ROR is your gross profit (GP) divided by the sales price (SP). Your gross profit equals the sales price less your purchase price (PP), shipping supplies (SS), postage (P), and marketplace commissions (C). This strategy works best with lightweight books (under one pound) so the shipping credit received from the marketplace covers postage and handling. Consequently, for the purpose of this exercise I'm eliminating shipping supplies and postage from the equation since they're a wash. Therefore, the formula to calculate Gross Profit looks like this:

$$GP = SP - (PP + (C * SP))$$

The formula to calculate the Rate of Return looks like this:

$$ROR = GP / SP$$

Return on Investment can be calculated by dividing the Gross Profit (GP) by your purchase price. Therefore, you get this formula:

$$ROI = GP / PP$$

One final formula and I promise I'll stop with the numbers. Once you've determined your ROI, annualize the number to project how well your investment fares if you're able to repeat the results multiple times per year. I'll explain more about why annualized returns are important in a moment, but for now multiple your ROI by the number of investment periods in a year (IPY). We'll figure out how many investment periods there are in a year later. For now, here's the formula:

$$Annualized\ ROI = ROI * IPY$$

With these four simple formulas in mind certain purchasing decisions can be made based on the probable financial outcome. What you want is to turnover your inventory quickly. Popular titles should be sold as quickly as possible before inevitable price erosion from competition reduces bestsellers to penny book status.

Less popular titles need to be purged or quickly sold off through a book sale as soon as they're in danger of becoming unprofitable, recouping the original purchase price if possible.

Contributing to the murkiness of this mad dash to push inventory out the door are incremental profits. The strategy is this: during the course of a normal scouting day, train yourself to buy every single book with a sales ranking below 10,000—no matter how small the profit.

Books sporting a sales ranking below 10,000 rarely take more than seven to ten days to sell if they're priced competitively. Like I said, it's the closest you're ever going to get to a guaranteed profit in this business. With inventory turnover of less than ten days, even small profits balloon to astronomical annualized RORs.

Let's take a few real-life examples of field experiences to illustrate how you can obtain maximum cash flow from your investment capital. For all the examples that follow I assume the shipping credit you receive from the marketplace is adequate to pay for postage and packing materials to ship the book.

Suppose you scan a book with a 5,000 sales rank that costs you $1 to buy and you sell it five days later on the Amazon marketplace for $2 even. If you apply the ROR formula after factoring in Amazon's 15-percent sales commission, it doesn't seem too impressive. The numbers work out like this:

$$GP = SP - (PP + (C * SP))$$
$$GP = \$2 - (\$1 + (\$2 * 15\%))$$
$$GP = \$2 - (\$1 + \$0.30)$$
$$GP = \$2 - \$1.30$$
$$GP = \$0.70$$

You make a 35-percent ROR because your gross profit of $0.70 divided by the Sales Prices equals 0.35. Express this decimal as a percent, and you have the ROR. The formula works out like this:

$$ROR = GP / SP$$
$$ROR = \$0.70 / \$2$$
$$ROR = .35 = 35\%$$

Big deal, you say, it's still only $0.70 profit. True enough, but now lets look at your ROI and see what a shrewd scouter you are. You calculate your ROI like this:

$$ROI = GP / PP$$
$$ROI = \$0.70 / \$1.00$$
$$ROI = 0.70 = 70\%$$

Things are looking a little better. When you calculate the return on actual invested capital you get a 70-percent ROI. Now that's impressive. But it's still only $0.70 right? Yes, but let's look at one more number and calculate your annualized ROI. Since the book sold in only five days you calculate there are exactly 73 five-day investment periods in a year. The formula works out like this:

$$\text{Annualized ROI} = \text{ROI} * \text{IPY}$$
$$\text{Annualized ROI} = 70\% * 73$$
$$\text{Annualized ROI} = 5,110\%$$

Where else can you (legally) earn an astonishing FIVE THOUSAND PERCENT return on your investment? If you find it please eMail me so I can get in on the action! "But wait!" you protest. "We're still only talking about $0.70!"

True enough again, but when you consider the fact that it only took five days to make the sale you can now take that same $1 investment and do it again, and again, and again. In fact, you can do it 73 more times throughout the year and turn every $1 invested this way into $73 within 12 months.

Just think what that means.

Set aside $100 and invest it this way every five days. At the end of 12 months you've turned $100 into $7,300 *without investing another dime.* That's a little over $600 per month in additional cash flow on a *single* $100 investment! *For a home-based operation, $600 more than covers fixed overhead with money to spare.*

How much additional effort is involved in pursuing this cash flow technique alongside your normal scouting routine? Next to zero, because once you scan the book you either put it back on the shelf or throw it into your shopping cart. Each action takes the same amount of effort. Therefore, your incremental cost is zero, but your incremental profit is $0.70 for the sale.

Of course it takes additional effort to pack and ship the book once it sells. But while you're flipping books every five days something else astonishing happens. You're building an inventory of higher ranked, slower moving, but highly profitable books too. That inventory consistently produces $8, $10, $12 and $15 bread-and-butter sales, day-in and day-out. In addition, you're building an inventory of $25, $50, $75, and $100 books that generate consistent *residual sales.* We're going to discuss residual sales in great detail in a moment. But what I want you to understand right now is that all these things happen to your inventory because you had the staying power of good cash flow.

Don't Ignore the Flip

One reason why I was able to buy so many books each month in the beginning was because I *relentlessly* went after quick flips wherever I found them. To see the cash flow benefits don't think about flipping, just do it until it becomes second nature. More than 25 percent of my purchases were flips. When you're flipping that many books, your new listing sales rate can exceed 60 percent per month. Consider that number for a moment. *Sixty percent of all the books you buy sell within 30 days.* Most retail business owners would happily sever their right arm for that kind of turnover.

Before you get too excited about flipping, please understand your actual results heavily depend on the quantity and quality of books available in your area. Having said that, any number of flips you make improve your cash flow.

Just because you flip doesn't mean you don't buy higher priced books too. The remaining 40 percent of your purchases are accumulating as ongoing inventory, most of which sell at premium prices. I haven't sold a $1,000 book yet, but I've sold a $440 book, several $300 books, and a slew of $100 to $200 books. Keep in mind that you flip in *addition* to building an inventory of high dollar books—not *instead* of building quality inventory.

Limitations of Flipping

If flipping books for incremental profits is so great, why not concentrate exclusively on flipping? Because of the basic reality that there simply aren't enough high turnover books in any given market accessible to the small independent bookseller to sustain an entire business. You can't earn a living selling $2 to $5 books exclusively. You need the higher ranked books for their superb profit margins.

As your high quality inventory grows, your average sale price begins to climb. A $3 average sale price quickly jumps to $6. Soon it'll pass $7 and not long afterward it'll hit $8 per sale. That's because as your inventory grows, 25 to 35 percent of your books sell for $8 to $100 or more. Another third of your sales fall between $5 and $8 per book. The remaining third of your sales are for books selling below $5. This is the normal sales distribution for the strategy I've described.

Depending on the effort and resources you put into your business you'll soon see a rising and almost entirely predictable income stream generated by your operation. You'll be amazed at how smoothly the pieces fall into place.

Pay Up for Higher Profits

Up until this point the focus has been on books you can acquire for a dollar or two and sell them for $10 to $50 online. But don't neglect the profit potential of higher priced books in the post-1972 market either. There are plenty of books you can buy for around $8 to $15 and easily sell for, say, $75 and up.

For example, I recently found a brand new used bookstore run by a non-profit that had been open for less than two weeks. A friend ran across the store's "Grand Opening" sale advertisement in the local newspaper. He called me up and invited me to go to the sale with him. Since he owns a brick and mortar (B&M) retail store and he doesn't sell on the Internet, there's little competition between us.

We showed up for the sale and I was initially disappointed at the limited number of books they carried. All together, I estimated they stocked less than 3,000 books. However, upon closer examination I noticed several dozen quality reference books on engineering, railroading, and art. Each book was priced between $10 and $12, but scanned as having an online value of $100 or more. I bought 40 books from the store that day for an average of $11 each. I was their largest customer for the day and the store employees were ecstatic to have raised so much money for their cause.

The woman in charge of the book sale approached me to thank me for my large purchases and during the course of our conversation revealed that she was a former B&M bookstore owner herself. She also mentioned she was largely responsible for acquiring the fine selection of books on display. She quickly identified me as a bookseller and asked if I sold on the Internet. When I responded that I did, she lamented that she knew she was leaving a lot of money on the table by not listing the donations they received online, but she just didn't have time to manage an Internet operation and fulfill orders.

I immediately proposed that she consider allowing me to sell her better inventory on consignment, thus earning more money for the organization without the hassle of staffing an Internet sales operation. I offered to split the profits 60/40 in my favor.

Naturally, she was interested in new ways of increasing revenues for the organization without increasing their workload and a deal was struck. Not only do I now have a new source of incoming inventory, I averted more competition for my Internet sales. It's a win/win for everyone.

Hold a Monthly Clearance Sale

Earlier we covered the importance of purging deadwood from your inventory. Here's a neat way to get paid for tossing out the old to make room for the new.

On precisely the first day of the last week of each month, run an automated repricing script with the price reduction governor bumped to 50 percent and your price floor reduced to $2 *on your oldest inventory with the worst sales rankings*. This competitively prices a larger portion of your stock. Only do this once! As soon as it's finished, lower your governor back to its original limit. In addition, increase your price floor back to its original level.

Let me be perfectly clear about this technique. I'm not suggesting you lower prices by 50 percent on your entire inventory. I'm suggesting you raise your downward price adjustment percentage to 50 percent on the part of your inventory that is the oldest and poorest ranked with the purpose of bringing it back in line with the rest of the market. Don't slash prices on your entire inventory by half and tell your friends and colleagues I told you to do it!

Almost immediately you're going to see a spurt in sales as books whose online prices dropped below your normal price floor sell off. That happens because you lowered prices to meet the market. Don't cry over those books because chances are the vast majority of them would have simply sat on your bookshelves for an eternity while competition relegated them to penny book status. There's always the possibility that some of them might see a price recovery. But not enough of them recover to offset the overall losses from books that continue to decline in price.

Not only do you clear out deadwood on a regular basis, but you give your month-end sales an extra boost and recover some of the capital invested in unproductive merchandise. This monthly exercise allows you to kill two birds with one stone.

Handling Slowdowns

Every industry operates in cycles and Internet bookselling is no exception. There are seasonal cycles as well as economic cycles. For example, during the four month period between October and January you'll experience a significant increase in sales of all kinds due to the Thanksgiving and Christmas holiday season. Throughout the year you'll experience mini-booms for specific media just prior to most major holidays.

Conversely, you'll experience seasonal and economic slowdowns throughout the year in a continuous series of boom and bust cycles. The summer months, for example, are typically slower for most booksellers than any other time of year. As I write this chapter, the country is experiencing one of the worst economic slowdowns since the great depression, and most of the booksellers I know are reporting major dips in sales revenue. To make matters worse, there are more Internet booksellers entering the market than ever before, making it doubly hard to find quality inventory.

However, my sales have remained relatively stable, and growing. Granted, they haven't grown as fast as before, but they haven't fallen either. Why? It's not that hard to figure out. As the economy worsened I increased my scouting to compensate. Before you claim I'm stating the obvious let me explain in practical terms why I'm not.

Prior to the economic slowdown I scouted four to five hours per day and brought in 40 to 50 books. As the economy worsened and competition increased, five hours of scouting would yield 25 books if I was lucky. To counteract changing economic conditions I began scouting eight hours per day to bring in 40 to 50 books to maintain my sales levels. In addition, I increased my minimum price while improving my repricing script to drop prices at a slower pace and increase prices at a faster pace. This helped my profits because I sold books at higher prices.

The recession continued to deepen and I continued to increase my listings to double what I was putting online compared to prior months. An Internet bookselling acquaintance I know from an online bookselling forum once posted that "Joe scouts like the devil is after him." The net result was that I maintained my sales revenue in a failing economic climate.

When faced with difficult economic conditions you'll need to step up your listing to maintain sales. Employ as many of the scouting and business building techniques in this books as possible. You not only need to scout consistently, you need to scout *more*. Go for incremental profits and flip like mad. It's hard work, but it may be just the thing needed to keep your business afloat.

Systematize Everything

The simplicity of Internet bookselling is surprising. In its most efficient form it should consist of a series of relatively minor actions that you repeat over and over again. Your day-to-day operations function like a baker using a cookie cutter to stamp out identical ginger bread men. Day after day the process continues, one cookie after another.

Sound boring? It should, because that's exactly what you want: a lean, efficient operation with as few variables as possible so you can ship large numbers of books to your customers with flawless precision and the highest quality. The way to achieve this economic bliss is to take the time to sit down and think through how you actually accomplish each task and document the steps. Once fully documented, your efficiency increases because your procedures are clearly defined and they soon become second nature.

World-renowned entrepreneur, author, and business coach Bradley J. Sugars gives another reason for systematizing your business. Sugars writes in his book *Instant Systems*:

> "I'm big on systems for another important reason: They allow your business to work without you. That's right. They will allow you to live your dreams, to do the things you want to do, and to spend your time pursuing other, more lucrative goals like increasing your wealth."[2]

None of the road trip techniques explained in this book can work without someone back at headquarters carrying the ball in your absence. That person will be far more effective if you've adequately systematized every aspect of your business in clear, easy-to-understand procedures. Solo operators must hire competent help if he or she wishes to go on road trips.

Write a Standard Operating Procedures (SOP) Manual

After you've systematized your business, take your documentation and store it in a three ring binder for safe keeping and easy access for everyone connected with your operation. This is an important step—no, it's an *essential* step in growing your business. As you reach out to others to assist you, whether they are family members, temporary help, or full-time employees, they expect to receive clearly defined parameters within which they can work. It's your job to provide those parameters.

Have you ever eaten at a McDonald's restaurant? Most of us have because they're everywhere. Did you know that whether you order a hamburger in a McDonald's in San Diego or one in New York they'll always taste identical? That's because every restaurant is maintained the exact same way. French fries are cooked in Phoenix exactly the same way they're cooked in Dayton. How are they able to achieve this amazing degree of consistency across thousands of restaurants? First, they systematized their franchises to the nth degree. Then they documented those systems in an SOP manual and drilled those procedures into their employees until they became second nature.

Michael E. Gerber, author of *The E-Myth Revisited,* suggests thinking of your business as the prototype of a franchise that will be replicated 5,000 times across the country. He calls it the "franchise prototype."[3] He wants you to design systems so simple they can be operated by people with the lowest possible level of skill; otherwise, it's impossible to replicate and you'll never free yourself from your business enough to focus your energy on growth.

Once created, your systems need to be documented, loose-leaf bound, and accessible by everyone working in your business. Training incoming employees is easier, and repetitive questioning from workers diminishes because the information they need is at their fingertips. There is no need to interrupt you. If you're the type who hates to document your work, that's a growth-inhibiting weakness that needs to be overcome.

I'm not suggesting you hire an army of employees to be successful. All I'm saying is organize your business as if it were going to be franchised and duplicated thousands of times across the nation. That means every procedure must be documented and stored in a binder for easy access. Drill those procedures into your brain until they're second nature and you can do them in your sleep. Your level of efficiency grows exponentially, and your profitability increases too.

The Importance of Determination and Commitment

I've painted a fairly accurate picture of the day-to-day requirements of running an Internet bookselling business. As you read about my experiences you may be thinking to yourself how easy it'll be to run your own business. I want to take this opportunity to caution you on how insanely competitive this business can be.

No one is more competitive than me. Others may be a bit smarter, have lots more money, or have better business and political connections. But no one is more competitive. Let me give you a couple of examples.

One rainy morning I awoke pumped and ready to hit the field because this particular day was half price day at a major thrift store on all merchandise, including books. I never failed to score 100 books or so on half price day so I was understandably excited. The stores opened at 7 a.m. on sale days, so I had to leave unusually early to get ahead of the expected heavy crowds.

I make note of the fact that it was raining only because rainfall is so rare in Phoenix. Whenever it rains here it's the topic of much conversation, but that day it was raining torrents. Thunder crashed across the sky and lightening arched as far as I could see. The storm was the top story on all the morning TV news channels, with talking heads warning everyone to stay indoors for safety. The warnings and admonitions only got me more excited. My wife was aghast.

"You're not going book hunting in that weather are you?" she cautioned.

"Of course, it's perfect weather for book hunting."

"Only insane people go out in weather like this!"

"That's exactly why I'm going," I tossed over my shoulder as I headed out the door. "There won't be much competition."

As it turned out, I was right. The weather was horrendous. Rain poured down in sheets; winds blowing so hard I could barely steer my car in a straight line. But at each stop there was hardly a soul to be found and I hauled away nearly twice as many books as I normally would. I encountered one other scouter halfway through the day (after the rains subsided somewhat) and he was using a cell phone lookup tool. He wasn't particularly friendly and quickly disappeared when he saw me zipping along with my PDA scanner.

In less than seven hours I scored 197 books—more than 70 percent of them low ranking and the majority of them in like new condition. However, I kept 17 for my personal library, leaving 180 salable books for less than a full shift.

I could have scored another 25 or so, but the weather slowed me down and I had to cut my scouting short because the Mrs. and I had plans for the evening with friends. I tried to weasel out, but I was duly reminded of what awful things would happen to me if I were late. I was tired and hungry anyway and actually ready to go home. Still, it was a good day.

Other times I've relentlessly scouted during the hot Phoenix summer when temperatures reach a blistering 120 degrees in the shade. Who goes out in heat like that? Me, and others like me who are serious about their businesses.

I'm not suggesting you be as driven as I am. Clearly, my kind of motivation approaches the extreme. I know that, but that's me. It doesn't have to be you. You may only work at your business a couple hours per day because that's all your schedule allows, or because you just plain don't want to work that hard. That's perfectly acceptable. You can still build a good business over time. It just won't happen as quickly for you as it will for those putting in more time and effort.

Only you can decide how hard to work at this. Only you control the level of success for your company. That's the beauty of Internet bookselling. It's completely customizable; flexible enough to fit both the most demanding and least demanding lifestyles. Yet it's lucrative enough to help you meet whatever financial goals you establish for yourself.

CHAPTER 8

Business by the Numbers

You'll be hard pressed to find a business that can be measured as accurately as selling books. With Internet bookselling, you can decide how much money you want to earn, determine the level of effort it takes to earn it, and know in advance how much capital is needed to get there.

Let me put your mind at ease. This chapter is not about accounting, although a few accounting principles are covered. If you need help with accounting, there are many books in your local bookstore or public library that thoroughly cover the topic. More importantly, sit down with your CPA and discuss the particulars of your business.

Instead, this chapter is about benchmarks I use to run my business. A more formal dissertation on the subject of benchmarking can be found in *The Benchmarking Book,* by Tim Stapenhurst. In his book Mr. Stapenhurst says,

> "Benchmarking is a method of measuring and improving our organizational performance by comparing ourselves with the best."[1]

I agree with Mr. Stapenhurst, and when I consider the performance of my Internet business I compare my relative results with the best in the industry: Amazon, Barnes & Noble, and a small army of the largest third-party sellers around.

Throughout this book you've been given a few assumptions that will make more sense in this chapter. We're going to settle on a few of those assumptions as benchmarks and use them as examples. The benchmarks used are based on more than 50,000 sales I've made over the last few years.

First, we'll assume your average revenue per sale is $14. Notice I said *revenue per sale* and not *sales price*. The average revenue per sale is quite different from the average sales price because average revenue per sale includes the shipping credit. We're focusing on revenue per sale because it's important to account for all income received from sales to accurately manage cash flow.

Presently, Amazon gives a $3.99 shipping credit for each sale. I'm going to round that number to $4 for the sake of simplicity. Let's assume the average sales price is $10. Therefore, $10 plus $4 equals $14 average revenue per sale because this is the total amount of money you receive from the marketplace. Your average selling price can be higher or lower depending on which end of the bookselling market you target. Generally, the shipping credit will cover the postage and shipping supplies for lighter weight books (under two pounds). Smart sellers can actually squeeze additional profit from sales by carrying more light-weight books (such as mass market paperbacks) and by getting shipping supplies inexpensively or for free.

We'll further assume a minimum 50-percent net profit margin on each sale. These numbers are what you'll typically see using the techniques in this book.

On the cost side, you need to consider fixed and variable costs. Fixed costs are unchanging, and remain the same regardless of changes in your sales. Rent, equipment lease payments, and insurance are examples of fixed costs. You can count on those expenses to remain static month-in and month-out.

Variable costs increase and decrease in direct proportion to sales. Selling costs, postage, shipping supplies, and office expenses are examples of variable costs.

For the purpose of the following examples, we'll assume $0.08 in fixed costs, and $7.79 in variable costs per book. I arrived at my fixed cost per book by dividing my total fixed costs by the total number of books in my inventory. Again, these numbers are based on years of actual sales data in my business. You'll understand why there's such a wide variance between the two in a moment. We'll further assume you're operating a home-based business and you don't have outside employees, so you don't have rent or employee expenses to pay.

Finally, we'll assume you have a standing inventory of 1,000 unique titles, you're purchasing 300 books per month using the scouting techniques in this book, and that you're selling 200 books per month. All these assumptions are realistic and obtainable by the average person with a reasonable supply of inventory in his or her geographic area.

Sales Projections

Not all sales and revenue are alike. It's important you understand that your sales come from two different revenue streams:

1. New listing sales.
2. Residual sales.

Each type of revenue plays an important role in your cash flow management. Therefore, you need to understand the source of each revenue stream and how to maximize profits from each one.

What Are New Listing Sales?

New listing sales are the direct result of your daily scouting efforts. These are the books you find in the field and bring home to be graded and listed online. Depending on your purchasing criteria 30 to 60 percent of your new listings sell within 30 days.

Based on several years of my own sales data, you'll find that your average selling price floats between $8.50 to $13 per sale with a gross profit margin up to 70 percent. Of course, variable expenses such as the cost of the book, marketplace commissions, shipping supplies, and postage affect your profit. Knowing this, let's look at the two components of sales revenue a little closer.

Here's where a thorough understanding of the mathematics of Internet bookselling serves you well. The idea is that you can decide in advance how much income you want to earn and mathematically predict how much effort it'll take to earn it by applying a few industry assumptions to your scouting routine.

For example, if you want to generate $700 per month in sales and you know that 33 percent of your new listings sell within 30 days, you need to list at least 150 books each month to meet your sales goal, assuming the following criteria are true:

- # Books Listed   150
- # Books Sold   50
- Average Revenue Per Sale $14
- Sales Ranking   Below 500,000

To get your monthly sales figure you multiply the number of books listed times the new listings sales percent times the average revenue per sale, or:

$$\text{Monthly Revenue} = (150 * 0.3333) * \$14 = \$700$$

I dropped all fractions for the sake of simplicity. But that's all there is to it. Well, almost all there is to it, but you get the idea. All you do is find and list 150 *quality* books per month to generate $700 in sales. By quality I mean books that are in Good to Like New condition, have decent sales rankings (under 500,000), and list for $10 or more online.

If you maintain a 50-percent gross profit margin you'll retain $350 per month in before-tax net profit. Do 150 books sound like a lot to you? It shouldn't. Many of you can find that many books practically sleepwalking in just a few days.

The story doesn't end there. A curious thing begins to happen after the first 30 days a new batch of books is listed; your inventory begins to swell. After listing your first 150 books and selling 50, you still have 100 left. The next month you list 150 more, except instead of selling 50, you sell 55 books. Instead of generating $700 in sales, you generate $770 in sales. Instead of retaining $350 in net profit, you retain $385. Where did the extra five sales and $70 in additional revenue come from? To coin a phrase, "Residual Sales."

What Are Residual Sales?

This is where the business gets exciting. We've talked about residual sales a few times so far but now we'll look more closely at them.

A curious phenomenon of Internet bookselling is that you earn money on past efforts without doing more than packing a few extra orders. It's been my experience that old inventory sells off at a rate of 4 to 7 percent per month, depending on demand. We'll continue our conservative approach and use 5 percent as our benchmark. Multiply 100 times 5 percent and you get five orders equaling an additional $70 in sales. So far so good, right? Wrong—it gets better.

Now you're sitting at the end of month two. You've sold 55 books and generated $770 in sales. You roll into month three with 195 books in your inventory

Table 8.1

SALES PROJECTIONS						
Month	**# Books Bought**	**Beginning Inventory**	**Ending Inventory**	**New Listing Sales**	**Residual Sales**	**Monthly Revenue**
JAN	150	0	100	50	0	699
FEB	150	100	195	50	5	769
MAR	150	195	285	50	10	836
APR	150	285	371	50	14	899
MAY	150	371	453	50	19	959
JUN	150	453	530	50	23	1,016
JUL	150	530	604	50	27	1,070
AUG	150	604	673	50	30	1,122
SEP	150	673	740	50	34	1,171
OCT	150	740	803	50	37	1,217
NOV	150	803	863	50	40	1,261
DEC	150	863	920	50	43	1,303

and you list another 150. By the end of the month instead of generating $770 in sales from selling 55 books you sell 60 books and generate $836 in sales revenue.

Whoa! Your gross sales revenue increased again, yet you've done nothing different for three months. If you punch these numbers into your own spreadsheet or calculator you'll find I've rounded the numbers for the sake of simplicity. But to seriously get your juices going, review Table 8.1 for a one year projection of what's possible using the scouting guidelines in this book.

As you can see, your sales and income continue to grow, yet you haven't changed a single thing you've done since day one. If you extend the table a bit it'll show that within 14 months your residual sales exceed your new listing sales, and you'll earn twice the money from the same effort, except for the additional time needed to pack and ship all those orders!

Scouting Time Estimates

I know you're eager to get your business off the ground, so let's deal with determining the amount of effort needed to acquire inventory for your business. Until you gain more experience and develop expertise with more advanced book buying methods covered in my follow-up book, *Advanced Internet Bookselling Techniques: How to Take Your Online Bookselling Business to the Next Level,* you're going to have to build your inventory the old fashioned way: by scouting.

Although you'll enjoy the thrill of hunting for hidden treasure in thrift stores, used bookstores, and libraries, you're going to discover that scouting is hard work. If you live in a climate like mine, when the temperature routinely tops 110 degrees, or in climates where the humidity makes you feel like you're swimming through the air, you'll understand what I mean. For those of you who live in colder climates, think snow and ice. But it helps to know you're scouting according to a plan designed to take you where you want to go financially.

As previously mentioned, you can expect to purchase five to ten books per location you scout. For the sake of this discussion, let's split the difference and say 7.5 books per stop. After factoring in your drive time, each location should take about an hour to cover. That gives you a maximum of 45 minutes at each stop. In an eight hour day you can generally expect to make eight stops and find 60 quality books to buy.

However, a number of factors can affect these estimates. For example, if your locations are clustered closer together, more stops per day may be possible. If locations are spread farther apart, you might not make all your stops in eight hours, and you'll have to extend your day. Also, the minimum sales price you choose determines how many books you ultimately buy because the higher your minimum, the fewer books you'll find that meet the hurdle.

Obviously, the amount of income you generate is governed by the amount of time you have available to devote to your business, but you can use these numbers as a guideline for estimating your income potential.

Inspecting and Listing Time Estimates

Now that you've found your books they have to be inspected and listed. The inspection process can be relatively quick, but depending on what kind of technology you use, the listing process can be somewhat lengthy.

The inspection process, as previously described, should take less than a minute per book. Therefore, if you bring home 60 books per day, it'll take about one hour to inspect them. However, as you gain experience you'll spend less time inspecting each book.

Depending on your set up and the specific book in hand, listing may take as little as ten seconds per book or it can take up to five or ten minutes. If you're equipped with a handheld scanner attached to your computer and the books you're listing all have barcodes, listing is a ten-second affair. If the books only have printed ISBNs, you'll have to manually key the numbers and that can take 30 to 45 seconds per book.

If you have a lot of pre-ISBN books, or a number of your titles are the only ones available on the Internet, further research is needed to determine the proper value before they're listed. Researching pre-ISBN books can take anywhere from 5 to 30 minutes each.

Let's assume you spend 45 seconds on average listing books because most of them are barcoded. Sixty books per day take 45 minutes to list after they've been inspected. After adding another 15 seconds per book for shelving you get a grand total of one hour per day. The combined effort of inspecting, listing, and shelving requires you to add an additional two hours to your day after purchasing 60 books.

Now you know how to figure your time commitment for a specific amount of scouting. The example above requires about ten hours per day. If you don't have ten hours per day to dedicate to your business, that's okay. Just work the numbers backward until your scouting effort fits your schedule. Then you'll know exactly how much income is possible from your business.

For example, let's say you only have ten hours per week to devote to your business. That means you can buy 60 books per week, or about 260 books per month $(60 \times 4.33 = 260)$. Using our previous assumption of $14 average revenue per book, your ten hours of effort will land $3,640 worth of inventory per week. That's not bad. You can still make a respectable part-time income scouting one day per week if you carefully build your inventory, as you'll soon see.

Packing and Shipping Time Estimates

One of the biggest mistakes beginning booksellers make is under estimating the labor and materials cost of the packing and shipping process. It takes a lot more time and effort than you think, if you do it right. Generally, a single individual can pack and ship about 12.5 to 15 orders per hour. This estimate includes pulling books from the shelves, cleaning them, and packing them up for mailing.

Notice I didn't include time for printing off shipping labels and packing slips. The reason I neglected to mention that step is because during the first few minutes of the printing task, the Pick List is produced first. You remove the Pick List from the printer and immediately begin pulling books from inventory as the shipping labels and packing slips continue to print. Thus you compress the time needed for order fulfillment by multi-tasking.

If you're selling 25 books per day, allow at least two hours for the packing and shipping process alone. Four hours are needed to pack and ship 50 books per day. For each hour you spend scouting add the appropriate amount of time for packing and shipping the orders you receive. Once you're able to predict your sales you'll have all the tools needed to figure out the labor equation.

Knowing the time commitments for your business in advance greatly simplifies writing a business plan capable of successfully guiding you toward your financial goals. You can plan your business around your own schedule such that it has the least amount of impact on your family or daytime work schedule. Eliminating the guesswork from your venture significantly increases your chances of success.

Adding It All Up

If you're going to give this business a try it's best you have a clear idea of what your time and resource commitments are before you get in too deep. Proper time management helps to maximize your income while minimizing the effort required. For example, if you only have two hours per day to spend on your business as a part-time effort, use the time commitment guidelines in this chapter to divvy up your available hours such that you acquire, list, and fulfill as many books and orders as possible on a weekly basis.

If you commit 20 hours per week to your business you can generate a larger income. Ten hours per week scouting should net 75 books. You'll need another hour and 15 minutes to inspect them, plus another hour and a half to list and shelve them.

Finally, you'll need nearly seven hours to fulfill the eventual orders. Assuming you have a 1,000 book inventory, Table 9.2 illustrates how the time commitment for running a 20-hour-per-week bookselling business works out:

Table 8.2

Part-Time Bookselling Commitment	
# Books Found	75
Hours Scouting	10.00
Hours Inspecting	1.25
Hours Listing	1.67
Packing New Listing Sales	2.00
Packing Residual Sales	4.00
Hours Weekly	18.92

Using the 20-hour-per-week guideline, and spending ten hours per week scouting, with the remaining ten hours spent processing books and filling orders, it's not unusual to generate $1,400 or more each month in gross revenue after two months. I used a new listing sales rate of 33 percent and a residual sales rate of 5 percent to arrive at this income level. That's about 28 sales per week starting from scratch. It'll take just over two hours per week to process 28 books. Add the residual sales from a 1,000 book inventory and your time commitment expands to just under 20 hours per week, and your income goes up another $500 per month.

Other than scouting, you don't have to perform these tasks in large blocks of time. Twenty-eight sales per week are just under four books per day. Scale down the guidelines and you find it takes less than half an hour per day to fulfill four book orders, and you can confine your scouting to weekends. Your time is your own and you can arrange your fulfillment activities to fit your schedule.

Compare part-time Internet bookselling to working a part-time job at a retail store to earn extra money. Your employer dictates your work schedule, your hourly rate, and raises. In my opinion, working for yourself wins every time.

If it seems like a lot of numbers have been thrown at you in this chapter, don't worry. You can download my time management worksheet from the "Downloads" area at *http://www.internetbookselling.com* with complete instructions on how to use it. Access is free if you're the original purchaser of this book. If you purchased this book used, you can buy a membership and start enjoying premium website benefits immediately, so logon and sign up today.

Cash Flow Management

For legal purposes, I want to repeat my warning found at the beginning of this book. I'm not a licensed financial planner nor am I an accountant. Seek out the services of a licensed professional when you need financial planning and accounting advice. The information I'm sharing with you is what I learned from my own personal experiences. Once you've consulted your experts and determined what financial and retirement goals best suit your particular needs, it's a simple matter to determine if Internet bookselling gets you there.

Guarding your cash flow is one of the most important things you can do for your business. I use two financial statements to get a quick snapshot of the health of my business. Those statements are the Profit & Loss (P&L) statement and the Cash Flow statement.

The P&L statement (also referred to as the income statement) is a standard financial document that shows how revenue and expenses were accounted for during a specific period of time. The Cash Flow statement (also called a statement of cash flows) is a financial document that shows the amount of cash generated through business operations and the amount of cash used during the same time period.

Many small business owners make the mistake of assuming that as long as their P&L shows a net profit, they're in good shape. That's a false assumption. It's the Cash Flow statement that gauges the true health of your company.

Cash is the lifeblood of your business. As long as you have cash you can weather the storms of market fluctuations. Spending more cash than you bring in each month is called your "burn rate." It means you're burning through your cash faster than you're making it. What you want is a positive cash flow in addition to a net profit on your P&L because as long as you're bringing in more cash than you're spending, your business is growing.

To control your cash flow be mindful of your expenses and don't withdraw more money from your business for personal use than your cash flow allows. A good rule of thumb is to limit your cash withdrawals to 50 percent of your after-tax monthly cash increase (that's the amount of money remaining after deducting tax liabilities from your profit). Doing so allows your business to accumulate cash that can be used for expanding inventory, or it can be socked away to help weather bad times. It's not a hard and fast rule as you'll see in a moment, but simply a suggested starting point for you to consider.

Breakeven Analysis and Profit Margins

Your breakeven point is when your revenue equals expenses. There is no profit and no loss. Determining the breakeven point for a given product can be distilled down to a couple of simple formulas. For example, to determine the breakeven price for a given book analyze the numbers like this:

$$Revenue = Fixed\ Costs + Variable\ Costs$$

To solve the equation assign fixed and variable costs to each book. Fixed costs are those costs you incur each and every month whether you make a sale or not. Good examples of fixed costs are marketplace subscription fees, inventory management system subscription fees, and lookup tool fees.

Variable costs are those costs you incur when you acquire books for sale. Your primary variable costs include the cost of the book, transportation costs such as the gasoline, commissions paid on each sale, shipping supplies, labor, and so on. Don't forget to include variable costs such as depreciation and maintenance on your vehicle. You should get those figures from your CPA.

Let's assign fixed costs of $0.08 per book and variable costs of $7.83 per book as a starting point. We'll discuss how to calculate those numbers a little later. But for now, let's calculate your per unit cost as follows:

$$\$7.91 = \$0.08 + \$7.83$$

Figuring out the unit cost doesn't tell the whole story. If you have fixed costs of $157 per month ($117 as calculated in Chapter 9, plus a $40 monthly Amazon marketplace fee), selling a single book isn't going to be financially rewarding. A number of books must be sold to breakeven. Therefore, a slight adjustment to our formula is required to figure how many books must be sold to cover all fixed and variable costs. In this revised formula, "X" represents the number of books sold:

$$Revenue(X) = Fixed\ Costs + Variable\ Costs(X)$$

That's better. Our adjusted formula tells us Revenue(X) equals the total amount of revenue received from selling "X" number of books. Fixed Costs remain the same and Variable Costs(X) equals the total variable costs incurred by selling "X" number of books. To find your breakeven point all you do is solve for "X":

$$Revenue(X) = Fixed\ Costs + Variable\ Costs(X)$$
$$\$14x = \$157 + \$7.83x$$
$$\$14x - \$7.83x = \$157$$
$$\$6.17\ x = \$157$$
$$X = 25\ books$$

Now you have your breakeven point. To cover your overhead you have to sell about 25 books before your business starts turning a profit. Beginning with sale #26 you add $6.17 to your bottom line for each additional sale because all of your costs have been covered. However, we're still not quite done with our analysis.

Presumably you want to withdraw money from your business for living expenses. Let's say your goal is to earn an extra $1,500 per month in addition to increasing your cash by $400 per month for future expansion. To meet those requirements you need to add $1,900 as a Cash Requirement to the expense side of the equation as a final adjustment:

$$\text{Revenue}(X) = \text{Fixed Costs} + \text{Cash Requirement} + \text{Variable Costs}(X)$$
$$\$14x = \$157 + \$1,900 + \$7.83x$$
$$\$14x - \$7.83x = \$157 + \$1,900$$
$$\$6.17\,x = \$2,057$$
$$X = 333 \text{ books}$$

Selling 333 books per month allows you to withdraw $1,500 in extra income plus retain $400 monthly in your business for reinvestment in future growth. All you do is figure out the effort required to find enough books to make those numbers real. If you're using the 50-percent rule of thumb, you'll limit your withdrawals to $750 and retain $1,150 in your business instead of withdrawing $1,500 because $750 is half of $1,500 and you still want to pay your taxes and retain $400 for future growth. Ultimately, you must decide what's best for your situation.

How to Achieve Financial Independence

Table 8.1 illustrated how you can gross more than $1,000 per month in less than six months. That's $500 per month in net profit. What if you need to gross more so you can put more money in your pocket sooner? One way is to try listing 200 to 300 books per month instead of 150. What would happen if you listed 500 books per month? In my second year of business I listed an average of 1,200 books per month and my income soared to nearly $14,000 monthly! Do you see the potential Internet bookselling offers?

Before you get too excited and drive yourself crazy trying to figure out all the numbers, logon to *http://www.internetbookselling.com* and visit the "Downloads" area to get a copy of my Sales Projections spreadsheet. Play with the numbers yourself until you find an income level that not only meets your financial needs, but fits your schedule. Once you determine the income level you want, the spreadsheet helps you figure out how much effort it'll take to earn it.

You can also approach it from the opposite direction. Based on your available time, resources, and energy, you decide the number of hours you can commit to the business and the spreadsheet tells you the amount of income you can earn.

To achieve financial independence, first decide exactly what "financial independence" means to you. For me, financial independence meant being able to pay all of my personal bills from income generated by my Internet bookselling business. Later, I refined my definition to mean being able to pay my personal bills in addition to setting aside a couple thousand dollars per month for retirement *from residual sales alone.* To accomplish my goal I need to build an inventory large enough for a 5-percent residual sales rate to generate the required income. Once accomplished, my scouting efforts are all gravy.

Your definition of financial independence can (and should) be completely different from mine. Does $2,000 per month supplement your family income enough to cover all your personal bills plus save a few bucks each month for a rainy day? Can $4,000 per month pay your personal bills each month? You're the only one who can answer those questions.

Find a quiet place and seriously think about the amount of money you need to live. Be honest and cut out the luxuries. There'll be plenty of time for that later.

Once you've determined your basic needs, add 20 percent to start yourself on the road to a solid retirement savings plan. If you're older and need to build your retirement nest egg faster, you may have to save more than 20 percent of your earnings. Again, your personal circumstances dictate the actual numbers. I urge you, no matter what your age, never save less than 20 percent of your earnings. To be safe, plan to save *at least* that amount to protect yourself from unexpected emergencies.

After you've determined you own personal threshold for financial independence and you've added a minimum 20-percent savings rate on top of it, add a couple of hundred dollars for a few luxuries if you want. Now, what is your number? Do you need $5,000 per month in sales? Does your goal require $10,000 in monthly sales? Both numbers are certainly achievable, but it takes time, energy, effort, and resources to get there. Do you have the resources to achieve your goal in a reasonable amount of time?

If investment capital is in short supply then scale back your operation to fit your budget. Again, don't violate the cash withdrawal rule of thumb by taking more than 50 percent of after tax cash flow. Reinvest your earnings in more inventory.

Using the methods I explain in this book you'll pick up fast-selling books to "flip" for quick cash. Simultaneously, you're building a strong base of "long-tail" inventory for generating steady residual sales for years to come. To achieve your financial goals all you do is determine what size inventory meets your financial needs.

I decided I wanted all of my income to come from residual sales. That meant I needed to bulk up on quality inventory as quickly as possible so my business would become self-sustaining. All I want to do is replenish sold stock at my monthly sales rate. In other words, I wanted to be in maintenance mode and no longer in growth mode.

For example, to pull $5,000 per month out of your business you'll need gross monthly sales of about $12,000 to do so without creating a negative cash flow. That's assuming a 50-percent gross profit margin and less than $2,000 per month in fixed overhead. Decide how much of the $12,000 will come from residual sales and how much comes from new listing sales. The more revenue coming from residual sales, the less work is required to maintain your income level.

If your residual sales rate is 5 percent and your average revenue per sale is $12, an inventory size of 20,000 books typically generates $12,000 monthly from residual sales alone. That means selling 1,000 books monthly, which is just over 33 books per day. Don't forget you need to replenish your inventory to maintain the proper quantity level so you'll have to *buy* 1,000 books per month to sustain your income.

The preceding assumptions are a bit simplistic because purchasing new inventory also generates new listing sales at a higher level, so the actual number of books that need to sell will be smaller. Also, as your inventory ages, residual sales will start to drop off.

In reality, you'll reach an equilibrium point unique to your business where no matter how hard you scout as a one-person operation, there's a ceiling you'll find impossible to breech without outside intervention. At equilibrium, the logistics simply start working against further growth for the small operator.

For me, my equilibrium was 12,500 books. Although I was able to buy up to 1,250 books per month from scouting alone, once I hit the 12,500 book level I discovered I couldn't grow my business any further because I always sold at least 1,200 books monthly. Throw in low yield days, occasionally getting sick, taking time off to tend to personal business, and my monthly scouting tended to equal my sales.

To grow further I needed to learn or develop more advanced methods of finding and processing larger amounts of inventory. I write about how to push past the equilibrium point in *Advanced Internet Bookselling Techniques: How to Take Your Online Bookselling Business to the Next Level.*

The math demonstrating how new listing sales interact with residual sales gets pretty complex. Therefore, I'll explain by example. Table 9.3 gives various inventory quantities needed to accommodate various income levels balanced against varying amounts of new listing sales versus residual sales. You can download this table from the "Downloads" area of my website at *http://www .internetbookselling.com* and play with the assumptions to match the availability of books in your local area against your personal financial goals. First, here are the assumptions:

New Listing Sales Rate:	33%
Residual Sales Rate:	5%
Average Revenue per Sale:	$14.00
Monthly Listings:	600 books

Table 8.3

NEW LISTING SALES VS. RESIDUAL SALES					
Starting Inventory	New Listing Sales		Residual Sales		Monthly Income
	Books Sold	Sales Amount	Books Sold	Sales Amount	
1,000	200	$2,800	50	$700	$3,500
2,000	200	$2,800	100	$1,400	$4,200
3,000	200	$2,800	150	$2,100	$4,900
4,000	200	$2,800	200	$2,800	$5,600
5,000	200	$2,800	250	$3,500	$6,300
6,000	200	$2,800	300	$4,200	$7,000
7,000	200	$2,800	350	$4,900	$7,700
8,000	200	$2,800	400	$5,600	$8,400
9,000	200	$2,800	450	$6,300	$9,100
10,000	200	$2,800	500	$7,000	$9,800

Very good money can be earned from buying as few as 600 books per month, but once your inventory exceeds 8,000 titles your inventory reaches a state of equilibrium. The number of books sold equal the number of books purchased. To continue growing, you have to increase the number of books purchased each month.

Buying Zones

After listing my first 100 books or so, I realized my sales were directly linked to the sales ranking assigned by Amazon for all books listed in their huge database. I also realized the cream of the crop in online book sales was for books sporting a sales ranking below 100,000.

To maximize my cash flow, I knew the bulk of my inventory had to consist of books with a sales rank below 100,000. I decided to find out what sales ranking level my inventory was developing so I could take steps, while my inventory was small, to skew the numbers in my favor.

I looked up the sales rankings of every book in my inventory and recorded them in an Excel spreadsheet. Then I developed a formula to count the number of books in each sales rank. This is what I found:

Inventory Sales Rank Ratios			
Sales Rank	**Qty**	**% of Inven**	**Zone Pct**
1–10,000	16	13.68%	
10,001–50,000	19	16.24%	
50,001–100,000	7	5.98%	35.90%
100,001–200,000	15	12.82%	
200,001–400,000	12	10.26%	
400,001–600,000	9	7.69%	30.77%
600,001–4,000,000	36	30.77%	
None (No Rank)	3	2.56%	33.33%
	117	100.00%	100.00%

I created three "buying zones" for my inventory. Zone 1 was what I called the "green" zone, since that's where maximum inventory turnover would occur; the higher the turnover, the higher the profits. Zone 1 consisted of books with a sales rank of 1 to 100,000.

I called Zone 2 the "yellow" zone since sales begin to cool off for books with ranks greater than 100,000. Zone 2 consisted of books with a sales rank between 100,001 to 600,000.

Finally, I dubbed books with a sales rank above 600,000 and books with no rank at all as belonging to Zone 3, or the "blue" zone because sales were so cold they seemed frozen compared to green zone sales.

By pure chance, 36 percent of my inventory fell into the green zone. Thirty-one percent fell into the yellow zone, and 33 percent fell within the blue zone. To perk up sales and drive higher inventory turnover I needed to change my buying habits.

Two options were available to me. Option 1 was to pick up the acquisition of green zone books so they grew at a faster rate than the yellow and blue zones. Option 2 was to slow down the acquisition of yellow and blue zone books until the green zone eventually dominated total inventory.

Since my immediate objective was to ramp up cash flow over the next couple of months my primary efforts needed to focus on increasing green zone book purchases while preserving the lucrative margins available with yellow and blue zone inventory.

To meet my objective I reset the minimum profit threshold on my scanner to $2 for books with a sales ranking of 1 to 10,000. Books with sales rankings of 10,000 to 50,000 were reset to $3, and books with sales rankings of 50,000 to 100,000 were reset to $4. This was only done for books I acquired from library shelves for which I only paid 50¢ or less. Acquiring fast selling books at those low prices would enable me to finance a significant increase in book acquisitions without making a large dent in my available cash.

The net effect of my efforts was that the number of "bread-and-butter" sales increased to where all of my fixed and variable costs were easily covered. Thus, I could afford to wait for sales of higher priced books (priced greater than $50) to materialize.

Turning Benchmarks into Dashboards

You've had a lot of numbers thrown at you and it may seem a bit overwhelming. To make sense of it all, it might help to organize your collection of benchmarks into a "dashboard" of measurement tools that monitor the health of your business. You can do that by producing charts and reports on a weekly or monthly basis that give you a visual representation of how you're doing.

Wayne W. Eckerson writes in his book, *Performance Dashboards*,

> "A performance dashboard is really a performance management system. It communicates strategic objectives and enables business people to measure, monitor and manage the key activities and processes needed to achieve their goals."[2]

Like other business owners I produce the traditional financial statements each month like the profit and loss, balance sheet, and cash flow statements. I also like to keep track of the number of books I list online each month along with the value of each book, the listing date (so I can track how long it takes for books to sell at various sales rankings), which categories of books sell the most (for example, mystery, science fiction, gardening, etc.), and the monthly new listing and residual sales rates. These are just a few of the benchmarks I track.

Ssssshhh—It's *Another* Secret!

I'll admit it: I'm having a lot of fun with this chapter. Whenever I explain to someone new to the business how incredibly simple it is to earn a decent income many are shocked. "It's too good to be true," they say. That's okay because this business is not for everyone. In fact, only a small number of people who buy this book will apply the techniques I describe in a meaningful way. Consequently, I'm genuinely not the least bit concerned about saturating the market by creating new competition or by giving away so-called "secrets."

Here's the bottom line: Americans are in economic trouble and I want to help. I don't care if I reveal someone's cherished secrets (which aren't secrets at all). If this book can help people keep their heads above water so they don't lose their homes, cars, or dignity, it's worth it. Or if my book helps them save for retirement, I'll publish everything I know about Internet bookselling and make it available to as many people as possible.

America is a big country, with a big economy, and enough opportunity for anyone willing to make the effort to achieve his or her goals. My goal is to make a positive contribution to the well-being of my fellow citizens through the information contained in this book.

CHAPTER 9

Tools of the Trade

E very profession has its own unique set of tools. Internet bookselling is no exception. Even a home-based business needs a certain amount of infrastructure to
operate efficiently. To be successful you must know what tools to use, how to use
them, and when. This chapter looks at the major Internet bookselling tools and
gives a brief summary of each one.

Accounting Procedures

If you have the benefit of a reasonable amount of start-up capital, plan to purchase a computerized accounting package right away. However, if you're starting
on a shoestring budget, manual recordkeeping works for a while. Regardless of
your financial circumstances, implementing a method to accurately track income
and expenses is crucial to running a profitable business. You don't need a complex
or difficult accounting system, but you definitely need a system.

If you're accounting-impaired, try visiting The Accounting Coach at *http://
www.accountingcoach.com* for amazingly clear explanations of accounting topics
of all kinds. *AccountingCoach.com* provides free online educational material to
help you learn accounting concepts by using hundreds of pages of explanations,
drills, exams, crossword puzzles, and a glossary of more than 1,000 terms.

Another great site to visit for accounting and bookkeeping help is Bean Counter
at *http://www.dwmbeancounter.com*. The site owners' motto is, "You don't have to
be a rocket scientist to learn and understand bookkeeping." He's right.

The Bean Counter site offers a dizzying array of tutorials, courses, tests, educational information, and quizzes. It also has an unbelievably wide selection of
links to free small business software of every description.

Manual Accounting

If you're starting with limited funds, a manual single entry bookkeeping system maintained with pencil and paper works. I recommend you pick up a Dome Monthly Bookkeeping System for less than $20 at your local office supply store.

Dome has been the leader in single entry bookkeeping systems since before I can remember. Their ledgers are compact and so easy to understand a teenager can do it. As your business grows you'll want a more robust computerized accounting package, but until you're ready, why incur the expense? Dome records are more than adequate for a start-up operation.

Computerized Accounting

After you've been in business six months, and you're following the guidelines outlined here, you'll generate consistent revenue and can afford a decent computer based accounting system. Doing your accounting on your computer vastly simplifies your life. For example, tracking your inventory may seem overwhelming, but putting it on your computer makes it straightforward and easy to understand.

There are many different computerized accounting packages for small businesses of all shapes and sizes. Here I'm going to discuss two of the biggest and best. They're both geared for the small business, yet robust enough to scale up to a substantial enterprise. You'll find more choices for accounting software in the "Resources" area of my website at *http://www.internetbookselling.com*.

Peachtree

Peachtree by Sage is an accurate and secure accounting package that provides the insights and control you need to manage your business more effectively. Helpful features like a Setup Guide, Preparation Checklist, Navigation Centers, Wizards, and an Online Tutorial make it easy to manage all aspects of your business.

The Peachtree system has been around a long time and is used by businesses nationwide. Their software receives good reviews from reputable sources such as *The CPA Technology Advisor* and *Accounting Technology*.

Website: *http://www.peachtree.com*

QuickBooks

Reputed to be the "#1 Small Business Financial Software,"[1] QuickBooks from Intuit is certainly the most popular small business accounting package across a multitude of industries. Whether your business is small, large, or somewhere in between, there's a QuickBooks version made specifically for you.

The intuitive business setup wizard gets you up and running in no time at all. Once setup, you'll breeze through data entry and generate dozens of financial reports at the click of your mouse.

Another reason for the phenomenal popularity of QuickBooks is the seemingly endless number of third-party vendors who supply a bewildering array of add-on products designed to streamline your business to peak efficiency.

Website: *http://quickbooks.intuit.com*

Wireless Look-up Software Services

There are a number of good software subscription services for cell phone and scanning devices on the market. Generally, you can expect to pay $600 to $1,500 for a device, software installation, and database subscription in a bundled package.

You can cobble together a less expensive package by purchasing used hardware from eBay and installing the software yourself, if you're technically inclined. To learn the exact cost of specific systems, I recommend you visit each respective website since any prices I print here would quickly become outdated. Now, let's look at the major services, both cell-phone-related and PDA, available today.

ASellerTool

ASellerTool offers a cell phone look-up service as well as a PDA scanner. I only mention the cell phone because if you purchase their PDA bundle you get the cell phone service for free. It's a good deal because you won't always have your scanner with you. However, most likely you'll always have your cell phone. If you unexpectedly happen upon a cache of books you can always use your cell phone to check prices. In addition, should your scanner fail in the middle of an important sale, you can use your cell phone as a backup.

Website: *http://www.asellertool.com*

BookDabbler

BookDabbler offers three levels of online subscription services to help you determine the value of a book. The services can be accessed via your Internet browser and your web-enabled cell phone. All you do is type in an ISBN or UPC code for any item and BookDabbler retrieves the market information from Amazon's website.

Website: *http://wap.bookdabbler.com*

BookHero

BookHero allows you to check Amazon.com merchandise for books, CDs, DVDs, and more. Unique features that come with BookHero are the ability to check up to 20 ISBNs at a time on PDAs and cell phones, to configure your display format for the information returned, track items bought, export the list into other applications, and view the image of products. It works with wireless PDAs and most Wireless Application Protocol (WAP) enabled cell phones.

Website: *http://www.BookHero.com*

BookScoutPRO

BookScoutPRO allows you to get real-time book prices on virtually any web-enabled mobile device including cell phones, PDAs, Sidekicks, Treos, and more. It also supports most barcode scanners. Prices are gathered from the major online retailers for new and used books to give the most complete pricing picture available. BookScoutPRO supports look-ups by ISBN, EAN, and UPC for books, music, movies, software, video games, and more.

Website: *http://www.bookscoutpro.com*

MediaScouter

MediaScouter quickly provides accurate Amazon pricing information. It does not require a mobile Internet connection or a cell phone. You choose the media you want based on customized scanning criteria including minimum price, sales rank, and so on.

As you scan barcodes, the program plays a distinct tone indicating which items can be resold for greatest profit. You can scan both ISBN and UPC barcodes. If an item does not have a barcode, you can type the number using a large touch number key pad.

One of the best things about MediaScouter is their world-class customer support. It's easy to get them on the phone and they're always more than willing to help me with whatever problem I have. In addition, users get to vote on which new features are built into the product. Now that's what I call truly taking care of your customers!

Website: *http://www.mediascouter.com*

Neatoscan

The Neatoscan service utilizes a barcode scanner, PDA, and earpiece to allow you to quickly and easily determine the value of books and other media while disconnected from the Internet. The software allows you to set thresholds dictating the kind of items to buy. For example, you can tell the software that you are only interested in items worth more than $5 and have a sales rank less than 250,000. Or you can tell the software you're only interested in high-margin items and set the threshold at $35 with a sales rank less than one million.

The Neatoscan development team acknowledges that all businesses have different requirements, and "one size fits all" solutions aren't always the best. Therefore, their systems are designed to accommodate custom versions of their software. At the time of this writing, they'll build just about any feature into the product you want for a fee. So if you're willing to pay the freight you can order up just about any kind of software modification you can imagine. See their website for details.

Website: *http://www.neatoscan.com*

ScoutPal

ScoutPal gives up-to-the-minute prices on your cell phone for books and other media listed on Amazon.com. Their wireless look-up service can report marketplace prices from Abebooks.com and PriceGrabber.com. At the time of this writing they also offered a beta version of a PDA scanning tool for instant database look-ups called ScoutPalDB at no additional cost.

Some of the unique features of ScoutPal include the ability to customize the content and format of your results, to alert you about pending pre-orders ("buyer waiting"), to give you the capability to search by Library of Congress number or title (that's *really* nice), and to display a "price graph" of pricing trends on your screen.

ScoutPalDB lets you scan just about any UPC barcode on the market. Sellers on eBay love this feature because in addition to books, you can find pricing on lawn mowers, tools, office equipment—you name it! The ScoutPal device allows booksellers to branch out and develop many different income streams. At $10 per month it's one of the best bargains you'll find in the industry.

Website page: *http://www.scoutpal.com*

Look-Up Tool Summary

Any of the services listed above will work fine for you. In my business, I use several of them to leverage the unique characteristics of each product to a specific task.

For example, in my warehouse I used ScoutPal for pre-screening bulk purchases prior to listing because it was easy to install on my equipment and because of its ability to recognize a wide range of products other than books and digital media. When scouting in the field I use MediaScouter because of their outstanding customer service and easy-to-read graphical interface. I can't tell you how many times I've encountered hardware or software problems in the middle of a book sale and got immediate telephone assistance from their technical support personnel to help get me back into the game.

Don't dismiss the idea of diversifying your product mix. While scouting you may find extraordinary deals on products that aren't books, CDs, or DVDs. It helps to have a tool that recognizes more than ISBN barcodes.

Internet Postage

Few things are more frustrating than spending two or three hours per week standing in line at the post office. Yet standing in line is nearly impossible to avoid until you automate your shipping operation by subscribing to an Internet postage service. An Internet postage service allows you to purchase postage online and print shipping labels from your computer.

Initially, preparing packages by hand is sufficient, but once you're shipping more than ten packages per week, it's time to streamline things a bit. With automated postage you eliminate the need to buy stamps, fill out delivery confirmation or custom forms, or get your international packages "round dated" at the counter.

Round dating is the round date/time stamp post office personnel use to manually postmark letters and international packages. Delivery confirmation is a service offered by the post office that certifies that a package was delivered to a specific address. We'll discuss delivery confirmation more thoroughly a little later in this chapter. All of the above tasks are seamlessly accomplished when you automate.

Another reason you want an Internet postage service is for something called "stealth postage" where the actual postage amount is not printed on the shipping label. Instead, the cost is hidden in a barcode that's scanned by the post office. Stealth postage is important because most marketplaces charge the customer a flat fee at the time of the order for postage and handling. Some marketplaces also take a cut of the shipping fee for themselves, leaving you with a reduced amount that may or may not cover the actual cost of shipping the item.

More than once I've gotten angry eMails from customers demanding to know why they were charged $3.99 for shipping, yet the postage indicia on the package read $2.41. They're simply not aware that sellers only receive $2.64 of the shipping credit from the marketplace to cover the postage expense. In addition, sellers shell out another 35¢ for packaging material plus another 75¢ to $1.33 in labor to pack the order for shipment. Applying stealth postage to outgoing packages eliminates the possibility of irritating your customers.

Finally, you can further streamline your shipping operation with a computer-attached electronic scale and special label printer for near total automation. The cost of stepping up to this level sophistication is about $500 or so for the equipment. If you don't have the money on hand to make the investment, build up more cash in your business over several months before upgrading your operation. To save money, you can pick up used equipment for under $250 on eBay.

Click-N-Ship

This is the web-based U.S. Postal Service online postage system allowing you to print postage for Express Mail, Priority Mail, Global Express Guaranteed, Express Mail International, and Priority Mail International labels. You can also create an address book to view your shipping history. A huge downside to this service is that you can't print Media Mail shipping labels. That's significant because more than 90 percent of your packages will use Media Mail (more about this later).

Website: *https://sss-web.usps.com/cns/landing.do*

Endicia

This service offers Standard and Premium flat-rate plans. The Standard plan gives you the ability to purchase postage online, access to discounted Priority Mail, discounted insurance for expensive items, free delivery confirmation for Priority Mail, discounted confirmation for all other classes of mail, address verification, automatic printing of customs forms, the capability to print postage on shipping labels and envelopes as well as send eMail notification to your customer indicating the package has shipped.

The Premium plan offers all the features of the Standard plan plus pre-filled customs forms for international shipments, XML integration (web programming), online package look-up, stealth postage, and the ability to print return shipping labels for customers who want to return a purchase. The Premium plan offers the best value for booksellers, especially since it includes stealth postage.

Website: *http://www.endicia.com*

PayPal Shipping

PayPal made its name as a fast, safe way for executing online transactions by sending and receiving electronic payments through eMail. Now they've jumped into offering shipping services to online sellers.

Internet booksellers who take PayPal payments can print a shipping label right from their Account Overview or History screen. With PayPal shipping you can create postage-paid shipping labels, purchase package insurance, and print packing slips. International shipping, delivery confirmation, and the ability to immediately void postage charges are available too.

Website: *http://www.paypal.com*

ShipStream Manager

This is a PC-based postage solution from Pitney Bowes purporting to be "a cost-effective way for your small business to send, track and confirm delivery of packages and over-sized flats."[2] Pitney Bowes has been around a long time and is an acknowledged expert in providing innovative mail handling technologies.

Website: *http://www.pitneyworks.com*

Stamps.com

This online postage system's Pro Plan allows you to print all denominations of postage on shipping labels and envelopes, Priority Mail discounts, free delivery confirmation, address verification, insurance discounts, and printing for first-class, Media Mail, and Express Mail. The stealth feature of Stamps.com is called "Hidden Postage" and comes with the Pro Plan.

The Premier plan includes everything in the Pro Plan, plus up to 21 percent off select Federal Express services and other benefits for advanced users. They also offer an Enterprise plan for larger organizations which includes all of the above in addition to the ability to network five or more locations together for comprehensive postage cost management capability.

Website: *http://www.stamps.com*

USPS Shipping Assistant

This is the U.S. Postal Service desktop computer program with the ability to create domestic, international, and Merchandise Return labels, and customs forms. You also use it to ship packages, compare rates, calculate estimated delivery times, verify deliveries, and request free Carrier Pickup service.

Website: *http://www.usps.com/shippingassistant*

Internet Postage Summary

I use Endicia Dazzle in my business because of its ease of use, the wide variety of third-party applications with which it integrates, and their telephone technical support. Dazzle also gives me the ability to write my own application to interface with it when I'm ready to fully customize my fulfillment process.

Inventory Management Software

There are dozens of inventory management software tools available on the market as you'll discover in a moment. Comparing all the different feature functions of the various products can be overwhelming, but there's no reason to feel paralyzed by the array of choices. Competing technology vendors constantly leapfrog each other in a never ending feature function war. With almost predictable regularity one vendor or another introduces a new feature that promises to blow away the competition—until the competition announces a similar feature a few months later and re-establishes the status quo.

As long as you choose a product containing the major features common to most inventory management system software, the specific vendor you select is a matter of personal preference for the way the vendor implemented the product's Graphical User Interface (GUI) and other subjective criteria. In other words, it "feels right" to you.

However, there are occasions when the vendor you choose doesn't keep up technologically for a variety of reasons. Maybe they don't have the staff to quickly innovate their product. Perhaps they're poor cash flow managers and they've run out of money. A vendor may even go out of business. Whatever the reason, be prepared to switch to another vendor. Also, don't be afraid to vote with your wallet if you have the unfortunate experience of choosing a vendor who is unresponsive to your needs.

Critical Feature-Functions

The features in the following list, in my humble opinion, are absolutely essential for an effective inventory management software solution. Although my opinion is based on 20 years of IT experience, it's still an opinion and should be weighed against your specific needs. But I consider each and every one of these features a deal-breaker. If a product doesn't offer all of these critical features, move on to another product.

1. Easy to Use. You shouldn't need a computer science degree to navigate a software program. The user interface should be intuitive and easy to learn. Do the icons make sense to you? Are they easy to find on the screen? Do the graphics contain sharp, recognizable images? Too many "no" answers to questions like these should send up a red flag.

2. Scalable. If a program can't handle at least 75,000 active listings it's probably under powered. You want a minimum level of robustness built into your software, even if you think you'll never max out the program's capability. With excess power in your software you'll be confident it has enough peak capacity to run your business without negatively impacting productivity.

3. Friendly, Basic eMail Support. Pay particular attention to a vendor's reputation for giving quick, friendly, and helpful technical support. By quick I mean that all your eMail should be answered within 24-hours. But don't be unrealistic. Asking a question at 4:59 p.m. on a Friday isn't likely to get a 24 hour response. More likely you'll receive an answer sometime on Monday.

However, any vendor who does answer questions outside normal business hours, especially on weekends, should be given special consideration. Many problems occur when it's least convenient.

Not only should the response be fast, it should be meaningful. Doesn't it drive you crazy when you send an eMail to a vendor with a specific question and you get back absolute nonsense for a reply? Usually it happens when a careless support person sends out canned responses to customer questions and the sender doesn't truly understand the problem. World-class customer service demands that the vendor actually read and understand customer inquiries and reply with helpful information.

4. Multi-Venue Management. This one requirement eliminates most inventory management systems on the market because *the product must be capable of supporting multiple marketplaces.* Period. End of story. Not open for discussion.

Many beginners make the mistake of listing their products on Amazon or eBay and think they're done. After all, aren't Amazon and eBay the two largest markets around? Yes, but a significant number of sales can be made on more than a dozen smaller markets, and those sales are often for higher dollar amounts. Even if you think you're going to stick to just one marketplace you always have the option of expanding to additional venues at a later time. Besides, several marketplaces don't charge a monthly fee and their commission rates are lower than the majors. You have nothing to lose by listing with them.

Having the ability to sell across marketplace venues is no trivial feature. *For your own sake, don't fudge on this important feature—you'll regret it, I promise you!*

You'll regret the significant loss of sales revenue, and you'll regret the nasty conversion costs you'll face when you finally wise-up and switch to a product capable of managing multiple marketplaces. I know these things for a fact because I made the mistake of starting out as a single marketplace seller myself. Don't say I didn't warn you.

5. A Streamlined Workflow. You want a product that manages your inventory with a minimum number of mouse clicks. The last thing you want is a long, drawn out procedure to process your daily orders.

If you like a particular vendor but their order processing function is clunky, tell them you're unhappy. Don't be afraid to pressure vendors by repeatedly asking them to streamline their software. There's no reason you shouldn't have the ability to process orders with one or two mouse clicks. They'll belly ache about how there's no demand for the feature, but don't you believe it. Tell them *you* demand it and you'll take your business elsewhere if another vendor provides it first. If enough sellers make enough noise we'll get software built the way we need it to run our businesses more profitably.

6. Point-and-Click Data Entry. Make sure the product supports bar-code scanning for data entry into your inventory database in addition to typing ISBN codes on your keyboard. Once the ISBN has been scanned or typed into the program, all the information needed to list the item should be automatically loaded by the software based on your own set of rules.

Truly savvy vendors allow you to automatically load general listing descriptions based on the condition of the book. For example, you can have a description for a "Good" book with no major defects pre-written and ready to drop into your listing at the click of a mouse. This feature alone slashes listing time by several hours every week, and should be demanded from vendors. Let them know you'll take your business elsewhere if a competitor offers it first.

7. Built-in Repricing. At the bare minimum, the product must have the ability to manually trigger a repricing script to reprice your inventory based on your own custom rules. Scripts are nothing more than small computer programs that reprice your inventory for you. There's a detailed discussion about repricing later in the book. For now, keep in mind that frequent repricing is an important part of your overall sales strategy.

Value-Added Features and Services

If you decide to scale your business up you'll eventually start signing up for premium service packages offered by vendors supporting your business. Many vendors offer more advanced versions of their products for an additional fee. These more advanced versions offer features, functions, and services not found in the basic products and the higher price is often justified.

Once your business is up and running you'll want to leverage those advanced features in your operation; the cost is well worth the added productivity and revenue gains. Below are a few of the added value features and services to look for when considering a vendor. These features are not deal breakers, but having them available should earn a vendor extra points.

1. Friendly Telephone Support. One premium service that's helpful is friendly telephone support. If the vendor being reviewed doesn't offer a premium service plan that includes telephone support, you might want to consider one that does.

There's telephone support, and then there's telephone support. Too many telephone support personnel are rude at best; treating customers as if they're interrupting "real" work. Before choosing a vendor spend a little quality time on bookselling forums and read what existing users say about the vendors you're considering. Also, don't forget to read what *former* users say about them as well. If there's an ongoing, underlying theme regarding unhelpful, rude behavior by the vendor you're considering—beware.

2. Automated Repricing. The advanced version of your inventory management system should include an automated repricing function. You want your repricer to automatically adjust your prices periodically so your books remain competitive. Automated repricing should take place with no manual intervention on your part.

This one feature alone can boost your sales 20 to 50 percent or more. However, be careful that your automatic repricer doesn't trigger a reverse bidding war with another repricer and engage in the dreaded "race to the bottom." Unchecked price slashing by two computers wipes out the profitability of your books, and that's not good for anyone.

Repricing strategies and how repricing increases sales are covered in greater depth later on. For now, just remember when automated repricing is used properly it can boost your sales significantly. Used improperly, it can destroy your bottom line.

3. Multi-User Version Available. A multi-user software application allows more than one person to use it simultaneously. Whether you plan to grow your business into a full-fledged commercial operation or plan to remain a home-based part-time concern, choose a product that's either network capable or Internet based to allow multiple users to access the system at the same time.

There are several reasons why you want multi-user software. For example, you can set up several computers to simultaneously perform different tasks such as listing, repricing, and order fulfillment. You may even want more than one person listing at the same time. Each task can be performed on separate computers by different people if your software is networked or resides on a common server. Splitting functions allow you to overlap workflow processes and be more efficient.

The Products

Only products meeting the entire list of critical feature functions are reviewed below. I've added comments to those products possessing one or more value added feature and service. For a more comprehensive list of major inventory management products for small booksellers, including the single marketplace products, read the "Inventory Management" report in the "Articles" area of my website at *http://www.internetbookselling.com*.

BookHound

Biblio.com and Bibliopolis teamed up to deliver this full featured database for independent bookstores and Internet booksellers. Marketplaces supported are Biblio, AbeBooks, Alibris, Amazon, and TomFolio. Multiple computers can be custom networked at an additional cost. The upload screen allows you to specify a percentage to add to or subtract from prices for items uploaded to the Internet, and you can globally edit your prices by a specific percentage. No automated repricing is available. Ongoing telephone support is available, but they prefer eMail.

Website: *http://www.bibliopolis.com*

BookSku

Not much was missed when the designers created BookSku. It's a full featured package complete with a streamlined data entry system that uses a barcode scanner or keyboard, and offers automated order fulfillment, automated sales and customer management, automated inventory management, online reporting, assisted marking, and automated repricing.

Marketplaces supported are Amazon, AbeBooks, and Alibris. Half.com and eBay stores are on the way. Multi-user support is included.

Website: *http://www.booksku.com*

ChannelAdvisor

Initially introduced as an eBay management tool, ChannelAdvisor has sprouted into a multi-faceted inventory management software solution. It's based on four core modules for targeted search engine marketing, comparison shopping sites, marketplaces, and rich media solutions such as online video, rich images, and other advanced capabilities.

Marketplaces supported are eBay, Google Product Search, Amazon, Overstock, your own website, and comparison shopping sites. Repricing and data entry automation are available.

Website: *http://www.channeladvisor.com*

FillZ

Originally developed by AbeBooks, FillZ (pronounced "fills") is now under the watchful eye of Amazon.com after its acquisition of Abe. FillZ sports an online data entry interface that uses a barcode scanner or keyboard, automated order fulfillment, automated eMails, automated inventory management, and online reporting. Its JavaScript based programming language automated repricing capability is to die for. If you can't write repricing scripts they'll do a bang up job for you at a reasonable fee. Premium users get their scripts written for free, along with automated script scheduling, telephone support, and faster servers.

Marketplaces supported are AbeBooks, Alibris, Amazon.ca (Canada), Amazon .com (United States), Amazon.co.uk (United Kingdom), Amazon.de (Germany), Amazon.fr (France), Barnes & Noble, Biblio, Chrislands, ChooseBooks, eBay Stores, eBay Express, eCampus, Gemm, Half.com, PlayTrade, TextbooksRus, TextBookX, ValoreBooks, and your own website.

Website: *http://www.fillz.com*

Mail Extractor

This order fulfillment and inventory management system automates order processing for half a dozen marketplaces, creates pick lists, invoices, and prints postage through Endicia Dazzle. It also sends customer eMails.

Marketplaces supported are Amazon.com (United States), Amazon.co.uk (United Kingdom), Half.com, eBay, and Alibris. They use a checkbox repricing function. No telephone support is offered on their website, although a fax number can be found. Their primary means of support is eMail.

Website: *http://www.mailextractor.com*

Monsoon

Frequently called the Cadillac of inventory management software, Monsoon packs a dizzying array of feature functions including a knock-your-socks-off intelligent data entry system that uses a barcode scanner or keyboard, automated order fulfillment, automated sales and customer management, automated inventory management, online reporting, assisted marketing, automated repricing, and a secure, networked multi-user environment.

Marketplaces supported are AbeBooks, Alibris, Amazon.ca (Canada), Amazon .com (United States), Amazon.co.uk (United Kingdom), Amazon.de (Germany), Amazon.fr (France), Barnes & Noble, Blackwell, Borders, eBay, Half.com, and Play .com. World-class telephone customer support rounds out the services offered by this company.

The rich environment of Monsoon comes with a steep price, costing up to three times more than competitors. However, if you decide to grow into a mega bookseller and want to go first class, Monsoon is an excellent choice.

Website: *http://www.monsoonworks.com*

Prager Software

Their 1-Click listing technology makes data entry easy. In addition to inventory management Prager has a synchronization module that alerts you to discrepancies between your inventory database and the marketplaces. They also offer a pricing program for fast price look-up of up to 20 books at a time.

Prager claims to support 18 different marketplaces, but their website fails to identify which ones. Repricing is triggered manually. They don't offer telephone support and there's no eMail support. Help is offered through the Mantis trouble ticket system.

Website: *http://www.pragersoftware.com*

The Art of Books

This is a complete inventory management system that offers automated data entry with a barcode scanner or keyboard, automated order fulfillment, automated inventory management, online reporting, and semi-automated repricing.

Supported marketplaces are AbeBooks, Alibris, Amazon.ca (Canada), Amazon .com (United States), Amazon.co.uk (United Kingdom), Amazon.de (Germany), Amazon.fr (France), Barnes & Noble, Biblio, Chrislands, ChooseBooks, eBay Stores, eBay Express, eCampus, Gemm, Half.com, PlayTrade, TextbooksRus, TextBookX, ValoreBooks, and up to five custom venues.

There is no telephone or eMail support. Help is obtained through support tickets and Live Chat.

Website: *http://www.theartofbooks.com*

Inventory Management Software Summary

When looking for inventory management software pay close attention to the Critical Feature Function list. All of the above meet the list requirements, but some may be a better fit for you than others. For example, solutions that support the greatest number of marketplace venues should be favored. FillZ, AOB, and Monsoon are the leaders in marketplaces supported.

I use a combination of FillZ for order management across multiple marketplaces and my own proprietary inventory receiving system for listing books online. There's nothing wrong with the product listing component of FillZ. I simply have unique requirements for my business for features that aren't available in any product on the market. But I've gotten along with FillZ for a number of years with no problem.

You can read about my system in my follow-up book, *Advanced Internet Bookselling Techniques: How to Take Your Online Bookselling Business to the Next Level.* Go to *http://www.internetbookselling.com* for more information.

Global Positioning System (GPS) Tools

Scouting for inventory is going to require you to get to know your local area. It's one of the cooler parts of this business. Soon, everywhere you go you know someone, or someone knows you. If you're not thoroughly familiar with your area, then definitely purchase a GPS device to help you navigate your way around town.

The Global Positioning System consists of a ring of navigational satellites orbiting the planet. These satellites continuously broadcast radio signals that provide location and time information to anyone equipped with a GPS receiver. There are many commercial retailers who sell GPS receivers in a multitude of price ranges, the most popular being Garmin, known for its catchy jingle that's played every Christmas season (give a, give a, give a, Garmin!).

I use the GPS service that comes with my Verizon cell phone. All I do is punch in the address I want, and the phone automatically goes into speaker mode and guides me to my location with audible turn-by-turn directions. I use the GPS when trying to find new locations I haven't yet visited, when following-up on leads, or when I get lost. Otherwise, I use Microsoft Streets & Trips to make maps of my routes.

My phone GPS has gotten me out of trouble on more than one occasion. I even travel with it and it has worked extremely well in more than a dozen states. Having a GPS is particularly valuable on road trips. We'll talk more about road trips later.

What Does It Cost?

I bet you're just dying to know how much all this fancy hardware and software will set you back, aren't you? To be honest, surprisingly little. Properly equipping yourself with the right technology costs far less than lost revenue from an inefficient, error-prone operation.

Except for your computer and PDA scanner, no additional hardware is required to go into business. Putting together the "nice-to-have" technology to get your business up and running, and producing maximum profit from day one, costs approximately $600 up front. This means a new out-of-the-box Zebra label printer and Endicia 25-lb. computer-attached electronic scale. You can find lower prices on eBay for used equipment. You may even get the some eBay sellers to give you support.

Once you're up and running you'll spend another $30 to $117 in monthly subscription fees for the following software:

Inventory management system	$10—$50
Online postage	$10—$17
Wireless look-up tool	$10—$50
Total	$30—$117

The faint of heart may be paralyzed by those numbers. However, the techniques described in this book recover up-front costs in just a few weeks, or at most two or three months. Monthly subscription fees are paid by the business's sales almost from day one. It all depends on the effort you're willing to put into your venture.

CHAPTER **10**

Organizing Your Business

rganizing your new venture is relatively easy. But there are certain questions to consider before proceeding. For example:

- What do you name your company?
- Will it be a sole-proprietorship, corporation, partnership, or Limited Liability Company (LLC)?
- What are your financing options?
- What do you know about bookkeeping?
- What responsibilities do you have to federal, state, and local taxing authorities?
- How much additional insurance, if any, is required?
- Where do you store your inventory?
- Finally, what supplies and equipment do you need day one?

There may also be special considerations for your local situation such as hostile zoning restrictions against home-based businesses imposed by your city, county, or state government, or even by your homeowners association. Luckily, most municipalities and other governing authorities recognize the vital role small entrepreneurs play in our economy and the majority of such restrictions were eliminated years ago. However, it's always better to be safe than sorry, so a quick check with your local chamber of commerce, zoning office, and homeowners association may spare you a great deal of grief down the road.

Choosing Your Business Name

It's time to decide what to call your new company. There's a large body of opinion about how to name a company. But I don't want you to lose any sleep over it. Give your company a name that's pleasing and meaningful to *you*. So long as the name is not obviously offensive to any group of people, does not infringe upon the name or trademark of another company, and meets your state and local requirements, it should be fine. If the name conveys your business focus, all the better. One other suggestion: keep it short. People tend to remember shorter names over longer ones.

Ever hear of Wendy's? The legendary Dave Thomas named his fast food franchise after his daughter. What does the name Wendy have to do with selling hamburgers? Not a thing. But it's cute—and it works. Wendy's hamburgers are also square, but that's another story too.

I once knew a gentleman who was so inspired by Dave's approach he decided to name his company after *both* his daughters, Wendy and Tara. Thus, WenTara Printing & Graphics was born. That idea also worked, and he sold plenty of printing.

The examples are endless. Logon to one of the bookselling marketplace sites and you can review the user names of thousands of third-party sellers. You'll get lots of ideas.

At this stage of your business, I wouldn't worry about what it's called. As a third-party seller, it's unlikely you'll generate repeat sales. That's because the people buying your books are not your customers. They belong to the marketplace venue on which you sold the books. The depth and breadth of your inventory is where you make your money. What you call yourself is close to irrelevant beyond the state and local registration requirements.

Of course, if or when you decide to expand into a full-time operation generating hundreds of thousands of dollars in sales your company name takes on new meaning. For example, generating a significant revenue stream from your own website requires an entirely different business model than selling through established marketplace venues. Name recognition and branding take on strategic importance, and significant capital is needed for advertising and marketing to drive traffic to your site.

As a large enterprise, repeat sales become a regular occurrence; you'll have your own website, logo, corporate image, brand, and so on. If your existing name is unsuitable for a larger company, the conversion won't be a major effort. For now, have fun and choose a name you personally like that's legal and in good taste.

Your Business Address

Years ago conventional wisdom counseled home-based entrepreneurs to use their home street address as their mailing address. The reasoning was that a street address conveyed a more stable business image to the public. This advice made perfect sense for a traditional Mail Order business, especially before the Internet became such an important part of the economic landscape. That opinion has changed in recent years.

These days, many individuals and businesses direct all their mail to a U.S. Post Office box or private mail box. I've always used a Post Office box to run my business with no adverse effects. I recommend you do the same. Plan to rent one of the large boxes because once you're in business you tend to receive more mail than the typical household mailbox accommodates. In addition, a few of your customers' packages will be returned by the Post Office marked "Return to Sender," "Refused," or "Unclaimed." Returned books tend to fill up a lot of space in your mailbox.

One final benefit of directing mail to a Post Office box is that it prevents customers from coming to your home to pick up orders or to complain. Occasionally, it can be downright unsafe, especially if the customer is dissatisfied with a purchase.

Writing a Business Plan

There are several key reasons for you to write a business plan. First, organizing your ideas in writing helps to crystallize your vision. For example:

- You'll be forced to consider exactly what kind of business you want from the start.
- It makes you decide what legal structure is best for you.
- It spells out how you'll finance your business.
- You'll know how inventory is acquired.
- Your marketing plan is established.
- Your competition is identified.
- It helps you consider many other vital details you might miss without sitting down to commit your ideas in writing.

Second, a formal business plan helps you manage your operation. In your plan, you set benchmarks to gauge if you're on target. By closely monitoring your financial statements, and comparing them to projections in your business plan, you can avoid a financial catastrophe.

Finally, banks won't lend you money without a well written business plan. Although I don't recommend you start your business with borrowed money, you may eventually decide to apply for a Small Business Administration (SBA) loan to expand your operation. If you sit down with your banker with a written business plan already prepared, you instantly impress him or her by demonstrating you're a professional who can be trusted. Anything less puts you at a disadvantage.

Rhonda Abrams captured the essence of the need for a well written business plan when she succinctly wrote in her bestselling book, *Business Plan in a Day*, "An effective business plan saves you time and money by focusing your business activities. It can give you control over your finances, marketing, and daily operations. A good plan can also help you raise the necessary capital to build your company."[1]

Business Plan for Booksellers

There are many excellent books about how to write a business plan, and there is an abundance of software programs available that virtually automate the entire process. You'll find a list of some of the resources I used to create my own business plan in the Appendix. Clickable links to business plan resources can also be found in the "Resources" area of my website.

In addition, I strongly urge you to contact your local Chamber of Commerce and make an appointment with a Service Corps of Retired Executives (SCORE) representative.[2] That person meets with you one-on-one and helps you develop your business plan for free.

As a point of reference, I'll summarize the elements I used in my business plan to give you a starting point for writing your own. But before writing your business plan read this entire book to get an understanding of how the business works. Doing so gives you a few ideas about what goals to pursue. By the end of your first reading, you'll know exactly what to put under each sub-heading of your plan.

Remember, the primary purpose of the business plan suggestions in this book is for your own personal use and to help you stay on track. If you ever decide to seek third-party financing, buy one of the many business plan books found in leading bookstores, or check one out from your public library.

Executive Summary

The executive summary provides a concise overview of your vision and where you want to take your business. Describe whether your business is a hobby, a part-time money-making opportunity, or a full-time business.

Briefly state how you plan to bring your vision from concept to reality. The executive summary should be brief—no more than two pages. Any more than that and it's not a summary.

After completing the detailed portion of your business plan, go back and re-work your executive summary to ensure it accurately captures the essence of your plan since you will have likely incorporated additional ideas during the detailed writing.

Management

In this section, take stock of your personal abilities and motivations. Briefly describe any notable talents you bring to the table. Honestly list your strengths and weaknesses. Give your thoughts on how you'll bridge gaps in your skill set by leveraging the expertise of others. Also, articulate how you'll maximize your strengths. After performing this exercise, you'll have a better understanding of your skills and gain more confidence in your ability to manage your business.

Professional Support Team

No man (or woman) is an island, and you're going to need help from a strong support team of competent professionals. In separate paragraphs state the names of your attorney or legal services firm, accountant, insurance agent, and bank representative. Give a brief biographical background of each one. Include their addresses and phone numbers and the reasons you selected each particular person.

Product Line

In this section, list the products you intend to sell. Obviously, you want to list books. But also list CDs, DVDs, and VHS tapes. But if you decide to offer other types of products, list them here as well.

Market Analysis

Identify your competition, and discuss how you plan to gain a competitive advantage. One thing I learned from experience is that your true competition is going to be other small Internet booksellers who live and work in your local area—not other sellers on the Internet.

Other Internet sellers are competitors for sure, but the real competition for a small operation such as yours is for inventory. The savvy scouter scores the most valuable items in the best condition. You want to be the savvy scouter and let your business model deal with the online competition.

Business Model

Use the business model section to describe the nuts and bolts of how your business will function. Describe each of the inventory sourcing techniques you intend to employ.

Using the information in Chapter 9, project how much inventory you plan to acquire each week. Discuss your listing and repricing strategies. Will you specialize in specific subject matter books, or will you provide a wide range of general interest nonfiction titles? Will you aggressively pursue CD, DVD, and VHS sales from the outset, or gradually incorporate these other media into your inventory as you gain more experience? How does your customer service differentiate you from your competition?

Include information about your premises; how and where will you store your inventory? What technology will you use to operate your business? What kind of accounting system will you use?

In addition, map out your sales and marketing strategy. For the small independent bookseller, your strategy is relatively straightforward. Later, I'll recommend which online venues to use initially. Then you'll learn when and how to expand into additional marketplaces.

Your business model doesn't need to be complex—just thorough. There are as many different ways to implement a business model as there are entrepreneurs to do it. Your model must not only fit your specific circumstances, it must do it profitably. Take care of the details and the details take care of you.

Profit and Loss Projections

You need a realistic picture of your potential profits and cash flow. Therefore, you must develop financial forecasts reflecting your income and expense projections for your first three to five years in business.

Take stock of your personal finances and estimate how much start-up capital you intend to contribute to get the business started. What are your ongoing sources of revenue? What will be your expenses? Document any assumptions you've made to support your numbers.

You're probably wondering how you can make a profit and loss forecast, even a basic one, when you have no experience with bookselling. Fear not—just use the benchmarks given in Chapters 8 and 9 to measure your progress. Although you want your plan to be thorough, you don't want to get so wrapped up in the details you lose sight of the big picture. Benchmarks are general guidelines for use as tools to warn you when you deviate from your plan.

For example, your average cost per book should settle around $2. That doesn't mean you won't find plenty of inventory under $2 per book. Nor does it mean you never pay more. It only means that after the dust settles, if your average cost per book is significantly more than $2, consider re-evaluating your purchasing criteria (if you're following the business model in this book). If you choose to pursue a different model, your cost structure could be higher or lower. Also, your cost structure is heavily dependent upon the average cost of inventory in your local area.

Similarly, if your average sale per book is less than $10 then your pricing strategy may need scrutiny—unless you've settled on a business model that stresses high volume over high prices. There's nothing inherently wrong with either approach. Just be certain you thoroughly understand the business model you're developing and let the benchmarks guide your progress.

Closing Statement

A closing statement isn't necessary for most business plans, but it's an excellent idea to include one to wrap up your thoughts. In your closing, briefly summarize in one concise paragraph the essence of your plan. State why you believe it'll be successful and give your potential creditor one final reason to get involved.

A Final Word about Your Business Plan

Whether your business is a hobby, a part-time money-making opportunity, or a full-time occupation, a clearly written, detailed business plan improves your chances of success. Please don't skimp on this important exercise! I once read that a business without a plan is like a ship without a rudder. Don't let your business drift aimlessly in the treacherous waters of the marketplace. You need a compass to guide your fledgling enterprise. If you run your business without planning your strategy, your chances of failure are greatly increased.

After your plan is written, periodically review it to gauge your progress. Get out your calendar and mark down a date that's three months from your start-up date. Mark another date six months out, and another date a year from the day you start your business.

On those dates assess how well your plan is working. Ask yourself the following questions:

1. Where was I right in my projections? Why?
2. Where was I wrong in my projections? Why?
3. What objectives did I have that were not accomplished? Why?
4. What do I need to do differently?

Write down the answers to each of the above questions, and then update your business plan with any necessary mid-course corrections.

Financing Your Business

Let's talk about finances. You're better off clearly understanding how you'll bankroll your company before you go any further, because answers to the "money question" dictate how you address most, if not all, of the many other questions you face during the start-up phase.

Sorry, You're Going to Need Some Money

Contrary to what you may have read or seen on late night television infomercials, starting a business requires money. The lure of bootstrapping your fledgling enterprise on a shoestring budget may make terrific advertising copy, but your business crawls along at a snail's pace. The last thing you need is a cash flow crunch just as success starts knocking on your door. The amount of start-up capital needed depends on how aggressively you plan to grow your business. Once you've written a detailed business plan you'll have a fair idea about the amount of money you need.

I know a bookseller who lives in an area where it's difficult to find inventory. Yet, she sold 10 books in her first month of business for $225 after listing a total of 82 books online. Her listing and sales numbers for the first six months were as follows:

Table 10.1

HER FIRST SIX MONTHS			
	LISTED	**SOLD**	**SALES**
January	82	10	$225
February	82	20	$337
March	42	27	$910
April	95	21	$591
May	38	19	$378
June	87	26	$458

Even now, she lists fewer than 200 books per month, but managed to maintain sales exceeding $1,000 for all but one of the last 24 months.

If your goal is to consistently make a few hundred dollars *profit* per month, your capital and labor demands are fairly reasonable. Thousands of small Internet booksellers working part-time from home do it every day. For such an operation, you can build an initial inventory of only 300 books in your first couple of months and list less than 200 additional books in subsequent months for replacement inventory to earn several hundred dollars in steady monthly income. The upfront investment for an operation of this size is modest.

Conversely, if your goal is to earn two or three thousand dollars per month, a larger amount of start-up capital is required. By quickly building up an inventory of 1,000 to 1,500 books, you'll need at least 300 to 500 books monthly for replacement inventory to meet your goal.

For truly daring readers with the objective of establishing a full-time business as your primary source of income, you need serious resources right out of the gate. A full-time operation with employees and heavy equipment to run an efficient operation requires a totally different business model that's discussed in my follow-up book *Advanced Internet Bookselling Techniques: How to Take Your Online Bookselling Business to the Next Level.* The model explained in this book lays an excellent foundation upon which to build a full-time business.

Regardless of your ultimate financial goals, I urge you to start small. Remember baby steps? There's no need to dive into this business and immediately start investing big money. Take a few months to figure out what you're doing before you expand. Internet bookselling is the only business I know that allows you to begin with little risk and enjoy handsome upward potential. From the beginning of your venture, get into the habit of practicing sound risk management to protect your capital.

Raising Cash at Home

Unlike many other beginning entrepreneurs, you probably already have salable merchandise in your possession right now in the form of your own personal collection of books. When I started my business, I listed more than $500 worth of books in a matter of hours just from my personal library. One sold for $175 just a few days after being listed! It was a great way to raise capital and boost my confidence at the same time. How many books do you currently own? Some of them may sell for perfectly good money.

In addition to books, what other things can you sell? How about DVDs, CDs, and VHS tapes you haven't watched or listened to in years? Those items can be ready sources of cash that are easy to access. The nice thing about money raised from selling personal items is that it never has to be repaid.

Savings

The next place to look for start-up capital is your savings account. If you were to withdraw money to support your business would it cause financial hardship? Can you get the car repaired if you have an emergency breakdown? Could you still pay the plumber if a pipe burst?

The obvious advantage to self-financing your venture is that you're not incurring outside debt. Notice the distinction I've made here. I said, "outside" debt. When I started my business, I split my capital in half. One half I invested directly into the business as start-up capital. The other half was a loan to the business. I drew up a formal loan agreement with a five-year term and monthly payment plan at the prevailing market interest rate for personal loans. Yes, I incurred debt at the outset; but it was personal debt to me, and not to a third-party.

It felt nice to write myself a check each month for the interest and principal payment instead of to a bank or credit card company. The payments I received went into my savings account to earn further interest. It just doesn't get much better than that.

Another advantage was I was able to write off, as a business expense, the interest I paid myself. Of course, the inverse is also true. I had to declare that interest as income on my personal tax return. You can never outrun Uncle Sam!

Make sure you create what the IRS calls an "arms length" transaction. Done properly, this money never has to be paid back to anyone but you. That means drawing up a formal loan agreement and making regular payments to yourself from your business checking account. This is how I financed my business. Consult with your tax advisor to help you decide how to finance yours.

Credit Card Debt

Another source of ready capital is a credit card. Notice I said, "card" and not "cards." The last thing you need is a lot of high interest credit card debt to burden your progress. Still, a credit card with a credit limit high enough to finance your business may be just the ticket for you.

One advantage to using plastic to finance your start-up is that you don't have to worry about going through the bank approval process. You're already approved when you qualified for the card. Plus your monthly payments are low, maybe as little as $15 depending on your outstanding balance. The big disadvantage is the interest rate, which can be as high as 29 percent—ouch!

Tread carefully when thinking about using a credit card to finance your business. It can be done, but make sure your sales cover the payments. Being able to accurately determine how large a debt load you can comfortably carry is another good reason not to cut corners on your business plan.

Home Equity

Do you have equity in your home? A home equity line of credit could be a handy source of start-up capital. Once again you don't have to ask permission to use these funds (except of course, from your spouse). The payments are usually quite reasonable with interest rates far lower than most credit cards.

Ask your tax advisor about the possibility of using up to three-fourths of the borrowed funds as a loan to your business. Then draft a loan agreement to yourself with payments covering the entire payment to the bank and let your business pay off the loan. Don't forget to declare any interest you earn on your personal income tax return. Also, the interest on the line of credit may be tax deductible.

Another reason to use an equity line of credit is that it can be drawn upon as required, so you never have to borrow more than you actually need at any given time. Limited borrowing saves interest expense and avoids high monthly payments. The cash you save in interest payments can be used to expand your business.

Family Members

Do you have relatives willing to invest in your venture? Armed with your business plan and the results from your Fast Track sales, you may convince supportive family members to provide the start-up capital you need.

Be professional in your presentation, just like if you were going to a bank asking for money. Let the power of your business plan make your case. Your plan shows your family how profitable you expect your venture to be and demonstrates exactly how you'll realize those profits. A well-written business plan lets them know this isn't a half-baked scheme, and they have a reasonable expectation of recouping their investment.

Also, demonstrate to them you've already invested a substantial sum into your idea and have gotten an excellent return. Back up your claim by showing them the sales and profit figures from your Fast Track results and early listing efforts. All you're asking them to do is help you expand.

Bank Loan

When I founded my company I wanted to dip my toe in the water before jumping off the high dive, so I used the Fast Track method and started with minimal risk. I purposely avoided borrowing from a bank. However, you may eventually want to consider this option.

Once you've been in business for a while and developed a solid track record of steady profits, you may decide to expand by taking out a Small Business Administration (SBA) loan to raise additional capital.

"The U.S. Small Business Administration is an agency of the federal government, established in 1953 to assist small business enterprises. One of the most important programs operated by the agency is the loan guaranty program, which provides a financial guaranty to qualified, eligible businesses to enhance their ability to obtain long-term capital financing from the private sector."[3]

Borrowing money from a bank can be difficult for a start-up, especially when the economy isn't doing particularly well. Consult your SCORE representative as well as read a few good books on SBA financing, like Charles H. Green's, *The SBA Loan Book*.

Friends

I saved this funding source for last because it's the least desirable option of all. Even if you have wealthy friends willing to invest in your business you might want to think twice. When money becomes an issue between friends, the friendship usually takes a beating. I've seen it happen too many times not to feel queasy about approaching friends about borrowing money. It's socially awkward, particularly so if the friend turns you down.

In my mind, the only exception is if a friend approaches you to become a part owner in the business and he or she is interested in being an active participant who brings skills to the table you don't possess. A partnership could be particularly desirable when you each have complementary skills. For example, you have the brainpower to run the operation, but he or she has the capital. You're good at scouting, attending book sales, and negotiating lower prices from suppliers, while your partner is a whiz at accounting or computer programming.

Choosing a partner is just as important as choosing a spouse. If you find the right one, life can be bliss. If you end up with the wrong one life can be, well, you know. I'll discuss the advantages and disadvantages of partnerships more thoroughly below. For now, just remember what the honorable knight said to Indiana Jones in *The Last Crusade,* "Choose wisely."

Getting Legal Assistance

Do you need to hire a lawyer to start your new business? I used the services of a legal assistance firm and it was more than adequate. If you're starting your business on a small budget and you choose a simple legal structure such as a sole proprietorship or Limited Liability Company (LLC), you may feel the same. However, if you're the least bit nervous about jumping into the water, by all means schedule an appointment with a competent business attorney.

Deciding on a Legal Structure for Your Business

Now that you've chosen a name for your business, make it legal by selecting a structure for your company, and getting the name registered. The legal structure you choose is one of the first important decisions you make and it should not be made lightly. Do you want to remain a small hobby operation or do you have plans to grow into a full-time concern? This is one area where the services of a competent professional pays, so consult with your accountant and perhaps a legal advisor to help select the structure that's right for you before making a final decision. Meanwhile, here's a quick summary of the various legal structures to consider.

Sole Proprietor

The simplest and least expensive form of business ownership is the sole proprietorship. Usually, the owner will file a fictitious name statement with state authorities to register a "Doing Business As" name. All income flows directly to your personal income tax return. You are captain of your ship. You have complete ownership of all assets and command dictatorial decision-making authority.

Along with the dictatorial power of a sole proprietorship comes total liability for actions by the company and any of its employees or agents. If anything nasty happens, you and your assets are personally and financially on the hook.

Sole proprietors also have more difficulty raising funds for their company as well as getting credit from suppliers without being personally liable. While being a sole proprietor is the simplest of all legal forms, it's also the most financially, and legally dangerous.

Partnership

There's strength in numbers, so perhaps a partnership works for you. When two or more people share ownership in a business it may be easier to raise capital for later expansion. The talents and energies of multiple people can be focused on growing the company faster than is possible for a single individual. And like the sole proprietor, income flows directly to the personal tax returns of the partners.

The downside to partnerships is that many of them don't work. Conflicts arise that eventually cause the partnership to dissolve. For that reason, a legal agreement needs to be drafted by a competent attorney spelling out how the partnership is to be managed from the beginning. It must be clearly understood what each partner contributes to the arrangement to ensure the success of the company.

For example, which partner provides the capital? Who has sales or management responsibilities? Does one of the partners have industry or government contacts? Whatever the partners contribute must be clearly set down in writing to avoid serious problems in the event the partnership dissolves.

Don't forget what I said earlier about getting into partnerships. It's just as difficult to choose a good partner as it is to choose a spouse. Choose wisely and never form a partnership without the help of an attorney.

The C Corporation

The C Corporation (or just "corporation") is the granddaddy of all legal entities. It's the most complicated and most expensive legal structure you can choose. From a liability perspective it's also the safest. Corporations have shareholders, and thus the corporation, not an individual shareholder, is liable for the actions of the organization, its employees, or agents. In extreme cases of fraud or gross negligence the corporate veil can be pierced, so forming a corporation is no guarantee of complete protection from legal liability.

Corporations are also subject to double taxation. All income earned by the corporation is taxed at the corporate rate. Income distributed to corporate owners (shareholders) as dividends is further subjected to personal income taxes. Since dividends are paid by corporations with after-tax dollars, paying a second round of taxes by individual recipients of those dividends amounts to double taxation.

Why consider a corporation? For starters, as I've mentioned, corporations provide superior liability protection. It's also easier for corporations to raise money than other legal entities. But unless you plan to go full-time and build a large business you'll find that the cost of maintaining a corporation quickly eats up your profits. Also, never attempt to form a corporation without the help of a competent attorney.

Sub Chapter S Corporation

At one time, the S Corporation was extremely popular with entrepreneurs who wanted the liability protection of the corporation, but didn't want the administrative and tax burdens the corporation carried. However, it seems to be falling out of favor due to the rise of the Limited Liability Company. Consult your tax and legal advisors for all the pertinent details about the S Corporation.

Limited Liability Company (LLC)

When I formed my company I chose the LLC as my legal structure. Like the S Corporation and C Corporation it's designed to provide liability protection from lawsuits. Simultaneously, it provides the tax efficiencies and operational flexibility of a partnership. The LLC is a little more complex to establish and maintain than a sole proprietorship, but it's far less complex than a partnership, C corporation, or S corporation to form and maintain.

The LLC offered me the best of both worlds—limited liability and reasonable tax obligations—without significantly increasing my downside. As with any business entity, liability protection doesn't exist when fraud or misrepresentation has taken place. And taxes are paid at the personal rate instead of lower corporate rates paid by C corporations. However, the LLC escapes the double taxation trap of C corporations.

The LLC is relatively easy to set up, and easier to administer. Please consult with your CPA or attorney for assistance.

Hiring an Accountant

A good accounting firm is worth its weight in gold to your business. Your accountant is not just another service provider. He or she should be an integral part of your advisory team. Your accountant can help you safely grow your business to the level you want. Your accountant should work with you to establish monthly and quarterly sales and profitability goals against which you can measure your progress. Your accountant is also the 800-pound gorilla that keeps the tax man away.

A good accountant helps you set up your books by reviewing your chart of accounts and advises you on choosing appropriate expense categories for your bookkeeping system. If you operate your business part-time, and you're still holding a day job, your accountant can show you how to reduce tax withholdings by your employer in anticipation of business tax deductions you plan to take on your tax return, and increase the amount of your paycheck. It's like getting a tax-free raise!

Your accountant advises you on effective ways to track expenses such as:

- How to keep a mileage log (some accountants may even give you one).
- Under what circumstances are certain travel expenses deductible?

- Which expenses require a receipt and which don't?
- Is it to your advantage to take a home office deduction?

Discuss with your accountant the best way to withdraw money from your business for personal expenses. Also, plan to discuss year-end tax strategies around October of each year—well ahead of the April 15th deadline.

Sales Taxes and Licenses

As previously mentioned you have certain federal, state, and local licensing and taxing responsibilities. For licensing requirements, check with your local Chamber of Commerce for a packet on how to start a business in your state. While you're at it, make an appointment with a SCORE representative to help you. Your packet lists all the regulatory bodies with which to register and make your business legal.

Most states have a sales tax that must be collected by merchants at the point of sale. Internet companies are treated just like mail order companies in that sales taxes are only collected on sales for items shipped to a destination within the state in which the company resides.

When buying books for resale from retail stores you can escape paying state and local sales taxes on your purchase if you have a copy of your resale certificate on file with the merchant. Conversely, you're responsible for collecting and paying state and local sales taxes on Internet sales with a delivery address within your state. Sales with a delivery address outside your state are currently not subject to any type of sales tax.

Why You Need Insurance

Don't make the mistake of thinking you can go into this business without protecting yourself with insurance. Guard your inventory from loss or damage— even if it's stored in a spare bedroom or in your garage or basement.

Most homeowner policies allow you to attach a rider to insure valuable items. A few homeowner policies may even insure small business assets up to $10,000. Check with your insurance agent and review the particulars of your policy. If you're a renter and have renters insurance, you may be protected too. Again, check with your agent.

Ask your agent to ensure you have enough life insurance to replace your income should the unthinkable happen. Having adequate life insurance is a good idea whether you start a business or not.

In addition, ask your agent about "Key Personnel" insurance. Key Personnel insurance is an extra layer of protection for your business should something happen to you. It can be used to pay off major creditors so they don't go after the personal assets of the surviving owners of the business.

Finally, there is business continuation insurance, employee theft, employee liability claims, and the list goes on. A competent insurance agent can advise you on all the various types of coverage needed for your business structure.

Where to Get Help

There are numerous federal, state and local government agencies dedicated to helping small business owners. Consult with your local Chamber of Commerce to learn about special programs that may be available in your area. In addition to the Chamber, contact the following organizations for free business resources.

Service Corps of Retired Executives (SCORE). As previously discussed, this non-profit organization bills itself as "Counselors to America's Small Business" and for good reason. Although the headquarters for SCORE are in Herndon, Virginia, and Washington, D.C., the organization has 370 chapters throughout the United States with an army of 11,000 working and retired volunteer counselors nationwide. You can receive personal, one-on-one mentoring, telephone support, and attend local workshops for solving business problems. The mentoring and advice hotline is free, but you normally pay for workshops. They have many helpful articles and ideas on their website at *https://www.score.org*.

United States Small Business Administration (SBA). On the SBA website, you'll find a wealth of useful information on virtually all aspects of starting and running a business. The SBA is best known for providing loan guarantees to small businesses that can't otherwise qualify at commercial banks. The national SBA office is located in Washington, D.C., and you can reach them at 202-205-6665. However, your local SBA office may be better suited to address your specific needs. Visit the national SBA website at *http://www.sba.gov*.

CHAPTER 11

Physical Inventory Management

Okay, you're in the book business. That means you're going to handle lots of books—perhaps thousands of them every month. For an efficient operation, plan ahead for how you'll get books from the field to your bookshelves, in as few steps as possible.

Preparing Your Storage Area

Decide right away where to store your inventory. When I started out, I happened to have a long hallway that stretched from the master bedroom to the laundry room. It was wide enough for me to line both walls with five-shelf bookcases; six on one wall and seven on the other, enough for about 2,000 books. It was perfect, out of the way, climate controlled, and a great conversation piece for visiting guests.

"Wow. You sure do read a lot!" they would exclaim.

"Yeah, right."

The only downside to this arrangement was that, to get from the front of the house to the laundry room, I had to walk sideways down the hall to squeeze between the bookcases. (After I finally removed the bookcases and relocated them to my first small warehouse, for a while I'd still instinctively turn sideways to walk down the hall even though there was plenty of room!)

Once the hallway was filled to capacity, my books spilled into the garage. I built four huge bookcases from cinder blocks and 2" × 8" × 8' boards. Each bookshelf held about 800 books. I'll talk more about the bookcases later, but storing books in my garage presented a few climatic problems in the Arizona heat, as you can imagine. So I installed a floor model air conditioner to keep the garage at a book friendly temperature most of the time. It wasn't quite as perfect as having them inside the house, but my wife would have killed me if I tried to expand beyond the hallway. Bookselling can sometimes be hazardous.

I know booksellers who dedicate a spare bedroom to storing their books. That's just as good as my hallway; maybe even better. A standard 10 × 12 room should easily accommodate 2,500 to 3,000 books. Just line the walls with bookcases, then fill in the rest of the room with more bookcases butted back-to-back.

Bookcases lining the walls should be anchored to a stud to prevent them from tipping over. Bookcases in the middle of the room should be anchored to each other to prevent swaying. They should be further anchored across the top with a 2 × 4 either to a wall or to the tops of bookcases lining the walls. This is particularly important if you have small children. The last thing in the world you want is to have a child climb a bookcase and have it topple over onto the little tyke. A bookcase filled with 150 to 800 books weighs between 300 to 960 pounds and can easily crush a small child. In fact, you're better off not storing your books where children are present. Don't take chances, be safe!

Another safety concern comes from overloading an upstairs room with thousands of books. I've gone into the homes of booksellers trying to sell me their entire inventory and seen upstairs floors buckling under the weight. The last thing in the world you want is your ceiling collapsing down around your ears with tons of books landing on your head. When I kept books in my home they were always at ground floor level for safety reasons. Besides, I never liked the idea of lugging books up and down the stairs anyway.

Essential Supplies and Equipment

Your equipment needs will vary with the scale of operation you choose to start. I'm going to assume your plans are modest and you only require a minimal amount of supplies and equipment. At a bare minimum have on hand:

- Four 5-shelf bookcases. (Each one holds about 150 books.)
- A desk or sturdy table.
- A comfortable chair.
- A computer.
- High-speed Internet service.
- A telephone (one with a speaker is nice).
- A TV stand with wheels and shelves.
- A small complement of office supplies:
    1. Scotch tape.
    2. Scissors.
    3. Pens and pencils.

- Size 1.75" × 0.5" REMOVABLE address labels for SKU numbers.
- A starter compliment of shipping supplies:
    1. Bubble mailer sizes #0, #2, and #6.
    2. Packing tape.
    3. Tape gun.
    4. Goo Gone or Bestine.
    5. Several clean cloths for cleaning books.
    6. White erasers.
    7. A 320-grain sandpaper block.
- A generous supply of flat rate priority mail envelopes (available for free from the post office website).
- A generous supply of large and small flat rate priority mail boxes (available for free from the post office website).
- Eight USPS mail tubs to transport outgoing mail (available for free from your local post office).

Let's go over the list. Having several sturdy bookcases is obvious, though some small booksellers keep their books in boxes. Personally, I would find it maddening to constantly sort though boxes of books, but if money is an issue you have that option.

You can buy decent bookcases at your local Wal-Mart Super Center. I used the Mainstays 5-shelf unit with the Alder wood finish. I chose the Alder wood finish because I liked the classic look. You assemble them yourself and they hold about 30 books per shelf. The cost is under $30 each so buying four units gives you enough capacity to store around 600 books for about $150 with tax. Seven units give you enough capacity to store about 900 books for under $250.

You can also buy used bookcases from Goodwill and The Salvation Army thrift stores on sale for under $10 each. You'll buy them piecemeal as they become available, but you might get lucky and find several at one location. I once bought four of them for $7.50 a piece. While you're out scouting in thrift stores, take a couple of minutes to quickly stroll through the furniture section of the store. Be on the lookout for folding tables, desks, chairs, and bookcases. You'll be amazed at the bargains you find.

The TV stand is a little less obvious but, in my mind, an essential piece of equipment that makes an inexpensive book cart. I'm sure you've seen the little cheap particle board TV stands with the fake oak finish and plastic wheels in every major office supply store on the planet. Sometimes they have doors that hide the shelves (not recommended because they only get in the way). They cost about $50, and if you get the model with two shelves underneath you can store bubble mailers there for easy access.

Today I use an industrial strength book truck from Brodart to haul my books around, but back when money was more of an issue, the TV stand "cart" was a cheap alternative. I used the makeshift cart for piling up my books as I pulled them from inventory for shipping. Since the books were stored in SKU sequence, I simply removed a book from the shelf, placed it on the cart, and pushed the cart to the bookcase holding the next book I needed to pull.

You need a workspace, but I assume you already have a desk or workstation for your computer. This will do fine. If you don't have a computer (and presumably a desk), then you can't do this business. You simply can't sell books on the Internet without a computer.

Believe it or not, people have actually asked me if they needed to buy a computer to sell books online. Since I'm already stating the obvious, I might as well mention you need Internet access too. I recommend high speed DSL service or high speed cable. I chose cable, and I bundled my telephone into the deal as well to earn a discounted rate. So my cable TV, telephone, and Internet access all come on one bill, and is automatically deducted from my checking account each month.

You can buy 8,000 removable address labels for SKUs for less than $35. Use a spreadsheet to print the labels. For a complete explanation on how to use a spreadsheet visit: *http://www.internetbookselling.com*. You can download a sample Microsoft Excel spreadsheet from the "Downloads" link to use as a template.

CAUTION!

Make sure the labels are **REMOVABLE**. If you start sticking permanent address labels on books, you're going to have a huge mess on your hands trying to get them off after they sell. In fact, to avoid damaging the dust jackets or covers of older books, removable labels should not be stuck to them. Instead, stick them on the top edge of the book pages.

The above shipping supplies are the bare minimum you want to have on hand. The remaining office supplies and equipment are self-explanatory. If you have the money, pop for the additional items in the following Nice-to-Have section before buying any other goodies. Also, when you buy shipping tape, buy the thicker 2ml kind. It's not only sturdier for shipping, it's easier to handle in the mail room. The price difference between the thinner, cheaper tape and the better stuff is practically nil.

Nice-to-Have Supplies and Equipment

As soon as you're able to raise more working capital, here are a few additional items that help your operation run smoother:

- A second desk or folding table.
- Multiple telephone lines.
- A second computer.
- Additional office supplies:
    1. Book repair kit.
    2. An electric pencil sharpener.
- Additional shipping supplies:
    1. Bubble mailers #4.
    2. Bubble wrap, small and medium bubbles.
    3. A supply of multi-dimensional boxes.
- Automation equipment and systems (more about these later):
    1. Shipping label printer.
    2. Integrated postage scale.
    3. Global Positioning System (GPS).

For the sake of efficiency, have a separate table or desk to stack the books you're currently listing. It's difficult to perform administrative tasks at your desk when piles of books are in the way. Put them on a separate table and keep them there.

As your business grows, you'll discover you need more than one telephone line. For maximum efficiency, consider a separate line for personal calls, incoming business calls, outgoing business calls, and a fourth line for faxing.

Make your single computer system last as long as possible. When you decide a second computer is necessary, set up a simple Local Area Network to share resources such as files and printers. Computers are relatively cheap these days, and a second one saves lots of time. Never forget, time means money.

I nearly put the book repair kit under the Essential Supplies and Equipment heading. I decided not to because it's better if you get into the habit of avoiding books requiring a lot of repair in the first place. There will be occasions when you buy books without noticing a minor flaw that can be repaired without too much fuss. In general, major repairs aren't worth the effort unless the book is valuable. Even with expensive books, weigh the diminished value of a book that's been repaired against buying books that are in good to excellent shape from the start.

Nevertheless, a book repair kit for minor repairs is nice to have. You can find book repair kits suitable for small sellers at *http://www.brodart.com* for a reasonable price.

I also nearly put the automation equipment under Essential Supplies and Equipment. In reality, it's not actually "essential." However, it'll definitely make your bookselling life easier. As your business grows, automation equipment pays for itself again and again. You'll wonder how you ever managed your business without it.

Don't think you have to run out and buy the items on the "Nice-to-Have" list all at once. If you're appropriately capitalized and those items fit within your budget, by all means go for it. But at this stage of the game they're not essential. You're better off spending your capital on more inventory.

Storing Books

Every new bookseller is confronted with the challenge of figuring out how to manage physical inventory. Just what does one do with all those books? Developing a physical inventory management system and organizing your books in a manner that allows quick and easy access makes your operation more efficient and profitable.

Earlier in this chapter, I discussed the use of removable labels printed with SKU numbers for tracking books. Let's delve into that topic a little deeper.

The easiest and fastest way for beginners to implement a SKU system is to use a series of consecutive numbers printed on removable labels. The SKU is uploaded to marketplaces when books are listed for sale. After a sale is made, the SKU of the book sold is included with the notification you receive from the marketplace. Since books are arranged in numerical order on your bookshelves, it's a simple matter to find books on your Pick List for later packing and shipping. We'll delve a little more deeply into how this all works in a moment.

Filling the Gaps

As books sell, gaps appear on your bookshelves where books were removed after being sold. To keep your books from leaning over and warping or possibly falling off the shelf, spend five minutes each day sliding the remaining books on each shelf to the left to close the gaps. Place an inexpensive bookend at the end of the row to hold them in place. This keeps your books standing upright on the bottom edges as they were designed, and avoids unnecessary damage to the spines and boards. It also makes it easy to add additional books to the far right of the shelf.

Every couple of months go through your bookcases and fill the gaps at the end of each shelf by moving books from lower shelves up to the higher shelves. I call this process "consolidating" inventory. Periodically consolidating your inventory reduces the need to build or buy more bookshelves, thereby conserving cash and space.

This system works quite well for your first few thousand books. Beyond that level, physically moving books between shelves and between bookcases is a major effort. When you acquire that many books you'll need a more advanced physical inventory management system that doesn't involve shuffling them around.

Nevertheless, I continued using sequential SKUs until my inventory grew to about 10,000 books. Every couple of months I'd hire a couple strong young men from a temp agency such as Labor Ready to do the heavy lifting, because my old bones had become much too brittle to move them around anymore. With 10,000 books, the job took two people a good eight hours to complete. At $14 per hour, I had a bi-monthly expense of $224 just to consolidate my inventory.

While the consecutive numbering system worked quite well when my inventory was small, it became increasingly more costly over time. For the sake of simplicity, you may want to use the consecutive number system until you get tired of shuffling books around. Or you may want take a smarter route and adopt a more flexible system that doesn't require you to physically shuffle books at all.

A More Sophisticated System

The following method for managing physical inventory uses a location code, and you won't ever move books from shelf to shelf. You'll only have to slide books to the left at the end of each day, or even every other day to compress out gaps that appear when sold books are removed. Eliminating gaps is a simple procedure that shouldn't take more than ten or fifteen minutes, even for a 20,000 book inventory.

Label each bookcase with a numeric identifier. If you have seven five-shelf bookcases, label each bookcase 001 to 007 consecutively. Use a three digit book-case number to allow for future growth and for meaningful sorting by inventory management software.

Next label each bookshelf with the bookcase number and shelf number of 01 to 05 respectively. Use a two digit shelf number for meaningful sorting by future inventory management software as well. The combination of bookcase number and shelf number is your location code. Thus, bookcase one, shelf four, has a location code of 001-04. Bookcase three, shelf two, has a location code of 003-02.

Finally, each book is assigned a numerical value just like in the consecutive numbering SKU system discussed above. The location code is added to your con-secutive number scheme as a prefix.

As a practical illustration, let's say a book has a SKU number of 0033257. Then, if it's on bookshelf three, shelf two, the location code and SKU number of the book combined will be 003-02-0033257. With the books stored on the shelf in numerical sequence all you do is run your finger down the line of books until you come to 0033257.

Make sure you buy *removable* labels instead of *permanent* labels or you'll create a real mess for yourself. Visit Online Labels at *http://www.onlinelabels .com/Products/OL25WR.htm* to see an entire line of label products for a variety of purposes. For SKU labels order product OL25WR – 1.75" × 0.5" Return Address Labels and make sure the selection says "removable." They come 80 labels to a

1 - 2

This is unit one, shelf two, with books using the location code. Finding books is easy with this system.

sheet, so a package of 100 sheets lasts a long time. If you have any doubts, give them a call to confirm you're ordering the right material.

As you scan each book into your inventory software, the system automatically assigns a SKU number to each. For books that don't have a barcode just punch in the ISBN on your keyboard. For pre-ISBN books, you may need to create a catalog page on the marketplace before it can be listed. Once all your books are entered into the system, print the book titles along with the SKU and affix the appropriate label to each book before placing it on your bookshelf.

You can choose to not stick a SKU label on every book, because books on the shelves can be sorted in alphabetical order by title, by author, or not sorted at all. Since you're only dealing with one shelf, it's a simple matter of scanning the titles for the one you want.

As books sell, gaps appear just like before, except now all you do is move the books from right to left and leave an ever growing space on the far right end of each shelf. When new books are listed, you simply add them to the end of the shelf to fill the space. This system eliminates the need to consolidate shelves, thereby saving a great deal of time, not to mention wear and tear on your back.

I actually started out using the Post-It Note system and it worked great until I had about 500 books in my inventory. Before long I found myself spending huge amounts of time doing nothing but writing numbers on Post-It Notes and cutting them up with scissors. I told myself there had to be a better way, and it wasn't long before I discovered removable address labels.

I created a simple spreadsheet with formulas that automatically incremented a sequential set of numbers that perfectly aligned with my sheet of labels. Since the labels were laser printer ready, it was a simple matter to print tens of thousands of numbers at a time with the press of a button. You're welcome to get a copy of the spreadsheet I used for several years from the "Downloads" link at *http://www .internetbookselling.com*.

If you choose not to SKU every book, insert an 8½ × 11 sheet of colored index card paper between every 15th book or so with the SKU of the book to the left of the card written on both sides of the outer edge of the sheet in big, bold, dark numbers. This trick gives you the ability to segment your shelves into smaller groups of books that need eyeballing for sold titles. Combining the unit and shelf numbering system with the SKU card allows you to eliminate the need for SKU labels entirely. This is the method I currently use in my business.

State-of-the-Art Inventory Management

In highly sophisticated inventory management systems, available space is tracked via a computer that automatically decides which gap to fill with books as you list. When your business becomes successful enough to afford such a system— congratulations! You've hit the big time. Your physical inventory management can be almost completely automated, and you'll be as efficient as humanly possible. Until then my friend, keep track of the gaps and manually decide where to direct newly listed books. However, keeping track using the methods described above is ridiculously easy, requiring five to ten minutes of your time prior to each book listing session.

If your inventory gets so large that the time commitment to track the gaps becomes too costly, eMail me and I'll be happy to consult with you on designing a large scale inventory management system integrated with your online listings, manifest system, and computerized conveyor network to automatically carry pulled books to assigned packing stations for shipment. Just make sure you have the bucks to pay for all the technology; not to mention my fee!

Seriously, though, either one of the methods outlined will suffice for 99 percent of the readers of this book. I started with the consecutive numbering system, and I now use the location code system.

As my final bit of advice on this topic, if you intend to grow your business into a large company, you probably want to consider using the location code method immediately. My personal experience with converting from the numeric system to the location code system was a bit painful, and there's no sense adopting the simpler system if you know in advance you're going to convert to a more sophisticated one down the road.

Conversely, if your plans are to keep your business under 5,000 books, the consecutive numbering system works fine. Just prepare yourself for a lot of shuffling of inventory around every few months or so as large gaps appear on your shelves from selling books.

Heavy Duty Bookcases

I wish I could take credit for the idea of building bookcases from cinder blocks and planks, but I originally got the idea from Michael Mould after reading his book, *"Online Bookselling: A Practical Guide with Detailed Explanations and Insightful Tips."*[1] I wrote to him and he sent me a file with his bookcase design. It uses 8" × 8" × 16" cinder blocks and 2" × 8" × 8' planks for shelves. It's sturdy and inexpensive to construct.

Here's a side view of two cinder block bookcase units. Structural integrity is maintained by attaching each shelf to the 2″ × 4″ × 8′ stringers on both ends, and across the tops with three inch wood screws.

This is what an entire unit looks like. It's two bookcases attached to a center panel.

After trying them, I decided I wanted a design that used less floor space in a warehouse setting, so I modified the construction to what I currently use to store my inventory. It uses most of the same material, but I take two cinder block bookcases and join them in the middle with a 1" × 16" × 8' panel to make a single unit. The shelves of the two bookcases are attached to the center panel for added strength. On the ends, I use a 2" × 4" × 8' strip for connecting all the shelves to make them immovable.

Finally, I lay another 2" × 4" × 8' wood strip across each end of the tops of all units to connect them together for even more stability. Recently, I began substituting 6" × 8" × 16" cinder blocks for added shelf space for books. By using thinner blocks, I can fit up to 100 books per shelf, or 2,000 books per 20-shelf unit. That's a 25 percent increase over the original design.

Unlike free standing bookcases, it's all but impossible to topple these monsters by accidentally bumping into one. To knock these bookcases over you must purposely and repeatedly slam your body into them full force to have any effect. It's not that I don't think there are people careless enough to do such a thing, but it's important you know that this design is pretty solid. Still you don't want small children or careless adults climbing them because accidents can happen, and if one should topple over onto a person the weight of the bookcase will cause serious injury, and perhaps even death.

Members of my free Internet bookselling forum can download a detailed schematic and parts list for a single bookcase as well as the double bookcase design I use. Go to the "Downloads" area of my free website, *http://www.internetbook selling.com* for download instructions.

One unit is actually two bookcases attached to a 1" × 16" × 8' center panel. The bookshelves are attached to the center panel as well as to the 2" × 4" × 8' stringers on each end of the unit.

Shelving Your Books

Over time, books experience wear-and-tear, even while sitting on a shelf. They incur shelf-wear every time you shuffle them around, remove an adjacent book, or add a book to the shelf. If they're leaning to the left or right with the top edge of the board resting against another book, they can warp, or the spine can become cocked. Moisture, humidity, extreme heat, and direct sunlight can damage them as well.

There are numerous things you can do to protect your inventory and keep your books in excellent shape until the day they sell. For starters, keep your books in an environmentally controlled space. Don't allow moisture from a leaky roof, swamp cooler, or open window damage them. Also, try not to subject your books to dramatic temperature swings.

Ideally, books are stored upright resting on the bottom edge with the spine facing out. It's best if they're sandwiched between books of the approximate same height and width to prevent bulging at the top or lead edges. Expensive books should be further protected with Mylar covers to reduce shelf-wear and other damage. You can buy Mylar covers from Brodart at *http://www.brodart.com*, or call them at 1-888-820-4377 and request a printed catalog of their library equipment and supplies.

You can further protect highly valuable books by bubble wrapping them before putting them on the shelf. Bubble wrapping prevents almost all shelf-wear in addition to protecting against moisture, dust, and corner damage from dropping the book. Always handle your books with care and your buyers will reward you with great feedback.

CHAPTER 12

Your Future in Internet Bookselling

The bookselling industry in all its forms is rapidly changing thanks in no small part to the exponential growth of the Internet. The mom-and-pop corner bookstore has now burgeoned into a global enterprise with customers worldwide. Even the smallest Internet bookseller can be an international player. Nevertheless, the lone book scout making his or her rounds can still earn a comfortable living provided he or she is willing to work hard and systematically build the business.

That doesn't mean there aren't challenges. Digital offerings of bestselling titles are becoming more popular every day. Amazon's Kindle and the Barnes & Noble Nook reader are good examples of how books are being digitized and downloaded into mechanical devices for a fraction of the cost of physical books. And eBooks written for a variety of PDA tools are becoming more common.

In an article written for the IOBA, Erwin H. Bush says, "Three key trends in book publishing that will significantly alter the future of bookselling are Print on Demand (POD) publishing, eBooks and Audiobooks and changes in the publishing marketplace."[1]

Meanwhile, Steve Weber writes in his book *The Home-Based Bookstore* an even more dire prediction:

> ". . . new printing technology has already changed the economics of niche titles. Print-on-demand (POD) enables publishers to efficiently print single copies of books for which there has not been enough demand for a new edition. In the future, it's possible that no title

would ever have to go out of print. A book could simply be printed each time a customer orders one. This could reduce the value of scarce used books and shrink the territory for sellers specializing in out-of-print books."[2]

Despite encroachment on the printed word by digital technology, I believe the market for used books supplied by small Internet booksellers will continue to flourish for some time. No doubt there will be industry changes, market swings, and technological revolutions, but the savvy entrepreneur adapts to changing market conditions and thrives.

The entrepreneurial spirit longs to be free. Internet bookselling strips away the corporate straightjacket of arbitrary dress codes, rigid schedules, management bureaucracy, and mind numbing sameness of thought and behavior.

As an Internet bookseller you leave all the negatives of corporate life behind and make your own way in the world. You make your own rules, call your own shots, and break free of the drudgery of being controlled by others. Internet bookselling is a wonderful life indeed. Through hard work and perseverance you can make a better future for yourself and for your family.

Does this all sound too good to be true? Nonsense! Tens of thousands of small Internet booksellers are doing it right now. If you don't believe me, go to Amazon .com, Alibris.com, or Half.com and look up any book and see for yourself how many third-party sellers there are selling used copies. Many of those people are making good money—people just like you, entrepreneurs dreaming of a better life who have the willingness to work hard to get it.

Continuing Education

I've tried to be as thorough as possible in this book. As mentioned in the Warning and Disclaimer, this book is not intended as a replacement for other works on the topic. Instead, it's meant as a supplement, and as such I've avoided duplicating material found in other books where I didn't feel I could add a unique perspective to the discussion.

I strongly recommend you develop the habit of allocating a block of time each day for reading bookselling articles found on various websites like *http://www .BookThink.com*, the Amazon.com bookseller boards, and my own blog and forum, which you can access from *http://www.internetbookselling.com*.

Start contributing your thoughts to bookselling blogs and forums. Form friendships with other booksellers you meet online and in person while scouting in the field. Share ideas and form alliances with some of them. Study closed auctions on eBay of book lots that sold for high prices to learn how to creatively sell penny books you can't profitably sell individually. Finally, buy books from other authors about the bookselling industry to round out your knowledge.

Keep Improving Your Technology

Books are physical, tangible products, but it's technology that drives Internet bookselling. Always look for innovative ways to cost effectively add to your technological infrastructure. Learn all you can about your equipment because it'll help you increase productivity, force costs down, and enhance profits. Find better and more useful ways to use your inventory management software, online postage service, scanning devices, integrated scale, label printer, laser printer, fax, phone system, and digital camera.

One of the best resources around for increasing your knowledge about all things digital is a subscription to the Kim Komando "Kim's Club" podcast of the nationally syndicated Kim Komando radio show.

Each week you get treated to a 90 minute download of her weekly broadcast, as well as a daily "digital minute" mini broadcast by Kim. Plus you can sign up for a free "tip of the day" eMail that'll give you tons of ideas about how to make your life and your business more productive. Finally, her website is bursting with fascinating computer hints, tips, and tricks of every kind.

I like to download my daily and weekly podcasts and let them play in the background while I list books for sale. I always pick up something useful every time I listen. It's a great way to stay current on the latest technologies for about $50 per year.

Check out Kim Komando at *http://www.komando.com* for extraordinary free resources and podcast subscription information. Also, use the station locator feature to find a radio station near you that carries her broadcast. With more than 450 affiliates carrying her show, there's bound to be a radio station in your hometown.

Members-Only Forum

As a service to my readers I've created a website where purchasers of my books can meet and discuss bookselling topics and share ideas to help each other build stronger businesses. It's a "member's only" website for the original purchasers of my books. If you purchased a used copy you can optionally buy a lifetime membership. For complete details go to *http://www.internetbookselling.com* and sign up today.

Since I'm a full-time bookseller I'm constantly learning new techniques and strategies that help me grow my business. I actively participate in forum discussions and I'm always happy to answer your questions on any aspect of bookselling.

My intention is for the forum to be a friendly and safe place for advanced and novice members alike to freely discuss all aspects of this fascinating business. I freely share my knowledge on the forum because I want it to grow into the largest and friendliest meeting place for booksellers in the industry.

There's a code of conduct you'll find published on the rules page of the forum that's strictly enforced. The rules reflect my desire to foster an intellectually stimulating atmosphere that encourages maximum learning and participation for all members. You can help make it happen by registering and joining existing discussions or starting topics of your own. Please report all rule violations to me via eMail for swift action.

The Future Belongs to Those Who Prepare for It

I once read that luck is nothing more than opportunity meeting preparation. Business and investment guru Robert T. Kiyosaki says, "Luck is Laboring Under Correct Knowledge."[3] Are you ready to create your own luck?

Now that I've explained how you can earn a living selling books on the Internet, are you prepared to go out and seize your opportunity? I can't promise you'll earn a million dollars in this business. What I *can* promise is when you sell your first book you'll know that a better future is possible because you'll have taken the first step toward wresting control of your life from others.

You're about to embark on what may be the most rewarding journey of your life. Work hard and work smart and there's no reason why you can't enjoy great success. It can happen for you if you follow the methods in this book. In fact, if you follow these methods plus the tips I give on my website, it almost *must* happen. I welcome you to the most exciting business opportunity I've ever found, and I look forward to meeting you in the field and online.

Good Hunting!

Appendices

The following Appendices contain a subset of the many useful resources you'll find in the members-only area of *http://www.internetbookselling.com*. The resources listed here are ones you'll use most often. However, there are many more resources listed on the website.

The website is updated on a continuous basis, whereas this book is only updated with each revised printing. Most likely there are resources on the website that weren't known to me when the book was last printed. Consequently, the website will always be more current.

Another reason to go to my website for resources is convenience. Some of the referenced URLs are quite long and clicking a link on the website is an easier and faster way to access the resources than retyping the URL from the book.

If you're visiting a website listed in the book and the URL is long, just try typing the portion of the address that takes you to the home page of the reference, then navigate to the desired information from there. It's still slower than clicking through from the resource links on the website, but it'll reduce the chances of making a typo.

If you're a supplier to the bookselling industry and you'd like to be listed in the revised edition of this book, please contact me through my website with a description of your product or service, your web address, telephone number, and physical address. Not all suppliers are listed in the book, but the chances are good you'll be listed as a resource in the "Member's" area of my website.

If you're a reader and you discover a resource you think might be a good addition to the book, please contact me through my website about the resource. I'll make every effort to include it in the revised edition of the book, or in the "Resources" area of my website.

Finally, if you discover broken links in the book or on the website, please contact me so I can either revise the information or delete it as a reference. I'll do everything possible to ensure the accuracy of the resources, but if you help me, the job becomes easier. Thanks!

Appendix 1

IOBA Book Terminology

The Independent Online Booksellers Association (IOBA) publishes an alphabetized list of common book terminology you'll find helpful when listing books for sale. It's reproduced here with their permission as it appears online. For easy online access, visit the IOBA website at *http://www.ioba.org/terms.html*. There's also a link to the IOBA Book Terminology from the "Member's" area of my website.

ABA – In the U.S.: American Booksellers Association (for independently owned bookstores with a store front location selling new books). *In the U.K.*: Antiquarian Booksellers Association (the U.K. equivalent of the ABAA).

ABAA – Antiquarian Booksellers' Association of America (the U.S. equivalent of the U.K. ABA).

ABAC – Antiquarian Booksellers' Association of Canada (Canadian equivalent of the U.K. ABA).

ADVANCE REVIEW (or READER'S or READING) COPY (ARC) – A special prepublication copy mainly for review purposes—sent to reviewers and others prior to publication date. It is often referred to as an ARC. It is usually softbound in wrappers, which may be similar to dust jacket art of the first trade edition, and occasionally there are textual differences between an advance review copy and a first edition. It is sometimes issued as a hardcover as well with a review slip laid in by the publisher. This is preceded by an uncorrected proof copy printed for author's corrections, publicity, and promotion—usually published in plain wrappers and which may have substantial textual differences from the finished published book.

AEG – All Edges Gilt. See "Gilt."

ALS – Autographed Letter Signed.

ANTIQUARIAN BOOKSELLER – A term, in today's usage, that describes a bookseller whose stock in trade is primarily old, rare, and/or collectible books.

ASSOCIATION COPY – A book once belonging to the author, or signed or annotated by the author to someone closely associated with the author of the book or the book itself in some way. Also, a book inscribed by its author to a famous person, or owned by someone of interest.

AUTHORS EDITION – Book authorized by author, usually foreign editions, around the turn of the last century when many titles were pirated or "unauthorized."

BACKSTRIP – A strip used by binder to reinforce the back of folded sheets in the binding of the spine.

BAL – Bibliography of American Literature.

BDS – Boards.

BIBLIOGRAPHY – A reference work detailing known published titles on a given subject or by a given author.

BIBLIOPHILE – A lover of books.

BINDING – Material used as a protective cover for a book (e.g.: leather, cloth, buckram, paper, etc.).

BINDING COPY – A book whose text block is complete and serviceable, but the current binding is defective or incomplete. (Note: Technically, what we call bindings on most books today, where the text block is glued in [in a hardcover book the text block is glued to a cover by some mull and end sheet paper, and in a softcover book normally the text block is glued directly to the spine of the cover], is actually a casing. Bindings were actually sewn to the collected gatherings. The two terms—binding and casing—are, however, starting to be used interchangeably today.)

BIOPREDATION – An attack on books by living matter, which may include insects or mildew.

BLIND (Stamped or Tooled) – Impressed into paper or binding with no color, leaving an impression only.

BOARDS – The front and back covers of a hardcover book.

BOOK CLUB EDITION (BCE, BOMC, etc.) – Editions published by book clubs (i.e.: The Book-of-the-Month Club, Fireside Book Club, History Book Club, The Literary Guild, etc.).

BOOK JACKET – Separate paper covering for the book. Also referred to as the dust jacket or dustwrapper.

BOOKLET – A small book, often only a few pages long and bound in wrappers.

BOOK PLATE – An ownership label, usually placed inside front cover. Many have become collectible due to the designer or owner; others actually lower the value of books printed in the last 50 or so years.

BOOKWORM – A worm (in a larval grub state) which harms books by feeding on their binding or leaves. Also a term for a person devoted to books.

BROADSIDE **or** *BROADSHEET* – Large sheet of paper printed on one side only.

BUCKRAM – A heavy weave of binding cloth.

BUMPED – Refers to the corners or spine ends of a book that has been damaged by being dropped, or carelessly handled or shelved.

CASE – The covers enclosing a book, usually made of thick cardboard, and normally covered in cloth, paper, or leather.

CANCEL – Due to errors or defects in printing, a book may have one or more pages sliced out of the text block by the publisher after it has been bound. The new printed matter pasted on to the resulting stub(s) by the publisher is referred to as a "cancel" or "cancellans."

CHAPBOOK – Small, inexpensive books produced from the 17th century until today, originally sold by "chapmen," peddlers, and hawkers.

CHAPTER BOOK – Fairly modern term referring to books for older children which are organized into chapters, as opposed to "picture books," which often are not.

CHIPPED – Small pieces broken off of a dust jacket or binding.

CIRCA – (abbreviated: *ca*) Refers to an approximate date when actual date is unknown.

CLOSED TEAR – A tear with no material missing.

COATED – Paper is smooth and polished; something has been applied to the surface to make it appear glossy.

COCKED – If, when looking down on the head of a book, the corners are not square it is said to be cocked or rolled. Also known as a spine slant. (Note: Cocking "can" also involve a book's spine being slightly twisted or non-vertical at either end that is not severe enough to cause spine slant.)

COLLATE – To verify completeness of a book by examining it carefully (e.g.: all illustrative plates are present, no leaves are missing, etc.).

COLOPHON – Details of the printer's typography or the publisher's symbol, often found on the last page of a book and sometimes referred to as such when a printer's or publisher's "device" is found on the copyright page. Sometimes states the number of copies printed, and in the case of a limited edition, will cite the copy number and may contain the signature of the author, illustrator, or publisher.

CONTEMPORANEOUS BINDING – Up until the 19th century, books were published unbound, with the understanding that the new owner would have his books bound at his leisure. This term refers to bindings done the same year or within a few years of the publication of such a book. (Note: Formerly known as "contemporary binding," but in today's usage that has come to mean a more modern binding; a rebind.)

COPPERPLATE – Illustrations produced when the original printing plate was engraved on copper; this method was introduced before the end of the 15th century. They to some extent replaced the woodcut, which regained considerable popularity later on.

COPYRIGHT PAGE (c., cp) – The page that normally appears on verso of the title page, containing the artistic property protection.

CWO – Check or cash with order.

DAMPSTAIN – A stain left on a cover or pages that have been exposed to water.

DECKLE EDGE – Uneven and uncut edges, often found on books printed on hand-made paper and not trimmed by the binder, and sometimes simulated by binders on regular paper.

DEC – Decorated.

DENTELLE – A lace-like pattern on a border applied to the inner edge, usually gilt (was sometimes used on the outside in France in the 18th century).

DESIDERATA – A listing of books desired.

DEVICE – The printer's or publisher's imprint, sometimes referred to as a colophon, usually found on the copyright page when present (uncommon now). Sometimes indicates a first printing.

DIMPLE – A small indentation on covers or pages. Considered a defect, if not part of decorated covers.

DING – A small bump or dent leaving an impression, sometimes caused by careless handling or storage.

DISBOUND – A book that has been removed from its binding (and the binding is usually no longer present).

DOG-EARED – Worn or ragged, usually referring to the edges of pages and binding. Corners of pages turned down like a dog's ear.

DS – Document signed.

DUST JACKET **or** *DUSTWRAPPER (DJ, DW)* – The separate paper covering for a book. While originally intended for protection (and sometimes originally made from cloth), these have become an important part of modern books, often including information about a book not found elsewhere.

ED – Edition or Editor.

EDGES – The three outer sides of the text block when a book is closed: fore edge, top edge or head, and bottom edge or foot.

EDITION – All of the copies of a book printed from the same setting of type, at one time or over a period of time, with no major changes, additions or revisions. Minor changes, such as the correction of some misspelled words, or the addition of a dedication, or similar minor alterations, may be made and the revised copies are still considered as part of the same edition, simply being described as different states or issues.

ENDPAPERS (EP) – The double leaves added to the book by the binder that become the pastedowns and free endpapers inside the front and rear covers. These pages are an integral part of the construction of a book, holding the text block and case together. The lack of them drastically shortens the value and life of a book.

EPHEMERA – Printed material of passing interest in everyday life (e.g.: advertising, ticket stubs, photos, postcards, programs, some booklets and pamphlets, etc.).

ERRATA – A list of errors and their corrections or additions to the printing, found after book has been printed, usually on separate sheet or slip of paper. The plural of erratum. (Note: If the slip of paper does not make a correction, but rather supplies additional information, it is called an "addenda slip.")

EX-LIBRARY (EX LIB) – Deaccessioned from a public library or collection.

EX-LIBRIS – From a private library, as opposed to a public library. Could also indicate a bookplate or a stamp.

EXTRA-ILLUSTRATED – Extra illustrations added to the book after publication, normally done by the owner of the book, not the book's publisher.

FAIR – A book that is very worn, but all of its important parts, and dust jacket, must be present. May be soiled with tears, endpapers missing, etc. Such defects must be noted in descriptions.

FINE (F) – A book that has no defects in book or jacket, but not as crisp as it was when new.

FIRST EDITION – The first printing of a book, done from the original setting of type. The collectability of the first printing of the first edition was established in the early days of printing, when the lead type used in the presses would quickly wear away, compromising the readability of the book being printed. (Note: Technically, this term is used to describe any of the printings of a book, done from the original setting of type, at any time until the type is so altered as to constitute a second edition [see "Edition"]. In the world of literature and Modern Firsts, the term is used differently, and means the very first printing of those copies, done at the same time. A second print run, though it is technically still the "First Edition," is not what is meant by the phrase in the world of collectible Modern Firsts.)

FLEXIBLE BINDING – Limp, leather/plastic covers which are flexible.

FLY-LEAVES (FL) – Plain papers at front and rear of book after endpapers.

FOOT – The bottom edge of the text block.

FORE EDGE – The right edge opposite the spine.

FORE EDGE PAINTING – A painting on gilded fore edge, which can only be seen by fanning pages (or slanting the book's binding quite a lot—not recommended!). Although fore-edge paintings can be found on manuscripts dating back to the 13th century, the art became popular in the 17th century, and is still being widely practiced today by artists working on 18th and 19th century books in the old styles.

FOXING – The brown age spots thought to be caused by impurities in paper (e.g.: acid, exposure to humidity, etc.).

FREE ENDPAPER (FFEP: Front Free Endpaper; RFEP: Rear Free Endpaper) – Front and rear blank pages added by the binder.

FRONTISPIECE (Frontis) – The illustration facing title page.

GATHERINGS – The printed sheets, after folding, which are put in order and bound in sequence. Also known as signatures.

GAUFFERED EDGES – A pattern tooled on gilt edges of a book.

GILT EDGES – Page edges cut smooth and gilded (covered with a thin layer of gold leaf).

GLASSINE – Transparent paper sometimes used as a dust jacket to protect a book.

GOOD (G) – A book, or dust jacket in average used and worn condition—complete with all its parts. Note all defects in descriptions.

GRADING – Guidelines used to properly describe condition of books.

GUTTER – Inner margins of two facing pages. Can also refer to the outer indentation that is created by the joining of the boards and spine.

HALF BINDING – A book that has had its spine and corners covered in one material such as cloth or leather and the rest of the front and rear covers covered in another, such as boards or cloth. For instance, a book with a cloth spine and corners and covers of paper-covered boards is termed "Half-Cloth"; a book with a leather spine and corners and cloth or paper-covered boards is termed "Half-Leather."

HALF-TITLE (fly title) – The page, preceding the title page proper, normally listing only the title of the book and no other information. While always present in modern books, it is sometimes lacking in older publications because it was originally designed to be removed before custom binding.

HALF-TONE – A gradation of tone (between light and dark) of an image by minute, closely spaced dots. Used in photography and graphics.

HARDCOVER – A book whose case is made of stiff boards, as opposed to wrappers.

HC – Hardcover.

HEAD – Top edge of the text block.

HEADBAND – Band of silk or cotton affixed to signatures when bound together to form a text block for strength or, more often, decoration of the spine ends.

HINGES – Where the sides of the binding meet the spine (interior) of a book.

IDEAL COPY – When a number of copies of an edition of a book are compared to each other, a bibliographer may set out to determine how the book's publisher initially wished it to appear before the public. If so determined, that copy becomes the standard copy of that edition, to which all other copies can be compared. Thus, when a book is said to be "missing a page," it is assumed that the ideal copy of that book always contains that particular page.

ILAB – International League of Antiquarian Booksellers. Includes 20 national associations representing 30 countries.

IL, ILLUS – Illustrated.

IMPRESSION – All the copies of a book printed during one press run. During the hand-press period, when type was reset each time a press was used, this term was synonymous with edition.

INCUNABULA – Books printed between the invention of moveable type and 1500, coined from the Latin word cunae, meaning "cradle."

INSCRIBED – Signed by the author or someone associated with the book, but with more wording than simply a signature.

IOBA – Independent Online Booksellers Association. A trade association of online booksellers.

ISBN (International Standard Book Number) – A unique machine-readable identification number, which identifies any book unmistakably. One-hundred fifty-nine countries and territories are officially ISBN members. However, as with many man-instituted technologies, the system is not perfect; occasionally one will find two (or more) titles with the same ISBN.

ISSUE – A change, textual or otherwise, made after the book has been published. (e.g.: The first issue of Mark Twain's *A Connecticut Yankee in King Arthur's Court* has an "s"-like ornament between "The" and "King" on page 59. In the case of many of C. S. Forester's books, sheets were printed, but not bound at the same time; when they were, sometimes years later, they were bound in differently colored bindings. The color of the binding then became an issue point.)

JOINTS – Where the spine joins the sides of the book (exterior). Sometimes referred to as the "gutter."

LAID IN – Paper/photograph/print is laid in (not glued down).

LAID ON – See "Tipped In."

LAMINATE – The thin plastic layer covering the dust jacket of some books.

LIMITED EDITION – Small number of copies of a book published. Books are usually numbered such as "100/500" meaning number 100 of an edition of 500.

LITHO – Lithograph.

LOOSE – When a book has been read carelessly or too often, and has become loose and sloppy in its binding.

LTD ED – Limited Edition.

MANUSCRIPT – The original pages of an author's work, written in the author's hand or typed.

MARBLING – A process of decorating paper, in which the result resembles the veins of stone marble.

MARRIED – When the parts of a book or set are supplied from different copies of a book to form a whole, such as the dust jacket from one copy is "married" with a copy of the same book without a jacket, or Volume One is "married" to Volume Two, purchased separately, to form a complete set.

MULL – The cloth that reinforces the hinges and is pasted directly to the body of a book and is hidden by the spine.

n.d. – No Date; no publication date is supplied in the book.

n.p. – No Place; no place of publication is supplied in the book.

OBVERSE – The front or main surface of anything.

OCLC (Online Computer Library Center) – A non-profit cooperative organization of libraries that serves to share data and make cataloging easier. OCLC includes more than 43,000 libraries in 86 countries, and provides quick information to booksellers and collectors about which libraries have a copy of a particular title. Access to OCLC is by fee-based subscription service, most commonly available at libraries.

OPEN TEAR – A tear that may have some material missing.

OUT-OF-PRINT (OP, OOP) – A book no longer available from the publisher. It is no longer being printed and no new copies remain available for sale.

OWNER'S INSCRIPTION – Words written by previous or original owner of book. Also known as *previous owner's inscription*.

PAGINATION – The numbering of the pages.

PANEL – Refers to borders in binding. Can also be used in connection with the main surfaces of a dust jacket.

PAPERBACK (ppb, pb) – A book bound with flexible paper covers; usually a term reserved for mass-market publications.

PAPER COVERS – Stiff, normally heavy weight paper (though usually flexible) covers into which a book is bound by various methods. Can refer to a temporary binding, a booklet or pamphlet, or a book in early (1800s) wrappers.

PAPER-COVERED BOARDS – Book binding (casing); front and back panels which have an outer paper surface glued to underlying stiffer and/or heavier material. The outer paper surface may be decorative or plain.

PARCHMENT – The skin of a sheep, goat, etc., prepared as a surface for writing or for use as a binding material.

PASTEDOWN ENDPAPER – The part of the endpapers that is pasted to the inside of the front and rear covers.

PLATE – A special page containing an illustration or other extra information.

POINTS – Peculiarities in a published book whose presence or absence helps to determine edition, issue, or state.

PBO – Paperback original.

pp (Pages) – For pages — to —. [A single page is p. and then the number.]

PPD – Postpaid.

PR – Printing.

PRESENTATION COPY – A book inscribed by the author to someone else of importance to the author, the book, or society in general.

PRICE CLIPPED – The price on the inner flap of a dust jacket has been cut off.

PROOF – See "Uncorrected Proof."

PROVENANCE – Evidence of the history of the ownership of a particular book (e.g.: auctions records, booksellers' records, book plates, and so on). The book may be important because of who owned it—perhaps a president or important bookseller, collector, royalty, or someone who may be related to the book in some way. Important in establishing the ownership of especially rare items.

PSEUDONYM/PEN-NAME/NOM DE PLUME (PSEUD) – An assumed name used to protect the anonymity of an author.

PUB – Published/publisher.

PUBLISHER'S BINDING – Binding provided by the publisher when supplying a book for a bookseller. This practice, while common today, dates from the 1800s.

QUARTER BINDING – A book with its spine bound in a different material than the boards (e.g.: a leather spine and cloth- or paper-covered boards).

READING COPY – A nice way of describing a book that is complete in text and plates, but so badly worn or soiled that in its current condition it is good only for reading, and cannot be considered "collectible" in this condition. Also tends to suggest that the book has faults that make it not worth rebinding, else it might be described as a "Binding Copy."

READING CREASE – A crease down the spine of a book (usually a paperback).

REBACKED – A repair, where the original spine or backstrip has been removed, the spine replaced, and the original reglued on top. Can be considered a defect, but more valuable than not having any of the original spine present.

REBOUND – A repair, where the entire binding has been replaced by a new one.

RECASED – A repair, where a book is taken apart and put back together using original pages, cloth, and endpapers. Usually done to tighten the sewing or to wash the pages, etc.

RECTO – A right-hand page, when a book is open and facing the reader.

REMAINDER – A new book returned to the publisher as unsold, then re-marketed at a much lower price.

REMAINDER MARK – A mark (rubber stamp, felt marker stroke, or spray, often on a book's bottom edge) signifying that the book was returned to publisher as unsold, and then offered for sale again later at a much lower price. Considered to be a defect by collectors.

RET – Returnable.

REVIEW COPY – A copy of a new book sent free-of-charge for purposes of review. Often includes a laid in review slip with publishing information. Not necessarily a first edition.

RUBBED – Where color has been worn from portions of the binding or dust jacket.

SHAKEN – The text block is loose in its binding; no longer tight, but not detached.

SHEETS – The pages that have been printed, but not yet folded, sewn, or gathered together for binding.

SHELF-BACK – The spine of a book.

SIGNATURE – A printed sheet of paper, folded to size and ready for sewing (i.e.: large paper folded in half, fourths, eighths, sixteenths, or thirty-seconds).

SIGNED (SGD) – Signed with a name only, and no other text included.

SLIPCASE (SLC) – A box built to house and protect a book, leaving the spine exposed.

SOPHISTICATED – Books that have had repairs that involve making additions to the original (e.g.: chips filled in and tinted to match the missing portion, replaced page corners, and so on).

SP – Spelling.

SPINE – The backbone, or back, of the book where the title (if present) is displayed when it is standing upright on a shelf.

STARTING – Hinges or joints beginning to show signs of becoming loose, either through wear or defective binding.

STATE – Variations within an edition, which are made *prior to publication*; can include:
- alterations due to stop-press insertions, damaged type, etc.
- the addition of errata leaves, advertisements.
- textual changes affecting page lay-out.
- some special-paper copies.

This term applies only in connection with the printed pages, and not variations in bindings (e.g.: a small number of copies of Ernest Hemingway's *For Whom the Bell Tolls* were erroneously printed without the photographer's credit on the back of the dust jacket. The presses were stopped midway through the first run, the credit was added, and the second state of the first edition resulted).

STICKER DAMAGE – A price sticker has been roughly removed resulting in surface damage to the underlying material.

STICKER GHOST – A sticker has been left on a book for some time, and the glue, reacting chemically, has discolored the surface.

STIPPLED EDGE – Color sprayed on a book's external edges.

SUNNED – Browning, yellowing, or fading of paper, dustjacket, or binding as a result of sun exposure.

TAIL – Bottom edge of the text block.

TAPE RESIDUE – Complications of cellophane tape that remains on the paper or a book's cover, resulting in brown stains or bits of tape adhering to paper.

TEG – Top Edges Gilt. See "Gilt."

TENDER – When the binding is loosening.

TEXT BLOCK – Pages containing the content of a book (text, illustrations, and so on) bound together; does not include endpapers.

TIPPED IN – Paper, photograph, or print glued down by only a narrow strip.

TITLE PAGE – The page that gives important information about the book (i.e.: title, author, publisher, date, etc.).

TLS – Typed Letter Signed.

TOOLING – The decoration of leather bindings.

TOP STAIN – The publisher's decorative colored stain, applied to the top page edges.

TP – Title Page.

TRADE PAPERBACK – When the cloth-bound trade edition and the trade paperback are issued by the same publisher, sometimes simultaneously, such issues can be quite a lot larger than paperbacks published for mass-market distribution if the same sheets are used. A large sized paperbound book.

TRADE EDITION – An edition sold through bookstores, as opposed to those meant for private or specialized distribution.

UNBOUND – A book that was never bound into covers, such as "unbound sheets" which were, for whatever reason, never bound by the publisher. Not to be confused with "Disbound."

UNCORRECTED PROOF – A pre-publication printing intended for editorial use, or occasionally to be sent out for review. Usually issued in plain colored wrappers.

UNCUT – Edges that are rough-cut, rather than being neatly trimmed by the binders.

UNOPENED – When folded edges of the pages of the bound pages remain joined together and have not been sliced open. Unread.

VOL, VOLS – Volume/Volumes.

VANITY PRESS/PUBLISHERS – Publishers and presses that publish books at the author's expense.

VARIANT – A copy of a book that varies in some way from the ideal copy. Can refer to binding color, illustrations, etc.

VELLUM – A thin sheet of specially prepared leather used for writing, printing, or as a binding material; considered superior in quality to parchment.

VERSO – The left page of an open book, when it is open and facing the reader. The back of a leaf. Also called the reverse.

VERY GOOD (VG) – Very light wear to book, and/or jacket; no large tears, or major defects. One of the most often used terms. Also see our page of descriptive terms.

W/O – Without.

WAF – "With All Faults." As in "Sold WAF." Usually found in connection with auction listings, but also some bookseller listings. Basically means that the book is in poor enough condition that whatever additional things you might find wrong with it that were not mentioned in the description are your tough luck and not a cause for return. Also "sold as-is."

WATERMARK – A faint identifying design, usually in quality paper.

WHIPSTITCHING – To sew a book's leaves by passing the thread over and over the spine. Often seen in early pamphlets.

WOODCUT – Illustrations produced when the original printing plate was engraved on a block of wood. One of the oldest methods of printing, dating back to 8th century China.

WRAPPERS **or** *WRAPS* – The printed or unprinted cover of a pamphlet or book bound in paper.

Library of Form Letters

As your business grows you're going to find yourself responding to customer correspondence on a daily basis. If you grow large enough your customer interactions can easily consume the better part of your day.

What you'll need is a method of streamlining your customer service activities without sacrificing the quality of your responses. One way to become more efficient is by developing a library of form letters that address most of the day-to-day issues. This minimizes the amount of time spent performing repetitive tasks. Organize your letters so the specific form you need is easily found.

For example, the most common question you receive will be, "Where is my order?" There can be a multitude of answers to that question; in fact, I have 22 different form letters to answer that one question alone. It only takes a minute or less to fire off a relevant, thorough response to each query because of my form library.

This Appendix gives you a few sample letters that answer the most common questions you'll receive on a day-to-day basis. These letters should form the basis of your own library and grow as your business grows. You can find even more sample form letters in the "Free Downloads" area at *http://www.internetbook selling.com*. You can also contribute letters you develop yourself to the website once you sign-up for a free membership.

Don't feel obligated to use the letters verbatim as they appear here and on the website. Make them your own with modifications that fit your personality and writing style.

As marketplace policies and procedures change, you'll have to adjust your form letters accordingly. For example, the recent change to Amazon's "charge when shipped" policy prompted several adjustments to my procedures and customer correspondence letters.

Post office changes in policies, rates and procedures will prompt adjustments to your operation as well. Be on the lookout for anything that requires changes to the way you do business. You don't want to appear like a beginner to customers by sending them inappropriate correspondence.

General Order Status Inquiry

As previously mentioned, the most common query booksellers get is from customers wondering what happened to their order. Good customer service practices dictate that you always inform buyers at the time orders are placed of how long it takes for shipments to arrive. That alone avoids a great deal of correspondence. However, many marketplaces forbid order notification messages to buyers because the marketplace sends one of its own. Always check marketplace policy before communicating with buyers.

Nevertheless, a certain percentage of customers won't take the time to read your notification, but take the time to write you a long eMail asking for the same information. You can minimize the time you spend answering these routine requests by sending the "first response" form letter.

Thank you for your inquiry.

Your order was shipped from my facility via standard Media Mail on _____ . Your tracking number is: _____ . An eMail was sent to you on the day of shipment to let you know your order was on its way.

Standard shipping normally takes 1–3 weeks to reach its destination and there may be longer delays during holiday seasons. You may track the status of your package by accessing the USPS website at: http://www.usps.com/ and entering your tracking number where it says "Track & Confirm."

I appreciate your business and I hope to be of service to you again in the near future.

Joe

Package Already Delivered

As previously mentioned, a certain percentage of customers won't receive their package for one reason or another. They'll write you a second time to let you know they still haven't received their order. After checking with the USPS tracking web page you'll often discover the order has already been delivered and the customer doesn't know it. Your response should be to send an eMail informing the customer that the package has arrived and that a minor physical search is warranted.

Thank you for your message.

According to the USPS online tracking system, your package was delivered on _____ . If you are unaware of its arrival, please check with other members of your family and perhaps your immediate neighbors in case another person received the package and forgot to tell you.

You may track the status of your package by accessing the USPS website at: http://www.usps.com/ and entering your tracking number where it says "Track & Confirm." Your tracking number is _____ .

I appreciate your business and I hope to be of service to you again in the near future.

Joe

A-Z Claim Response

After the customer searches for the package you may get yet another message that the order is nowhere to be found even though the Post Office says it's been delivered. In these cases, your best recourse is to advise the customer to file an A-Z claim with Amazon. If you shipped on-time, and you have a tracking number that indicates the package was delivered, you shouldn't have any difficulty defending your position.

Many booksellers advocate automatically refunding the customer for undelivered packages. That policy is certainly above and beyond the call of duty, and it's unnecessarily costly. You can still deliver world-class customer service without giving away the store. Advise customers to utilize the A-Z services if it's an Amazon sale and offer to help them through the process if they find it difficult.

Thank you for your message. I did additional research on your order today and determined that your package must be lost in the mail.

Unfortunately, I don't have a replacement to send you. I recommend you file an A-Z Claim with Amazon. The A-Z guarantee program protects buyers in situations like this. When you file your claim just explain that the Post Office failed to deliver your package. Amazon will contact me; I'll support your claim by providing the tracking number of your shipment and my shipping details, and Amazon reviews the claim before refunding your purchase price. If you have any questions about how this process works please do not hesitate to contact me for additional assistance. Rest assured your money is not lost and I'm truly sorry this transaction did not go smoothly for you.

Sometimes the Post Office delivers a package weeks or even months late, so your item may show up in the future. If that happens, please let me know, but feel free to keep it as my gift to you as compensation for any inconvenience this situation may have caused.

I appreciate your business and I hope to be of service to you again in the near future.

Joe

Refund the Customer

Sometimes circumstances beyond your control require you to simply refund the customer's purchase price. You may have to refund an order even if you have a tracking number, but the USPS tracking web page indicates the order is still in route and the estimated delivery date has passed.

Another time you may have to issue a refund is when you've shipped an order internationally and there is no tracking information available. If it's an expensive item hopefully you've insured it through your carrier to cover the value of the package. Otherwise, you may have to consider the loss a cost of doing business and move on.

Thank you for your message.

I researched the status of your package. If it hasn't arrived by now I can only conclude that your item is lost in the mail. Therefore, I'm refunding your entire purchase price.

Sometimes the Post Office delivers a package weeks or even months late, so your item may show up in the future. If that happens, please let me know, but feel free to keep it as my gift to you as compensation for any inconvenience this situation may have caused.

I appreciate your business and I hope to be of service to you again in the near future.

Joe

Cancelled Order

Finally, some customers have a change of heart and cancel an order almost immediately after it's been placed. As long as the book hasn't been shipped you're obligated to refund the order. Do so quickly and re-list the book in hopes of selling it again as soon as possible.

> Your order has been cancelled at your request. Please disregard any eMails you receive from me indicating your order has been shipped. A full refund will be reflected in your account within 24–48 hours. Thank you for your consideration. I hope to serve you again in the near future.
>
> If you like the way I handled this refund will you please leave me positive feedback? Your help with positive feedback lets other buyers know I'm an honest and reliable seller. Thanks!
>
> Joe

I want to make one final point about refunds. Whenever you issue a refund, always bend over backward to be gracious and never give the impression it's being given grudgingly. Remember, the customer still has the ability to leave negative feedback. If you're gracious and prompt with the refund you stand an excellent chance of getting positive feedback instead. Model your responses after the "send refund" or "order cancelled" form letters. Eventually, you'll create additional forms to handle refunds in your own style.

Address Change Denied

Occasionally, customers write you almost immediately after placing an order and request you send the book to an address other than the address of record maintained at the marketplace. It's against policy at most marketplaces to comply with those requests.

I send the "address change request denied" form when I receive these requests. If the customer responds back with a cancellation request before I ship the order I automatically honor the request.

Many booksellers change the ship-to address at the request of the customer in violation of marketplace policy. However, you do so at your own risk. If the order turns out to be fraudulent your account will be charged for the loss. If it happens often enough you may get your account cancelled by the marketplace venue.

Thank you for your message.

Amazon policy prohibits me from shipping an order to a location other than the address of record at the time of purchase or Amazon's A-Z guarantee will be invalidated. This policy exists for your protection against fraudulent use of your account. I apologize for any inconvenience this may cause.

Thank you for your business and have a great day!

Joe

Additional Damage Discovered

From time-to-time you may miss disclosable damage to a book that has been listed. Normally, overlooked damage isn't discovered until after the book has been sold and you're cleaning it prior to shipment. When you discover additional damage not included in the original online listing, notify the customer and give an updated description before shipping the book.

Eighty percent of the time the customer gives you permission to proceed with the transaction. Twenty percent of the time you'll issue a refund. Ninety percent of the time customers are appreciative of your diligence. Ten percent of the time they'll send you a few choice words. Use the "additional damage discovered" form letter to handle the situation.

I'm writing to alert you to a problem with your order so please disregard the previous notice I sent indicating your order has been shipped.

The problem is _____ .

I try hard to accurately describe the books I list online. If you look at my feedback, you'll see that the overwhelming majority of my customers report that the books I sell are in BETTER condition than what I describe in my listings. However, occasionally one slips by me with defects that I fail to notice.

Please accept my apology for this oversight. If you still want the book simply respond to this eMail authorizing me to proceed with filling your order and I will ship your book immediately.

If you do not want the book, I'll be happy to offer you a full refund of your purchase price.

I truly appreciate your business and hope this small error does not taint our positive relationship. I am looking forward to your reply. Thank you for your business!

Joe

Permission Granted to Ship Re-described Item

Approximately 80 percent of the customers you notify about undisclosed damage to sold books accept it anyway. Of course, that depends on the nature and extent of the damage, but the 80 percent figure is what I'm finding in my business. Count your blessings and do a better job inspecting your inventory in the future. Meanwhile, send your generous customer the "permission granted to ship" eMail thanking him or her for saving your bacon.

> Thank you for your understanding and I appreciate your business. Your book has been shipped. Your new tracking number is
> _____. Have a great day!
>
> Joe

Permission Denied to Ship Re-described Item

Conversely, you'll find approximately 20 percent of your customers won't accept a book with additional damage. They have every right to refuse the book, so don't get upset with them. You're the one who made the mistake. Your best and only course of action is to send them a gracious eMail apologizing once again for the error and promptly refund the purchase price. The "permission denied to ship" eMail helps to ease the pain.

> Thank you for your reply.
>
> Your refund has been issued as promised. I'm sorry this transaction did not go smoothly and I hope you'll give me another chance to serve you again in the near future.
>
> Joe

Customer Ordered Wrong Item

Sometimes a customer orders the wrong book for one reason or another that has nothing to do with you or your listing, but wants a refund. When that happens, check the catalog page under which your book originally appeared and verify it was properly listed and described. If so then you can legitimately withhold the original shipping charges for the book when you issue the refund. Use the "customer ordered the wrong item" eMail to instruct the customer to send the book back (at the customer's expense). Also, inform him or her that the original shipping charges have been deducted from the refund.

Thank you for writing.

I researched your order and found that the book I sold you was properly listed. If you click on the following link to the _(marketplace name)_ catalog page you'll find that the book is clearly listed as _____.

Nevertheless, if you're unhappy with your purchase you may return it to me at the address below within 30-days of receipt for a refund of your purchase price less the shipping fee of $3.99 since there was no problem with the listing and it was shipped in a timely fashion.

Please carefully pack the book so that I receive it in the same condition in which I sent it to you so you qualify for the maximum refund amount allowed subject to the conditions stated above.

Thank you for your business and have a great day!

Joe

GeneralShopper.com, LLC
P.O. Box 1800
Litchfield Park, AZ 85340

A Cornucopia of Bookseller Resources

There are hundreds of resources you may find useful in the day-to-day operation of your business. Many of them are listed throughout this book. Below is a recap of some of the resources mentioned previously, as well as a few additional resources you may find equally valuable.

For a more comprehensive list of resources visit my website at *http://www.internet bookselling.com*.

Book Fairs and Conventions

Chicago International Remainder and Overstock Book Exposition – *http://www.cirobe.com*

Seller's Conference of Online Entrepreneurs – *http://www.scoe.biz*

Spring Book Show – *http://www.springbookshow.com*

Book Repair Resources and Kits

Bookmakers – *http://www.bookmakerscatalog.com*

Brodart – *http://www.brodart.com*

Gaylord – *http://www.gaylordmart.com*

SicPress – *http://www.sicpress.com*

University Products Archival – *http://www.archivalsuppliers.com*

Vernon – *http://www.vernonlibrarysupplies.com*

Book Research Tools

Addall – *http://www.addall.com*

Amazon Advanced Search – Link found on any catalog page

BookFinder – *http://www.bookfinder.com*

BookFinder4U – *http://www.bookfinder4u.com*

Chambal – *http://www.chambal.com*

FetchBook – *http://www.fetchbook.com*

FindBookPrices – *http://www.findbookprices.com*
Google Search – *http://www.google.com*
Vialibri – *http://www.vialibri.net*

Book Scouting Resources

Book Sale Finder – *http://www.booksalefinder.com*
eBay – *http://www.ebay.com*
US Directory – *http://www.usdirectory.com*
Yellow Pages – *http://www.yellowpages.com*

Bookseller Forums

Amazon Seller Community – *http://www.amazonsellercommunity.com*
Book Think Forums – *http://www.bookthink.com*
eBay Booksellers – *http://forums.ebay.com/db1/forum/Booksellers/4*
Internet Bookselling – *http://www.internetbookselling.com*
Online-Bookselling – *http://www.online-bookselling.com*

Bookseller Organizations

American Booksellers Association – *http://bookweb.org/index.html*
Antiquarian Book & Ephemera Fairs – *http://bookfairs.com*
Antiquarian Booksellers' Association – *http://www.abaa.org*
Independent Online Booksellers Association – *http://www.ioba.org*

Industry Publications

Publisher's Weekly – *http://www.publishersweekly.com*
Firsts Magazine – *http://firsts.com*
Rare Book News – *http://rarebooknews.com*
Book Source Magazine – *http://booksourcemagazine.com*

Inventory Management Software

Art Of Books – *http://www.theartofbooks.com*
BookHound – *http://www.bibliopolis.com*
BookSku – *http://www.booksku.com*
ChannelAdvisor – *http://www.channeladvisor.com*
FillZ – *http://www.fillz.com*
Mail Extractor – *http://www.mailextractor.com*

Monsoon – *http://www.monsoonworks.com*

Prager Software – *http://www.pragersoftware.com*

Logistics

Google Maps – *http://www.google.com/maps*

MapQuest – *http://www.mapquest.com*

New Book Distributors and Wholesalers

Baker & Taylor – *http://www.btol.com*

Bookazine – *http://www.bookazine.com*

DeVorss & Company – *http://www.devorss.com*

Distributors – *http://www.thedistributors.com*

Ingram Book Co. – *http://www.ingrambookgroup.com*

Sunbelt Publications – *http://www.sunbeltbook.com*

Packing and Shipping Materials

Associated Bag – *http://www.associatedbag.com*

Bags & Bows – *http://www.bagsandbowsonline.com*

Browncor – *http://www.browncor.com*

eSupplyStore – *http://www.esupplystore.com*

Fast-Pack – *http://www.fast-pack.com*

Gator Pack – *http://www.gatorpack.com*

Hillas Packaging – *http://www.hillas.com*

Linton Company – *http://www.lintonlabels.com*

Office Depot – *http://www.officedepot.com*

Office Max – *http://www.officemax.com*

Online Labels – *http://www.onlinelabels.com*

Pack Secure – *http://www.packsecure.com*

Packaging Control – *http://www.multi-d.net*

Packaging Price – *http://www.packagingprice.com*

Pakoutlet – *http://www.pakoutlet.com*

Papermart – *http://www.papermart.com*

Quill – *http://www.quill.com*

Reliable Office Supplies – *http://www.reliable.com*

Shipping Supply – *http://www.shippingsupply.com*

Staples – *http://www.staples.com*
Trek Label – *http://www.treklabel.com*
Uline – *http://www.uline.com*

Remainder Book Distributors and Wholesalers

A1 Overstock – *http://www.a1overstock.com*
American Book Company – *http://www.americanbookco.com*
Bargain Books Wholesale – *http://www.bargainbookswholesale.com*
Book Closeouts – *http://www.bookcloseouts.com*
Book Depot – *http://www.bookdepot.com*
Book Sales, Inc. – *http://www.booksalesusa.com*
Bookazine – *http://bookazine.com*
BookLiquidator – *http://www.bookliquidator.com*
Books-A-Million – *http://www.booksamillion.com*
BooksNSave – *http://www.booksnsave.com*
Bradley's Book Clearance – *http://bradleysbooks.net*
East Tennessee Trade Group – *http://www.rhinosales.com*
Fair Mount Books – *https://www.fairmountbooks.com*
Great Jones Books – *https://www.greatjonesbooks.com*
JR Trading – *http://www.jrtradinginc.com*
LRA Books – *http://www.lrabooks.com*
Marketing Resource International – *http://www.mribargains.com*
Readers World Wholesale – *http://www.readersworldwholesale.com*
S&L Sales Company – *http://www.slsales.com*
Tartan Book Sales – *http://www.tartanbooks.com*
Warehouse Books – *http://www.warehousebooksinc.com*
World Publications – *http://www.worldpub.net*

Shipping Carriers

Dalsey, Hillblom and Lynn – *http://www.dhl.com*
Federal Express – *http://www.fedex.com*
United Parcel Service – *http://www.ups.com*
United States Postal Service – *http://www.usps.com*

Unclassified Resources

Faded Giant – *http://www.fadedgiant.net/html/signatures_quotes.htm*

Kim Komando – *http://www.komando.com*

Roman Numeral Date Calculator – *http://www.guernsey.net*

Verify Signatures – *http://www.tomfolio.com/autographs/AGIni.asp*

VistaPrint – *http://www.vistaprint.com*

Appendix 4

Notes

1. So You Want to Be an Internet Bookseller?

1. Headd, Brian. "Business Estimates from the Office of Advocacy: A Discussion of Methodology." U.S. Small Business Administration, Advocacy Small Business Statistics and Research. *http://www.smallbusinessnotes.com/pdf/rs258tot.pdf* (accessed May 15, 2010).

2. Amazon. "2009 Annual Report." Amazon.com. *http://phx.corporate-ir.net/External.File?item=UGFyZW50SUQ9Mzc2NjQyQyfENoaWxkSUQ9Mzc1Mjc3Mjc3M3jc3MjfFR5cGU9MQ==&t=1* (accessed August 4, 2010).

2. Getting Started

1. Pakroo, Peri H. *The Women's Small Business Start-Up Kit: A Step-by-Step Legal Guide.* Berkley: Nolo Press, 2010.

3. How and Where to Find Books

1. Publishing Central, "U.S. Book Production Plummets 18,000 in 2005, According to Bowker." PublishingCentral.com. *http://www.publishingcentral.com/articles/20060516-23-2748.html?si=1* (accessed August 18, 2010).

2. Ellis, Ian C. *Book Finds: How to Find, Buy, and Sell Used and Rare Books* (3rd ed.). New York: The Berkley Publishing Group, 2006.

3. Wikipedia. "RSS." Wikipedia.org. *http://en.wikipedia.org/wiki/RSS_feed* (accessed December 19, 2010).

4. How and Where to Sell Books

1. Anderson, Chris. *The Long Tail: Why the Future of Business Is Selling Less of More* (Rev. ed.). New York: Hyperion Books, 2008.

2. McBride, Bill. *Points of Issue: A Compendium of Points of Issue of Books by 19th-20th Century Authors* (3rd ed.). Hartford: McBride/Publisher, 1996.

3. Amazon. "Amazon Seller Community." Amazon.com. *http://www.amazonsellercommunity.com/forums/ thread.jspa?threadID=167119&start=0&tstart=0* (accessed March 5, 2010).

4. Basbanes, Nicholas A. *Among the Gently Mad.* New York: Henry Holt and Company, 2002.

5. ChooseBooks. "The Company." About Us. ChooseBooks.com. *http://www .choosebooks.com/showCompanyInformation.do* (accessed January 18, 2009).

6. eBay, Inc. "About eBay." eBay.com. *http://news.ebay.com/about.cfm* (accessed January 20, 2009).

7. eCampus. Home Page. *http://www.ecampus.com* (accessed January 22, 2010).

8. Gemm. "Welcome to GEMM!" Home Page. Gemm.com. *http://www.gemm .com* (accessed January 18, 2009).

9. ABookCoOp. "Frequently Asked Questions." TomFolio.com. *http://www .tomfolio.com/tomfolio/faq.asp* (accessed January 20, 2009).

5. How to Find and Sell Digital and Analog Media

1. Digital Innovations. "Disk Repair System." DigitalInnovations.com. *http:// www.digitalinnovations.com/fix-scratched-discs/skipdr-premier-disc-repair-system.html* (accessed March 25, 2009).

2. Wikipedia. "DVD Region Code." Wikipedia.org. *http://en.wikipedia.org/ wiki/DVD_region_code* (accessed March 5, 2009).

6. Fulfillment

1. Godsey, Joyce. *Book Repair for Booksellers: A Guide for Booksellers Offering Practical Advice on Book Repair.* Methuen: Sicpress, 2009.

2. United States Post Office. "Mailing Standards of the United States Postal Service, Domestic Mail Manual." *http://pe.usps.com/cpim/ftp/manuals/ dmm300/ full/mailingStandards.pdf* (accessed May 3, 2009).

3. Goodman, John A. *Strategic Customer Service: Managing the Customer Experience to Increase Positive Word of Mouth, Build Loyalty, and Maximize Profits.* New York: AMACOM, 2009.

7. Building Your Business

1. Kasdan, Lawrence (Director). 1988. *The Accidental Tourist.* [Motion Picture]. United States: Warner Brothers.

2. Sugars, Bradley J. *Instant Systems: Instant Success, Real Results. Right Now.* New York: McGraw-Hill, 2006.

3. Gerber, Michael E. *The E-Myth Revisited: Why Most Small Businesses Don't Work and What to Do about It.* New York: Harper Collins Publishers, 1995.

8. Business by the Numbers

1. Stapenhurst, Tim. *The Benchmarking Book: A How-to Guide to Best Practice for Managers and Practitioners*. Oxford: Butterworth-Heinemann, 2009.
2. Eckerson, Wayne W. *Performance Dashboards: Measuring, Monitoring, and Managing Your Business*. Hoboken: John Wiley & Sons, 2005.

9. Tools of the Trade

1. Intuit. "QuickBooks." *http://quickbooks.intuit.com* (accessed December 20, 2009).
2. Pitney Bowes. "ShipStream Manager." *http://www.pitneyworks.com* (accessed December 24, 2008).

10. Organizing Your Business

1. Abrams, Rhonda. *Business Plan in a Day: Get It Done Right, Get It Done Fast* (2nd ed.). Palo Alto: The Planning Shop, 2009.
2. Service Corps of Retired Executives (SCORE). "Find SCORE." *http://www.score.org* (accessed June 28, 2009).
3. Green, Charles H. *The SBA Loan Book* (2nd ed.). Avon: Adams Media, 2005.

11. Physical Inventory Management

1. Mould, Michael. *Online Bookselling: A Practical Guide with Detailed Explanations and Insightful Tips*. Seattle: Aardvark Publishing Company, 2006.

12. Your Future in Internet Bookselling

1. Bush, Erwin H. "The Future of Used Bookselling – An Observation." Independent Online Booksellers Association. *http://www.ioba.org/newsletter/archive/V10/eb.php* (accessed June 2010).
2. Weber, Steve. *The Home-Based Bookstore: Start Your Own Business Selling Used Books on Amazon, eBay or Your Own Web Site*. Falls Church: Weber Books, 2006.
3. Kiyosaki, Robert T. (Speaker). *You Can Choose to be Rich* (Cassette Recording). Scottsdale: Cashflow Technologies, Inc., 2003.

Index

 **Order Form**

 Fax orders: 623-321-5885. Send this form.

 Telephone orders: Call 602-233-2721.
Have your credit card ready.

 eMail orders: *orders@smallbusinesspress.com.*
See credit card information below.

 Postal orders: Small Business Press, LLC,
P.O. Box 1800-IBME, Litchfield Park, AZ 85340

	Price	Quantity	Total
Internet Bookselling Made Easy!	$23.95	_____	_____
_____	_____	_____	_____
		Sub-total	_____
Arizona residents please add 9.3% sales tax			_____
U.S. postage & handling (each item)	$3.99	_____	_____
International postage (each item)	$12.49	_____	_____
		Total	_____

Name: _____

Address: _____

City: _____ State: _____ Zip: _____

Telephone: (_____) _____

Email address:_____

Payment: ❑ Check   ❑ Credit Card: ❑ Visa ❑ MasterCard

Card number: _____

Name on card: _____ Exp. date: _____